D0000220

LITERACY IN EARLY MODERN EUROPE

To
Keith and Eva

Literacy in Early Modern Europe

Culture and Education 1500–1800

R. A. Houston

LONGMAN
London and New York

Longman Group UK Limited,
Longman House, Burnt Mill, Harlow,
Essex CM20 2JE, England
and Associated Companies throughout the world.

Published in the United States of America
by Longman Inc., New York

First published 1988

British Library Cataloguing in Publication Data
Houston, R. A.
Literacy in early modern Europe:
culture and education 1500–1800.
1. Education——Europe——History
I. Title
370′.94   LA621.4

ISBN 0-582-03080-3 CSD
ISBN 0-582-55266-4 PPR

Library of Congress Cataloging-in-Publication Data
Houston, R. A. (Robert Allan). 1954-
Literacy in early modern Europe,
culture and education 1500–1800
R. A. Houston.
    p.   cm.
Bibliography: p.
Includes index.
ISBN 0-582-03080-3
ISBN 0-582-55266-4 (pbk.)
1. Education——Europe——History.   2. Learning and
scholarship——Europe——History.   3.
Literacy——Europe——History.   I. Title. LA621.5.H68
1988
370′.94——dc19

Set in 10/12pt Baskerville Comp/Edit 6400

Produced by Longman Singapore Publishers (Pte) Ltd.
Printed in Singapore

Contents

Contents

Preface

This volume is an attempt to fill a considerable gap in the historical writing on the social history of education and literacy in Europe. Most countries have histories of national education, though some were written as early as the 1900s and many treat the period before the Enlightenment in a cursory manner. The best modern studies branch into reading, writing, the uses of literacy and the importance of oral culture but still deal with only a single country. At the same time they tend to emphasise particular aspects of schooling and literacy which have special relevance to one country, such as the struggle between church and state for control of education or the development of nationalism through vernacular publishing, and do not pick out the common features of developments across Europe or the way in which one nation's experience differs from another. An important gap therefore exists in the literature between Carlo Cipolla's slender *Literacy and development in the west* (1969) and Harvey Graff's monumental and densely-informative *Legacies of literacy* (1987). This book was substantially written before the appearance of Graff's book in the spring of 1987 and differs from it in important respects. First, it covers a briefer time period but deals with eastern as well as western Europe, using a wider range of literature in languages other than English and French. Second, it treats education and literacy in a thematic way rather than dealing with developments country by country, and it contains more on education, popular culture and the uses of literacy than Graff's volume. The aim is to provide a clear and interesting outline of the structures and trends in education, literacy and culture, *c*.1500–*c*.1800 for an undergraduate audience, and to bring a topic which is often treated peripherally in mainstream history to a central position by detailing its relevance to broader social, economic and political changes.

This is not so much a textbook as a set of arguments about the place of literacy and education in social structures and social change in Europe between the Renaissance and the Industrial Revolution. The central theme is that while education expanded and literacy improved enormously during these three centuries, the impact of change was tempered by the attitudes and social structures which obtained in the different societies of early modern Europe. The ideas of major authorities on the period – Eisenstein, Muchembled and Burke for example – have been incorporated, though explicit discussion of sociological and anthropological theories has been avoided in favour of a fundamentally *historical* analysis. Education is a hotly debated issue in the late twentieth century and the general lessons to be gained from an accurate understanding of historical context are considerable. Significant changes are highlighted, but the book is deliberately structured to emphasise continuities in the social history of education in the early modern period. The range of examples is drawn, as far as possible, from every part of Europe – Greenland to Transylvania, Finland to Portugal – though it should be recognised that the volume of writing on French education and literacy is, for example, huge compared with what has been produced on Spain. For the years 1976–80 the *Bibliographie d'histoire de l'éducation française* lists 6,598 theses, articles, books and reports. Subjects of study also vary between historical traditions: the elite culture of the Renaissance has been extensively studied for Italy but very little has been published on the extent of popular literacy.

I should like to thank those who have helped me with the research for this book. For Scandinavian language translations I am extremely grateful to Anna-Lisa MacDonald and Sirkka Upton. Paul Ries provided help in this area and many stimulating ideas about reading and the uses of literacy. The text was read by Peter Burke, Simon Franklin, Hamish Scott, Andrew Pettegree and Bob Scribner. Because of problems of accessibility for the general reader, unpublished works and theses have not been cited but I should like to give particular mention to Peter Burke, Dr G. Gömöri and Graeme Kirkham. Quotations are all in English and references in brackets refer to the consolidated bibliography at the end. References to certain parts of Europe suffer from anachronism in so far as countries like 'Italy' did not exist as single entities and other territories changed hands at various periods. The descriptions adopted will hopefully blend accuracy with ease of identification.

Rab Houston
Department of Modern History
University of St Andrews

CHAPTER ONE
Introduction

The European societies which gave rise to the cultural regeneration and intellectual innovation which we call the Renaissance enjoyed only very restricted levels of literacy among their populations. Writing was secret and scarce, printing in its infancy. Three centuries later, a new industrial age began to dawn in the north-west of a continent, many countries of which had achieved a majority of literate persons among their inhabitants. The reasons for this fundamental change from restricted to mass literacy, the process by which it took place and the implications for European society in the early modern period are the focus of this book.

The period is interesting because it marks an important transitional phase in European society and culture. Early medieval European culture had been dominated by what might be termed 'primary orality': writing and reading were skills which a very few professionals possessed, while the bulk of the population relied for information on what they could see and what they could hear, communicating through eyes and voices. Specialists monopolised reading and writing for peasants and kings alike; familiarity with documents was strictly limited and the ordinary man or woman had simply to listen. Late medieval Europe had no (known) purely oral cultures of the kind studied by anthropologists until recently, yet for most people seeing and hearing were more significant than reading and writing. Economic interactions took place face-to-face and religious experience was mediated to ordinary men and women by the words of a priest and the impact of visual symbols. Schooling was scarce, books and writing materials expensive, most literature was in Latin and there was an aura of inaccessibility attached to writing. As a result, literacy was restricted. By 1800 Europe was a very different place in economic, religious, political, social and intellectual terms, and it is conventionally assumed that the progress towards a 'modern' and economically developed world was aided by the dramatic expansion in education and literacy which had taken place during the previous three centuries.

Arguably, developed countries of the late twentieth century are now moving towards what might be termed 'secondary orality' where electronic communications media render the need for an individual to be able to read, write and count increasingly superfluous. Figures such as Marshall McLuhan have emerged to identify and explain the process and its implications. Yet, contemporary debates rage on the ways in which children should be educated, the role which the school should play in society and the overwhelming importance to the individual of high-quality literacy and to society at large of mass literacy. Historically, literacy tends to be associated with the development of abstract thought, broadening of the mind through vicarious experience, the intensification and extensification of intellectual exchange, personal independence of thought and action, economic development, democracy, even demographic change. Illiterates, on the other hand, are allegedly more restricted in their thought patterns, intellectually impoverished, culturally backward, isolated, inert, almost pathological (McLuhan 1973; Finnegan 1973). Illiteracy, in the words of Vladimir Ilyich Lenin, is 'enemy number one', while for Helvétius 'l'éducation peut tout' (Leith 1977:15).

Much writing on the history of education and literacy at earlier periods was occasioned by similar arguments and much of it was produced to make a specific political point about the need for literacy and the particular pathways which should be followed to achieve it. Such interchanges tended, for example, to occur at times of military failure or perceived political crisis, as in Prussia (1806–13) when commentators debated the role of education in reviving and creating national sentiment, Russia after 1856, England during the 1830s, France in the 1870s and 1880s or Spain after the First World War. They argued about why literacy had failed to develop, or why it was apparently in retreat, and about whether one agency or another, church or state, public or private, was the best method of controlling the provision of education (Furet & Ozouf 1982:1–4; Stone 1969:87–8). Traditional historical writing about literacy has, for its part, concentrated on schools and universities, print and publishing rather than on the extent of reading and writing and its social and cultural significance. This book deals with such aspects and emphasises the significance of interactions between church, state and people. The perspective is 'from below', reflecting a growing interest during the last two decades in the lives of ordinary people rather than in institutions and the elites.

The influences which bore upon literacy in the early modern period are neatly summarised by Lawrence Stone. 'The structure of education in a society is determined by ... social stratification, job opportunities, religion, theories of social control, demographic and family patterns, economic organisation and resources, and finally political theory and institutions'. (Stone 1969:70; Craig 1981.) To this list we can add the dimension of language, since it is easier to learn to read in the language of everyday communication than in an alien tongue, and easier if that language uses phonetic spelling. Because of the diversity of social, political and economic structures across Europe, it would be unrealistic to expect that any single combination of these could be used to explain developments over the whole continent. The relative signficance of the above factors varied over time, between different countries and according to the level of education. Educational theorists certainly existed in early modern Europe and we can study their writings to determine the prevailing attitudes to education among intellectuals, clerics and secular administrators who established the principles and guided the implementation of educational 'policy'. However, assessing the effect of education on pupils or the reasons why parents chose to educate their children is a good deal harder because of shortcomings in documentation. Direct evidence of attitudes and aspirations is rare and it is usually necessary to infer from prescription, casual allusion and from patterns of school attendance and literacy which fit in with the rest of the social context. Such inferences are, nevertheless, essential since 'an education incorporates three distinct things: a conscious cultural tradition, an educational ideology, and a curriculum' (Grafton & Jardine 1986:219). Much of this book depends on quantitative material which, in the words of Dr Johnson, 'brings everything to a certainty which before floated in the mind indefinitely', but statistical skeletons need to be fleshed out by more qualitative material when discussing meanings and understandings.

Much space could be used trying to define literacy. While we shall concentrate on one particular criterion, the ability to sign one's name, it is best to think not of literacy but of litera*cies,* of a variety of ways in which the products of a culture can be acquired and transmitted. First of all there is *looking* at a picture rich in visual imagery, with or without accompanying text, and deriving from it as much information as from a written or printed page. Single-leaf woodcuts are the best example of this medium (Scribner 1981a). Second is *reading* which can mean either private perusal by an individual or reading aloud, a practice which might bring the products of literacy to illiterates. Third comes *writing*, starting with simple abilities like signing a name but stretching through copying of set texts as far as composition of prose or verse, possibly even in Latin or another language not normally spoken by the writer. This rather advanced level is the test adopted by UNESCO for the modern world: a person, to be deemed literate, should be sufficiently fluent not only to make out words on a page or copy them out but also to read a newspaper or write a letter (Burnet 1965). Moving sideways a little, we find counting and high-level skills like navigation and the ability to convert foreign currencies.

The imperfect nature of early modern sources makes it necessary to categorise people as literate or illiterate, but it is essential to recognise that we are dealing not with one discrete literacy but a spectrum or hierarchy of skills. At the same time, the gap between literate and illiterate could be bridged by seeing and listening. What is more, literacy can be used for different purposes: to serve some practical or *functional* end such as economic need among tradesmen, in which case reading and writing would be advantageous; or to fulfil a *simple* religious need, where reading alone is all that is commonly required. In the words of Harvey Graff (1987:4), literacy 'is above all a technology or set of techniques for communications and for decoding and reproducing written or printed materials' or of Marshall McLuhan (1973:96), 'literacy is a uniform processing of a culture by a visual sense extended in space and time by the alphabet'.

A negative definition is also possible. Illiteracy could mean inability to read and write Latin (the medieval *illitteratus*) but the term might also apply to those unable to read in the vernacular or to those who could not write their name or a set phrase. The first known use of 'illiterate' in English was in 1556. The word *illettré* was scarcely used in north-east France or the southern Netherlands until the mid-eighteenth century when it was included in Trévoux's *Diction-naire universel* to mean someone who did not know anything about literature; *non lettré* meant without Latin. The word *analphabète* did not come into use until the late nineteenth century (Ruwet & Wellemans 1978:14). Sometimes a person might have learned to read one sort of handwriting or one print typeface (Gothic or Roman, for example) and therefore to have been quite at sea with a different way of presenting letters. The difference between Latin and Cyrillic alphabets could fox Europeans not acquainted with both.

4

Just as literacy can be defined in different ways, so can it be acquired by following a variety of paths. The most obvious would be attending a school held by a professional schoolmaster. But some teachers worked in the homes of the pupils they taught or in barns and outhouses; they moved to their pupils rather than the children coming to a building designated as a school. Children might learn in the home from parents or older children or kin. Unlike modern developing countries, literacy campaigns in pre-industrial Europe used schoolmasters, clergy, religious orders or parents but did not formally recruit children, youths, students or soldiers for the task (Arnove & Graff 1987). Schooling was more often an expression of social practices rather than a discrete phase of the life cycle lived out in the distinctive environment of a formal classroom. Furthermore, the school could be an expression of a desire for learning as much as it was an independent stimulator of literacy. Schooling must be seen in the context of social and economic life in early modern Europe as well as being regarded as an autonomous variable. Education and literacy created certain opportunities but they were themselves dependent on the societies in which they grew and can thus be treated both as agents of change and as indicators or even products of social developments.

Certain features about European societies before the Industrial Revolution should be borne in mind. First, the 'progress' of education and literacy was slow and frequently subject to reverses. Education was, to modern eyes, relatively disorganised and the scale of schools very small. Furthermore, the purposes of education and the uses to which it could be put seem restrictive and limited to modern observers. Second, we should beware of superficial similarities between twentieth-century experiences and historical ones and also between the countries of early modern Europe. The institutional frameworks, social norms and mental climate in which people lived between the Renaissance and the Industrial Revolution were very different from those of our own. The family and the local community were far more significant to everyday life, communications were rudimentary, technology primitive, life expectancy at birth short (thirty-five years on average), the role of magic and religion in everyday life pervasive – the latter was 'the idiom in which men thought' – concepts of 'liberty', 'democracy' and 'equality' as we understand the terms almost unknown. The societies of early modern Europe were varied both in their internal makeup and when compared with each other. Anything more than the broadest similarities in patterns and development should not be expected since there are bound to be inconsistencies, anomalies and contradictions in the structures of education and literacy and the way they changed. A sense of historical context is vital. Generalisations are possible but qualifications also have to be recognised.

This volume is divided into two principal parts. The first deals with the ways in which people became literate, both in and out of school, and analyses the educational hierarchy, teaching methods, teachers and the forces behind improvements in schooling in the early modern period. Alternative pathways to literacy are set alongside the demand for learning. A division is created by a chapter on sources for the study of early modern literacy and one on the extent of reading and writing between the Renaissance and the Industrial Revolution. In the second half, some of the uses to which literacy could be put are discussed, including substantial chapters on book production, distribution, ownership and reading. Language differences and their impact on literacy and communication are assessed. Finally, the significance of literate and oral communication to cultural stability and change is considered.

The early modern period witnessed substantial changes in political, religious, economic and social life. Yet alongside these developments there were also very significant enduring characteristics which tempered their impact. The central themes of this book can be summarised under these two headings, beginning with continuities. The educational hierarchy comprised an anarchic and geographically uneven variety of overlapping and sometimes competing components from the humblest village schools to grand colleges. The standard of teaching too was far from uniform but seems to have improved over time. Teaching methods and materials changed remarkably little during the three centuries and at both elementary and more advanced levels the pedagogic regime was often rigid and stultifying, designed to pass on an agreed body of knowledge and more or less fixed interpretations. Formal schooling was an important first stage in the learning process for many people but it was usually brief and basic. Learning was a piecemeal affair which might last throughout a person's life, the pace and timing determined by their religious, cultural and economic needs. 'Post-elementary' education was very much the preserve of the middling and upper classes, for whom it was an important way of preserving economic and social dominance. Order, stability and conformity were the watchwords of the authorities. Some observers argued that education was a good thing in its own right, but the over-riding aim was to offer an education appropriate to a person's established place in society.

This had profound implications not only for what was taught and how, but also to whom. One result was that women tended to be much less literate than men and the lower orders less educated than their social superiors. Access to education was determined by gender and social class, by parental attitudes and by its cost in a world where children were expected to contribute to the family budget from an early age. University education was the preserve of the middling and upper classes. Oral culture remained central to the lives of ordinary people even though the printed word played an increasing role. The masses retained an interest in simple religious and recreational literature at a time when the middling and upper classes were broadening their reading tastes. Most people read religious works and popular ephemera rather than major volumes of current scholarship. The range of books available expanded enormously between 1500 and 1800 but censorship by ecclesiastical and secular authorities continued to restrict what could be read. Understanding was shaped partly by what could not be read and partly by what was printed, whether ideologically neutral or in the form of overt propaganda. What is more, the process by which ideas were transmitted remained a complex one. Language barriers existed within as well as between countries, denying access to ideas and information to those who did not speak or read the language in which books were printed. Linguistic or dialect divisions were one facet of the cultural variety of early modern Europe. The spread of new ideas depended not simply on what was read but also on personal demonstration and on how literature was understood, illustrating that the impact of literacy was contingent on the existing mental and material environment.

Throughout the period, ecclesiastical control of education remained strong and religious emphases central to curricula. Yet the power of the state and the significance of secular concerns were growing. Many of the changes in education and literacy which took place between the Renaissance and the Industrial Revolution were the product of these developments. Indeed, we can outline the most significant changes between *c*.1500 and *c*.1800 by examining the agencies behind them. From the late medieval period the state began to play an increasing role in everyday life through its administrators who collected taxes, recruited soldiers, dispensed justice and enforced order and conformity. Such intervention increased noticeably during the seventeenth and eighteenth centuries and had two implications for educational change. First, the state's demand for trained officials had a direct impact on the increase in secondary education and on the expansion of the universities which occurred in the century after the Protestant Reformation in some countries and in the eighteenth century in others. Second, those forced to deal with the state had similarly to seek out basic and advanced literacy. At the same time, the state's drive for control over its subjects involved an insistence on linguistic uniformity and, notably in the eighteenth century, national campaigns which sought to structure education under government control and to extend literacy. Some of these campaigns were highly successful by the standards of the day but we should be wary of equating legislation with achievement. Nor should we exaggerate the spread of secularism since many of the developments in secondary education were brought about by groups such as the Jesuits and even in the eighteenth century the church provided many of the teachers and much of the drive behind day-to-day schooling.

Indeed the state was not the only force for change. The struggle between the Reformed Faiths and the Roman Catholic Church from the time of Luther created a powerful incentive for both religions to provide education and to insist on basic literacy and religious knowledge for their adherents. Individual men and women used reading and writing in their search for a satisfying relationship with God. Religious inspiration waned to some extent during the seventeenth century but was revived towards its end when the Lutheran Pietist movement began to regenerate education in countries like Prussia and Denmark. The third force behind change was economic. Population growth in the sixteenth and eighteenth centuries, urban growth, nascent industrial developments and the expansion of both internal and overseas trade involved growing numbers of ordinary people in market transactions for which literacy was immensely useful. To a considerable degree, most of the trends in education and literacy during this period, both positive and negative, were a function of political, religious and economic changes. There were, however, certain largely autonomous developments of which the invention and spread of printing by movable type was the most significant. This technological innovation made books cheaper and more available. Hundreds of millions of copies were printed between the 1450s and 1800, thus creating a huge potential for intellectual exchange and advance as well as for broadening the cultural horizons of early modern men and women. The development of printing was episodic and its impact, as with any innovation, took time and favourable circumstances fully to be felt. Changes took place in the intellectual climate too, notably in the age of the Enlightenment. The eighteenth century saw the extension of the humanist idea that education could be a good thing in itself coupled with the cameralist concept that the 3Rs made a nation's subjects more useful.

The people of early modern Europe were the final force behind change. The push of institutions had to be complemented by the demand created by individuals and social groups. One example is the growing demand for vocational and vernacular education from the end of the seventeenth century to replace the classical, humanist curricula which had dominated secondary schooling from the fifteenth century. Latin ceased to be the international language of learning and communication and was eclipsed by the vernacular languages of early modern Europe. Certain languages and dialects decayed as a result of a loss of faith in them on the part of certain social groups. Associated with this was a fundamental change in reading tastes away from religious and practical literature towards secular, entertaining material and from slow, intensive reading to swift and extensive devouring of novels and periodical literature, notably in the eighteenth century. Education and literacy opened up a Pandora's box for some of the people of early modern Europe since it was not always possible to control the uses to which reading and writing were put. This became obvious in the years of the English Revolution (1640s and 1650s) or of the French Revolution. Throughout, change was slow, uneven and not irreversible. Europe was culturally very varied and, arguably, became more so over our period both socially and geographically. These are the main threads which run through this book and which will be picked up as we examine the central issues of education, literacy and culture between the Renaissance and the Industrial Revolution.

CHAPTER TWO
The world of the school

TYPES OF SCHOOL

The diverse systems of schooling which exist in twentieth-century Europe share the characteristic of strict stratification according to age and curriculum. Access to a particular type of school or a certain class within a school depends on age and academic attainment. Over much of western Europe, education is funded by the state and complemented by a 'private sector' of fee-paying institutions and schools subsidised by secular or religious charities. By contrast, there was no planned, co-ordinated and unified 'educational system' in any European country between the Renaissance and the Industrial Revolution. Instead we find an anarchic jumble of different types of school whose functions sometimes complemented each other, sometimes rivalled or overlapped, and which fitted together into something resembling less an educational pyramid than a scholastic tower of Babel.

Varieties of school were legion in the early modern period. There were petty schools, grammar schools, poor hospitals, work schools, academies, evening classes, colleges, 'normal' schools (teacher-training establishments) and finally the universities. All of these did fit into a hierarchy of sorts, the ranks in which were distinguished principally by the level of learning which was provided. The most significant divide was between institutions which taught Latin, the international language of learning, and those which did not, but there were also differences based, for example, on the availability of writing instruction, arithmetic, philosophy, rhetoric, theology or technical training. The Latin/vernacular divide was paralleled by distinctions between the gender and social class of pupils. Some

10

schools were marked out by the background of the teachers – clergy or laity – others by gender – there were proprietary girls' schools in all countries and the upper reaches of the educational hierarchy were effectively the preserve of males. Funding was not an important distinguishing feature in most countries since the bulk of schools were financed partly by fees paid by parents and partly from charitable or official resources. Scotland's grammar schools were principally funded by taxation of local landowners, Ukraine's by the church or religious confraternities, England's by charitable endowment or civic coffers. To a considerable extent, the numbers in a school, the social composition of its children and its standing depended on the sort of education it provided.

The spectrum of size, curriculum and prestige between the most insignificant village school and the *collège* or university was enormously broad. At the lowest reaches were the tiny Spanish *amigas* or nursery schools run by women for children as young as three or four. Ranked among the most exalted were the state academies of eighteenth-century Russia, the Jesuit colleges, which were the closest thing in the seventeenth century to a 'national' (or even international) system, or the famous English grammar schools. In a sense, it is potentially misleading to group these together as schools though they can all be classed as formal institutions of learning. Any effort to divide schools into discrete categories is likely to be equally crude but necessary in order to make sense of the anarchic variety of educational institutions in early modern Europe. It is further clear that schooling was not distinct from everyday life and that while formal education helped to create literacy it was also part of the wider social forces which helped directly and indirectly to shape patterns of learning. These are discussed in a later chapter.

During the eighteenth century, most continental states set about reorganising and formalising the structure of education, sometimes codifying, sometimes extending existing provision. We shall deal with these campaigns at a later stage, but their present value lies in the explicit categories of school which they specified in educational regulations. Different types of school were designed to provide different skills for different social classes. Take the case of the *Allgemeine Schulordnung* promulgated for the Galician province of the Austrian Habsburg monarchy in 1774, shortly after it was annexed from Poland. A three-tier system was envisaged. At the lowest level, *trivial* or elementary schools were to teach reading, religious knowledge and arithmetic to boys from a peasant and artisan background. Next came the *haupt* (high) school which would be located in a town and provide the same education, plus writing, for bourgeois boys. Finally, the provincial capital was to contain a *normal* school for the purpose of training teachers. By 1789, Galicia had the Lvov normal school, 19 principal schools and 144 elementary ones, though even after the ordinance there were many other schools for Jews, girls and German speakers in the province, illustrating the great variety which existed in educational provision even at the end of the eighteenth century (Adler 1974:31–2; Krupa 1981).

The Danish schools laws of 1814, building on eighteenth-century ordinances, envisaged a similar hierarchy: elementary rural *almue-skoler*, urban *borgerskoler* along with vocational schools for craftsmen and tradesmen's children; secondary *real* schools, Latin schools and teacher-training colleges, all for middle-class boys. These school regulations often codified existing practice, and most countries had a hierarchy of this kind. Seventeenth- and eighteenth-century Finland had its elementary *pedagogier*, secondary *trivial-skolor* and elite *gymnasier*. And the north German city of Braunschweig in the second half of the seventeenth century possessed a hierarchy of schools headed by the three Latin schools, then two municipal vernacular schools, and finally some forty petty schools called *Winkelschulen* (Gold 1977; Luttinen 1985:31; Friedrichs 1982:372).

ELEMENTARY SCHOOLS

These categories are all approximate but it is useful to think in terms of a hierarchy or pyramid of institutions as we go on to examine the huge variety of schooling available in early modern Europe. At the base came the tens of thousands of elementary schools which existed in cottages and tenements throughout our period. Many of these have left no trace in surviving documentation, making it impossible to judge their numbers accurately. They were small in size, often seasonal to suit the rhythms of the harvest year, run by men and women alike, teaching very simple skills (usually religious knowledge and reading) to children aged roughly six (the age of discretion according to most thinkers) to ten. Polish school laws of the eighteenth century forbade the teaching of Latin in the elementary schools, and in seventeenth-century Scotland teachers were strictly enjoined to instruct only the very young or girls in reading, religion and practical skills which would help children of the lower classes to gain an honest living when they grew up. Some French, Italian, German and Spanish schools taught only religion at the most basic level. In sixteenth- and seventeenth-century Ukraine the simplest teaching came from parish schools run by the church or by religious confraternities. Pupils were few in number, less than a dozen on average in seventeenth-century Hungary, Germany and Poland. In some places these petty schools were illegal, but the failure of repeated attempts to eradicate them suggests that their low fees, local situation and humble ambitions suited the aspirations of numerous parents. Clandestine schools at Cracow in Poland during the 1770s could be run by almost anyone prepared to flout official regulations: a burgess and his wife, a town official, a bartender, a friar, a cathedral vicar. In seventeenth-century Braunschweig the teachers included a weaver, a soldier, a notary, a former clerk, a failed student, the widow of a Latin teacher, a sexton and the wife of a tax collector (Krukowski 1979; Friedrichs 1982).

The lowest level of the educational hierarchy was composed of petty schools ranging from glorified crèches to schools with the humble goal of teaching basic literacy. Most aimed to serve the needs of the lower orders, though some could act as stepping stones for boys from the lower and middling ranks to make their way into grammar schools. At the same time, the early modern period saw an increasing provision of schools especially for the poor. In the medieval period those whose parents were too humble in status and too straitened in circumstances to pay for tuition and who were lucky enough to receive any education did so along with the better-off, provided for by charity. Alternatively, specialist schools for the poor might be set up, such as the northern Italian Schools of Christian Doctrine. A voluntary teaching movement began in Italy in the late fifteenth century and was formalised by Castellino da Castello when he set up a confraternity to operate the schools in 1539. Schools of Christian Doctrine taught religion and basic reading and writing, but they did so for just two hours a day on Sundays and holidays using simple books such as the sixteen-page duodecimo *Summario della Vita Christiana*. Volunteers taught more than half the boys and girls aged four to fourteen at Bologna in 1568, and Rome in 1611 had seventy-eight Schools of Christian Doctrine with 10,000 attenders. These schools were particularly important in Italy since outside the major towns free schooling was much less common than in, say, England (Grendler 1984).

During the sixteenth century, the numbers of poor grew and they became a large and permanent class in all countries of Europe. Their betters saw them in a more menacing light and as a result there was growing social alienation between the middling and upper ranks in society and those who made up the rural and urban masses. Society was becoming more sharply divided and one reflection of this was the growing provision, notably in the larger towns from the 1520s, of poor hospitals and work schools to curb the turbulence of lower-class youth and turn them into useful members of an ordered society (Chartier, *et al.* 1976:48). The best-known examples of these specialist institutions for the poor are the hospitals or boarding-houses for orphans and the destitute, set up to take poor children off the streets, discipline them and train them to be productive and orderly members of society. As early as 1550 the poor house at Bruges in the Low Countries accommodated 230 children, but in French towns such as Paris and Lyon, the major development of the *hopîtaux généraux* came in the later seventeenth and eighteenth centuries. Paris' first formal *école de charité* was founded in 1636 and was soon emulated by others. The *hopîtal général* was a boarding school to which an elementary school was often attached, attended partly by its own inmates, partly by day pupils from the poor of the town. Commensurate with their purpose, the hospitals taught religion above all, followed by practical skills which would suit the children to find employment at their alloted social level and, almost as an afterthought, reading and writing. At Lyon in the later eighteenth century there were three work schools for boys and three for girls which they attended after receiving some basic education and which then trained them for apprenticeship or service. Regulations for the Blue- and Grey-Coat charity schools in the English city of York specified that five hours of the day were devoted to spinning and weaving, with reading, writing and the rules of arithmetic thrown in only as a 'relief from more painful tasks'. These prescriptions reflected a growing belief in the seventeenth century that the poor should be distinguished from the rest of society.

Indeed, virtually all schools for the lower orders included instruction in practical skills. For boys this would be some form of handicraft such as weaving or carpentry, for girls spinning and knitting. The merits of practical training as a way of reducing poverty and disorder among the lower orders were proclaimed from Seville in southern Spain to Stralsund in northern Germany during the sixteenth century, but it was the eighteenth century which witnessed the most marked proliferation of specialist 'work schools'. *Ecoles de filature,* begun in Normandy in the 1760s, were designed to fulfil the needs of both poor relief and education. In Ireland, the 'charter schools' of the 1730s, 1740s and 1750s were state-funded but run by a private, Protestant society whose aim was to proselytise the children of the Catholic poor and teach them 'useful employments and regular habits of industry' (Cullen 1980:199).

A growing number of work schools were attached to industrial enterprises. The English Lord Beaumont founded a school at his Coleorton mine in Leicestershire in the early eighteenth century, while in Finland landowners chose to attach *ruukikoulu* or factory schools to logging plants or foundries on their estates (Hufton 1974:167–8; Whittaker 1984:13). Individual landlords shared the views of civic authorities about the uses of practical education. One member of the Russian Kurakin family wrote to an overseer on his Ukrainian estates in the middle of the eighteenth century: 'I am sending twelve young sons of my serfs to learn their letters so that they can be made suitable for my service' (Black 1979:46–7).

These rather grand examples are not altogether typical of the sort of elementary education given to the poor. There were catechism schools which existed for only a few weeks in the year to instruct children about to receive communion. Many were hole-in-the-wall institutions with casual funding and an exiguous existence. During the 1560s there was a school in the *Patio de los Naranjos* outside Seville cathedral which taught reading and writing to poor boys. A religious confraternity paid the teacher's salary and a local bookseller supplied primers free so that the poor would not have to pay out in order to send their sons (Perry 1980:177). All these types of school shared a limited curriculum of religious knowledge, work, reading and possibly the rudiments of writing and counting.

Dependence on charity was common, and the bequest of Mr John Smarte of Rumford in Essex to the town of Stratford-upon-Avon in 1676 is typical of the sort of provision made by testators concerned about education. Smarte recognised that there were a number of prestige grammar schools but that there were few 'feeder' schools for the poor teaching basic English reading and writing. His bequest included a provision for an old woman to teach twenty boys and girls reading and one to pay for a writing master. Basic books such as twenty each of primers, psalters, catechisms and Bibles were to be provided and all education for the needy boys and girls selected was to be free (Richardson & James 1983:149). During the 1630s, Claire Rouille, widow of Jean Tronson, a tax administrator, left 200 livres to the confraternity of *Bon Secours* to provide basic religious and practical instruction to poor girls in the St Eustache parish of Paris. These schools were humble and very cheap to attend; sometimes they were free. Yet, even at this level there were plenty of parents too poor to afford to send their children. The French *petites écoles*, a step above the simplest schools, usually had bursaries attached to them to enable lower-class boys to attend. Because children from all social groups might attend a *petite école*, lower-class parents might be reluctant to admit their poverty and claim free schooling, or to send their badly dressed, dirty and scrofulous children to sit with their betters (Poutet 1971:94, 96).

For most children from the lower classes, boys and girls alike, this basic instruction in literacy and labour was as far as formal education went. Some boys might go on to an apprenticeship or possibly to a grammar school on a scholarship which might ultimately lead to a post as a minor official in church or state. That these individuals were rare is no accident. Attitudes to the education of the poor were stark and unambiguous. They should be trained as productive, godly and obedient members of society, and any education they received should not in any way alter the social order or their place in it. The men who dominated society had clear and firm views on the goals of education: it should preserve the distinctions in society rather than blurring them, and it should encourage the lower orders to accept their position rather than seeking to ameliorate it. There were, of course, subtleties in the exposition of these views and differences of opinion about whether educating ordinary people or keeping them ignorant was the best way of maintaining stability. Some thinkers began to advocate education as a good in itself during the eighteenth century (an idea which had existed even in the fifteenth century), yet the conservative consensus was overwhelming and so wholly different from the ostensible aims of schooling today as to require categorical statement.

Official attitudes to the education of the lower orders were remarkably homogeneous between countries and over time. Reports by bodies concerned with poor relief (such as the Italian *Carita dei Poveri* during the 1790s), deliberations of civic authorities, private correspondence among members of political and intellectual elites, debates in learned societies, articles in newspapers and periodicals, books and pamphlets: all contain evidence of a set of shared assumptions that education for any rank in society should be appropriate to the place of that stratum in the overall polity. Middling and upper classes should be taught to create wealth and to be faithful servants of church and state, lower classes to work and to obey. Specifically, the masses were to be orderly, godly, diligent, tractable and content. Or, as the French thinker Charles Rollin put it in the early eighteenth century, education was to create *'bons chrétiens, bons fils, bons pères, et bons citoyens'* (Black 1979:9).

The desirable ends of education for the poor fitted together into a coherent whole. Different interest groups tended to stress different aspects. The church, which had monopolised education during the medieval period and continued to do so in countries like Muscovy into the eighteenth century, was primarily concerned with moulding a population which shared its precepts. After the Reformation there was the added stimulus of protecting and propagating a new faith or defending Catholicism and defeating what French authorities termed 'the so-called reformed faith' *(la religion prétendue reformée)*. The prime aim was of course to save souls, but the approved method of doing so involved a rather rigid set of rules since the competing churches each tended to perceive only one path to godliness and salvation, though in countries as diverse as Russia and the Netherlands, Jews were allowed to keep their own schools. Religious emphases pervaded education throughout our period despite the growing power of the state and the development of more secular concerns. During the seventeenth and eighteenth centuries secular authorities began to take over the mantle of the church while realising that the ecclesiastical emphasis on obedience to God's Word or the prescriptions of a priest were of considerable importance to the creation of a disciplined population.

This connection between order and education is explicitly stated by 'the honourable council of this holy imperial city of Nördlingen' in southern Germany in an ordinance of 1652. Having 'had occasion to consider how remarkably much the common weal depends on well-conducted schools, and how one of the duties of rulers is to ensure that young people be diligently educated, with great circumspection and appropriate severity, and that they be habituated, aroused and encouraged to do what is good', the council set out regulations to preserve the peace and prosperity of the city with the help of its schools. Lack of schooling was perceived to be dangerous, leading, in the words of the States of Holland in 1596, to wanton idleness, improper behaviour and all sorts of foolishness. Proper education for the poor could, on the other hand, work wonders. The representatives from Seville to the Castilian Cortes (Estates) in 1548 argued that the creation of a House for the Instruction of Christian Doctrine there in 1546 meant that there were 'fewer thieves than before, less disease and contagious illness, and more doctrine and better example among the poor'. Religion, basic literacy and work training would preserve order, prevent mischief, acquaint the children of the poor with honest labour and make them strangers to the law courts and the poor hospital when they grew up (Friedrichs 1979:224; van Deursen 1978:58; Kagan 1974:19; Strauss 1978).

In addition to political order, enhanced social stability could be expected from the right sort of educational provision. The 1775 Austrian education commission envisaged elementary schooling raising a breed of 'citizen who was enlightened in accordance with his role in society' while the Parlement of Aix summarised the philosophy behind French charitable schools for the poor as that of providing 'an education which would make them useful to the public but without changing their status in society' (Becker-Cantarino 1977:41; Fairchilds 1976:88). Education for the masses was not a way of opening up avenues of social mobility but of preserving rank and degree in society by offering a training which would suit them for an appropriate role predetermined by their social origins.

Attitudes towards the place of ordinary people in the social hierarchy did not alter. However, a lively debate began in the later seventeenth century about the best means of achieving a loyal, obedient, pious and industrious population. During the eighteenth century the matter was the subject of informal discussion and formal debate by rulers and interested members of the elite: the landowners who made up the Tuscan *Accademia dei Georgofili,* for example. One camp asserted that a relatively extensive educational regime was the answer, the other that it was best to keep the masses in ignorance of anything except basic religious precepts. The debate hinged on the possibility that educating ordinary people could give them ideas above their station and could make them idle and discontented. The viewpoint of those who advocated a minimal education for the lower orders is summed up by the Englishman Bernard de Mandeville in his 1723 *Essay on charity and charity schools.* 'Reading, writing, and arithmetic are', he opined, 'very pernicious to the Poor ... Men who are to remain and end their days in a laborious, tiresome and painful station of life, the sooner they are put upon it at first, the more patiently they'll submit to it for ever after' (Watt 1972:42).

In the opposing camp were those who believed in the power of learning to elevate the minds of ordinary men to a level where they would share the attitudes of their betters. The Polish intellectual Poplawski enthused:

> Let us lead the peasants out of the gross darkness of ignorance by
> giving them the learning that is proper for them; certainly, as we

increase their willingness to work and make them more useful citizens of their country, so shall we make them better farmers when their reason, raised high as if awakened, will stimulate and whet their ability in every respect.   (Seidler 1977:343)

Like-minded individuals included Diderot in their ranks, but ranged against them were Voltaire, La Chalotais (a Breton magistrate who wrote extensively on the subject) and others. Importantly, nobody advocated an education which would treat middling and lower classes alike or which would do anything except conserve the existing social order (Trenard 1980; Chisick 1981).

Consensus about what was ultimately desirable for the masses was substantial. Utopian writers of the eighteenth century, able to depict their vision of a perfect society untempered by practical constraints, spoke of education controlled and funded by the state, geared to producing virtuous, upstanding individuals who would be loyal and useful members of society (Bridgman 1977:570–1). Concrete proposals often shared these emphases. Abbé Baudeau's educational plans offer an example of physiocratic thinking in the eighteenth century. His five social groups were to be found in five separate schools doing five different curricula. Heading the hierarchy were the princes at their colleges learning the principles of natural law, the rights of nations, history, political economy, mathematics, military sciences and modern languages; at its foot came the peasantry in their parish catechism schools. In fact and fiction alike, the projected schemes included everyone from the poor to the princes, the unifying principle being the sense of what was *appropriate* to the different classes of society. Spanish intellectuals of the seventeenth century urged that access to grammar schools should be restricted to the 'naturally superior' classes in order to fix the social order, and even the 'enlightened' leaders of eighteenth-century Spain tried to do the same (Grosperrin 1976:158; Kagan 1974:44, 47).

The concept of an appropriate training which would not upset the social apple-cart was not confined to the lower orders. It also informed attitudes towards the education of females throughout our period. Women's literacy was, as we shall see, everywhere inferior to that of males, a reality created by prevailing attitudes to the nature of the female sex and to what it was appropriate for them to learn. Men conventionally described females as intellectually and morally an inferior subset of humanity, endowed with less reason than men, easily influenced and thus in need of strong guidance. Women's place in society was as dutiful daughter, obedient wife, careful mother. If educated at all, girls were to receive a training which would prepare them for these roles. In the words of the Russian Commission for establishing public schools in 1783, 'the intent and the end of education for girls ... is to make them good housekeepers, true wives and trustworthy mothers' (Black 1979:163). Male aspirations for women are neatly summarised in the comments of Catherine the Great's adviser, Ivan Betskoi.

> We educate our daughters in reading, writing and diverse knowledge so that they can be useful citizens ... As mothers they will raise their children well. As wives they will fulfil their duties better. As grandmothers they will not fill their grandchildren with ignorant and superstitious tales about the devil and such. On the contrary their conversations will encourage worth [and] control passions.
>
> (Nash 1981:307)

These comments refer principally to women of the upper classes. Russia had its *Smol'nyi* institute from the 1760s, a glorified finishing school for gentlewomen. The refrain which runs through these comments is that women's education should enhance their social role and moral influence, rather than their academic potential. Mothers needed to be instructed in religion so that they could bring up their children to fear God, while religious and moral attitudes had to be instilled in servant girls who might otherwise infect the children of their noble and bourgeois employers with improper ideas.

The accepted attitude towards girls' education was not universally restrictive. Religious reformers took an interest in ensuring that women could read the same works as their spiritual equals. Erasmus wanted 'the weakest woman' to read the Gospels, equating them with such backward and heathen races as 'Scots and Irishmen ... Turks and Saracens', and pioneered, along with other Humanists such as Vives, a more sympathetic viewpoint on female capacities for learning (Millett 1976:561). Indeed, as early as the sixteenth century, some commentators took a more liberal view, though always within a conservative conception of women's place in society. The German Ambrosius Moibanus argued that girls were intellectually equipped to handle the same range of topics as boys, an idea which was followed up in the proposed 1574 *Jungfrauschulordnung* for the electorate of Brandenburg (Green 1979:98, 103). This outlook gathered strength in an increasing number of writings from the later seventeenth century. Rather than concentrating on training a housekeeper, nanny or ornament, writers such as Daniel Defoe advocated a broader education and the concept of wives as companions. Early English feminists like Mary Astell during the 1700s and Mary Wollstonecraft in the 1790s pointed to the circularity of the argument that women were inferior, therefore should not receive a full education, then using their poor educational standards to justify an opinion about their intellectual inferiority. The voice of women is rarely heard on this (or any other) subject, but the writings which do survive show a conservative emphasis: the German Anna Maria Schurman set out reasoned arguments for better educating women, but couched them in terms of a better preparation for their traditional roles.

Attitudes such as these determined the type of schooling which was available to girls. Schools for girls were essentially of two kinds: elementary ones similar to those for boys where work and basic literacy were the staple fare, and what might be called academies for girls but which were really finishing schools for the daughters of the upper bourgeoisie, gentry and nobility. Numerically, the former predominated. Indeed, most education for girls was in the lowest echelons of the school hierarchy. Only here was provision made on equal terms for boys and girls. The *grand chantre* of the cathedral chapter of Notre Dame in Paris controlled 334 elementary schools in 1789 of which 167 (exactly half) were for girls. At Lyon in the 1790s there were actually more petty schools for females than males: sixteen compared with eleven (Perrel 1980:79; Gutton 1970:471).

Boys and girls commonly sat together in the humblest schools. This was not altogether acceptable to the authorities who demanded segregation in the interests of morality and proper spiritual development. Spanish authorities laid increasing stress on this during the seventeenth century, and at all periods the older the children the stronger was the desire to divide classes according to gender. Girls' schools were not formally recognised by the authorities in Madrid until 1783. In charity boarding establishments for the poor, segregation was pursued obsessively by the administrators (Kagan 1974:27, 29; Fairchilds 1976:89). Separate education was provided for girls in Catholic countries by nuns. In rural parishes south of Lyon in France, the nuns of St Joseph set up groups comprising a handful of girls to teach them religion, housewifery and a little reading and writing. Indeed, at the lowest levels, educational provision for girls was sometimes more developed than for boys. Female religious orders proliferated in seventeenth-century France and some, though not all, took a keen interest in the education of poor girls: Ursulines, Béates, Filles de Notre Dame, Visitandines, Clarisses, Filles de la Croix, Soeurs de Nevers and many more. Grenoble, for example, had five 'free' schools, four convents and thirteen approved mistresses to teach girls compared with one 'free' school, a single *école des frères* and fourteen masters educating boys (Gutton 1970:475; Perrel 1980:75-9; Davis 1975:73).

The curriculum for girls was depressingly standardised across Europe. Religion, sewing, knitting, spinning, housekeeping, some reading and writing: such was the extent of education for the vast majority of girls. Beyond elementary learning, few ever progressed. Social and economic pressures might curtail their education as it did for their brothers, but so too did prevailing attitudes. Regulations for the English grammar school of Banbury (1594) forbade girls above the age of nine to attend, denying them any classical education, and girls were formally barred from the Latin and German grammar schools in seventeenth-century Braunschweig (Friedrichs 1982:374-5).

The proportion of girls who received *any* education was less than that of boys across most of Europe and throughout our period. A 1587 survey of Venetian schools recorded just twenty-eight girls in a total of 4,481 schoolchildren, and only 9 per cent of pupils in Russian state schools at the end of the eighteenth century were female. Of eligible boys, 62 per cent attended school in the Pyrenean diocese of Tarbes in the later eighteenth century; of eligible girls, a mere 2 per cent. The total of boys' schools in the Spanish region of Navarre outnumbered girls' by two to one in 1807. Attendance was less regular too: an Austrian report of 1781 on official schools in the Serbian and Rumanian provinces of the empire notes that half of boys at school were regular attenders compared with a quarter of girls (Alston 1969:19; Kagan 1974:29; Adler 1974:44). Attendance at school is discussed more fully below.

Attitudes to the education of girls were symptomatic of those towards the bulk of the population and informed the type of education given to those who attended the simplest schools of early modern Europe. The picture is not entirely gloomy. There are prominent, if atypical examples of women who transcended the limits imposed on them. And it is true that a higher proportion of girls were going to school in the eighteenth century than ever before. Less than one pupil in ten was female in the Polish diocese of Cracow during the early decades, but by 1792 the figure was 26 per cent (Litak 1973:65). There were almost no schools for girls in seventeenth-century Russia but again the situation improved during the eighteenth century. Yet, there were few opportunities for girls outside elite social circles to participate in educational advances in the 'secondary' sector, as we shall see in the following section on post-elementary education.

SECONDARY SCHOOLS

For the majority of children, schooling began and ended in the elementary schools which offered the basics of literacy. Some petty or elementary schools were only for the lower classes, but others were places where children of all social groups might associate. Boys and girls were present in approximately equal numbers even if they were segregated. Children were usually taught the 3Rs before entering a 'secondary' school. The situation in schools which went beyond basic instruction in reading, writing, religion and counting was different in important ways. The 'secondary' schools had more structured curricula and they were much more selective in terms of gender and social class. Girls were effectively, and sometimes explicitly, barred from the grammar schools and colleges of Europe and places were dominated by boys from the middling ranks in society. Most schools at this level contained some places for poor but gifted boys but these were few and far between. Again, the social composition and curriculum of these schools were dictated by prevailing social assumptions about the importance of education to different sections of society.

For the average parent, learning beyond the basics of religion and literacy for a son (still less a daughter) was an unthinkable luxury. Boys who did attend a 'secondary' school would probably have gone to one of the thousands of grammar schools dotted across Europe. In the fifteenth century in western Europe, Latin was taught principally in clerical schools but from the early sixteenth century new and more secular institutions modelled on Italian civic academies began to make their presence felt: the French municipal *collèges* and the German *Fürstenschulen* (Huppert 1984; Grafton & Jardine 1986). The core of the education which these provided was instruction in Latin grammar, literature and rhetoric, along with vernacular grammar and arithmetic. These schools were divided according to curriculum: the full *trivium* of Latin grammar, dialectic (formal logic and reasoning) and rhetoric (oral and written presentation) only being offered by elite institutions. Training was formal and literary.

In the countries of western Europe, Latin was the language of secondary education but in areas such as Muscovy higher learning was in Church Slavonic. In both cases the language was alien to everyday speech and was taught to a minority as an elite discipline. Examples from the Ukraine during the seventeenth century illustrate the sort of curricula which were offered. Grammar schools in this Polish dependency were principally funded by the church and urban religious confraternities. Prominent among these was the Lvov school, set up in 1586 and offering, at various stages in its development, Latin and Polish grammar, philosophy, theology, drama, music, arithmetic, dialectics and geometry. Moscow grammar school taught 66 of its 232 pupils Greek and the remainder Church Slavonic grammar in 1686; a year later it was remodelled into the *Slaviano-Greko-Latinskoe Uchilishche* which offered more variety. Spanish grammar schools were known as *Colegios* or *Escuelas de Gramática*, teaching grammar based on a late fifteenth-century text by Nebrija, Latin literature, religion, history, geography, mathematics, philosophy and rhetoric (Kagan 1974:31). The classical curriculum on offer across western Europe was fairly homogeneous though the precise range of topics within it, and indeed additional subjects, depended on the availability of teachers. Arithmetic was only taught at the Skálholt grammar school in Iceland for ten years of the seventeenth century during the residence of a master gnostic of its secrets (Hermannsson 1958:xxii).

The central importance of the grammar schools in early modern education and society lay in the classical curriculum they offered. Latin was *the* language of learning over all of Europe except for the eastern regions influenced by Muscovite, Byzantine traditions. It was used extensively in the law and the church, and it created a bond between those trained in its language and literature. In sixteenth-century Ireland it was used by clergy, scholars and nobility to correspond with each other and with their peers abroad. In Spain, Latin brought status and prestige to those with knowledge of it. And even in the revamped universities of eighteenth-century Germany, where vernacular teaching was becoming more common, a formal dissertation in Latin remained a central part of the examination process (Evans 1981:181–2).

Latin continued to be a passport to culture and status, but its importance declined during the early modern period. Ferdinand I's administrative reforms of the mid-sixteenth century involved a replacement of Latin with German in the courts of justice of Inner Austria, a development which had already taken place in Francis I's France. Agricultural literature followed the same trend as developments in administration. Reprints of ancient writings by Vergil and Pliny were in Latin, but 84 per cent of all new publications on farming and gardening during the sixteenth century were in modern languages (Burian 1970–1:84; Beutler 1973:1298–1300). The timing of this change differed across Europe but it was fastest between *c.*1650 and *c.*1750. Scottish and English secondary schools moved away from a classical, religious curriculum from the end of the seventeenth century and towards practical, secular training. This increasingly practical emphasis in education dates from the later seventeenth century as parents began to demand more vocational training for their sons and, as in the southern Netherlands, to boycott guild schools with their archaic curricula. The Danish school law of 1739 formalised this development by abolishing more than half the existing Latin schools (Dixon 1958:25).

Yet, we should not exaggerate the speed with which change occurred. The decline of Latin grammar schools in England after 1660 was only relative, the result of a growing number of non-classical and dissenting academies. Larger, more fashionable grammar schools survived and prospered as did those which adapted their curricula to new demands (O'Day 1982:196–216). Use of Latin as a comunications medium also persisted. Polish might be a literary language as early as the sixteenth century, but Latin continued to be used for theological treatises until the eighteenth. Latin obfuscation of legal proceedings was removed for a time in England in the 1650s but was restored in 1660 and not finally removed until 1733. Inventories of 100 Dutch theologians, scholars, lawyers and government officials who died in 1700 show that most learned books were still in Latin. It was only after the 1680s that the majority of books in the Frankfurt and Leipzig fair catalogues were in German. As an institutionalised medium of communication for education and politics, Latin survived in Hungary until the eighteenth century, and in Croatia and Slavonia until the nineteenth century (Tazbir 1982:52; Thomas 1986:101; Gibbs 1971:333; Kamen 1984:214; Kessler 1976).

Secondary education was funded by charity, civic treasuries, taxation of landowners, religious confraternities, the state, parental fees and by the various churches of early modern Europe. From their foundation in the middle of the sixteenth century to their forced dissolution in the 1760s and 1770s, the most powerful single force in post-elementary education was the Jesuit order. It is impossible to overestimate the importance of this dedicated order, for their methods, their schools and their example pervaded educational practice not only in Catholic countries but even in Protestant lands where they were illegal.

Jesuit colleges flourished in all the countries of Catholic Europe from the 1560s onwards. As early as 1559 they took over the 'liberal arts' university of Évora in Portugal. Seven new colleges were opened in Lithuania between 1580 and 1585, there were twenty in adjacent Ruthenia in 1620 and by 1630 somewhere in the region of 10,000 pupils had passed through Jesuit schools in the Polish kingdom. Between 10,000 and 15,000 boys a year went through Jesuit schools in Spain, and by the early eighteenth century one boy in every three who received any kind of schooling obtained it with the Society of Jesus. The Jesuits could boast more than a hundred academies in Italy by 1600 and the one at Padua taught nearly 1,000 students: five times the size of the arts faculty of the city's university (Martel 1938:225–8; Kagan 1974:51–8; 1986:174). When a school had to be revived, a backward region enlightened or a 'lost' land like Bohemia recovered for the faith, the Jesuits were the specialists for the job. The French *collège* at Amiens was gingered up by the Jesuits in the 1590s and the 1570s bishop Vilém Prusinovský called them in to found an academy at Olmütz in Moravia (central Europe), an establishment which quickly received the title of a university from the pope (Labarre 1971:17; Evans 1974:3–5). The French municipal *collèges* set up in the sixteenth century resisted Jesuit infiltration and control until the seventeenth century, but in some areas of Europe the terms secondary school and Jesuit school were synonymous: the *comté* of Nice before the reforms of Victor Amadeus II in 1729, for instance (Huppert 1984; Féliciangéli 1980).

The system of education which prevailed in most continental grammar schools, colleges and academies was that which originated in Renaissance Italy and was perfected by the Jesuits during the first century of their existence. Poland/Lithuania provides an example of the system in operation at its three main levels. The most basic schools offered five or six years of classes and were comparable with an English grammar school. Examples of such gymnasia included Lublin, Jarosław, Riga and Dorpat, though the last two had no rhetoric classes. Boys lived in a closed community under strict rules. The subjects they learned were of less importance for their intrinsic value than for the intellectual discipline of learning to speak and write in Latin about set topics relating to antiquity. The first six years of Jesuit education were spent in this fashion. 'Philosophy' – the formal, medieval, scholastic kind coupled with some mathematics and science – came only after this basic training and then only in some colleges. This marked the second level of college, whose philosophy courses provided logic in the first year, maths and physics in the second, ethics and metaphysics (where available) in the third. Complete colleges such as Vilna (made into an academy in 1578) and Poznań additionally offered theology courses (Litak 1978; Grafton & Jardine 1986).

Religion, humility and debating skills were to be the end product.

Jesuit activities covered all areas of life. In sixteenth-century Seville they not only provided formal schooling but also ran classes for actors who were to convey the message of the revived Catholic faith through the medium of dramatised religious plays. Their schools and colleges were usually free and the standard of teachers very high (Bailey 1977:106–7; Perry 1980:17). Jesuit methods were held in such esteem that Orthodox parents in Poland were happy to send their sons to the Catholic schools, while the illegal and clandestine Jesuit Latin school at Gouda in the Dutch Republic was even attended by the sons of Calvinist clergymen (Martel 1938:229–30; Van der Laan 1977:279).

The Jesuits were by no means the only religious order involved in education. In France, the second most important order was that of the Oratorians with some 400 teachers in 1762: one third the Jesuit total. In Hungary the Dominicans, Benedictines, Franciscans, Minorites and Promontors played their part. Indeed, during the eighteenth century, other religious groups became increasingly important. Jesuit education at this time was becoming more and more outdated, their religious and classical curriculum losing ground to new demands from parents and the state for practical, technological and secular training. Because of their loyalty to church and papacy rather than to secular authority, the Jesuits were becoming increasingly anachronistic to the developed absolutist states of eighteenth-century Europe. They had often come under attack from Protestants in the past: in Transylvania the Unitarians pioneered a takeover of Jesuit schools (including the college at Kolozsvár) following the Order's early expulsion from the area in 1603. In the eighteenth century, elements of Catholic opinion too began to cast doubt on their place in the church. New groups more suited to the changing intellectual climate flourished from the end of the seventeenth century, among them the Piarists and the Lutheran Pietists. In Poland and the Austrian territories these both stimulated Jesuit colleges, founded their own and, when the Jesuits were finally expelled, took over many of their institutions. However, the state campaigns of the eighteenth century were much more damaging. In some countries such as Italy the proscription of the Society of Jesus was a serious blow, albeit tempered both by the existence of other orders – the Summists and Barnabites took over in Parma, for example – and the drift of ousted Jesuit teachers back into their former posts under new guises. The university of Évora in Portugal was shut down in 1759 when the Jesuits left but was reopened with new statutes in 1772 (Doyle 1978:205–7; Evans 1979:133; Litak 1978:135–7; Marques 1972:414).

Alongside the *collèges* at the top of the hierarchy of 'secondary' education came the academies. One example from Ukraine in the seventeenth century is fairly typical. The Mohyla academy at Kiev, modelled on that at Cracow, had its own halls of residence and feeder schools. It offered a course of education lasting eight to twelve years, beginning with grammar and working up through rhetoric, history and geography to philosophy and theology in stages of one to three years' study. Some academies and colleges were glorified grammar schools, notably the lesser municipal *collèges* of France which often taught only the rudiments of Latin and French grammar, and many of the institutions in eastern Europe; others offered more specific training. Military schools are perhaps the best example of the latter. Venice had a training school for officers in the early seventeenth century but the first large military academy was founded in Savoy in 1677, the next of importance being at Berlin (1717). Those in Russia taught foreign languages, geometry, history, geography along with some residual trappings of the gentleman soldier such as dancing, heraldry and fencing. Russian technical training under Peter the Great was directly related to the needs of war with the Ottoman empire and Sweden. Mathematics at the Moscow academy was taught from Leontii Magnitskii's *Arifmetika* (1703), a text central to the whole educational programme in the school. All education there was practical and specific rather than theoretical: geography was in fact maps and surveying, astronomy was treated as the equivalent of celestial navigation. From 1731 the military academies were reserved for sons of the gentry and graduates could walk straight into a commission in the forces without any other experience (Alston 1969:8; Doyle 1978:244; Okenfuss 1973).

Academies throughout Europe were explicitly designed to defend aristocratic privilege and perpetuate their dominance of society. Some boasted curricula which were the equal of full-blown universities: for example, the Prussian *Ritterakademien* (knights' academies) of the eighteenth century. In France, students who wished to study arts subjects, notably philosophy, had, until the middle of the sixteenth century, to attend a university. Thereafter, humanist influence, a changing social environment and the competition between Catholic and Protestant stimulated the foundation in most major towns of local colleges where youths could follow a curriculum similar to that offered by university arts faculties (Brockliss 1978:517; McClelland 1980; Huppert 1984).

The more dynamic side of the academies represented in Germany contrasts forcefully with the stagnation of the Tuscan institutions during the seventeenth and much of the eighteenth centuries. These were not really teaching institutions. Described by one authority as 'clubs of upper-class dilettantes devoted to things cultural', Tuscan academies before the Enlightenment went out of their way to avoid involvement in current intellectual affairs and preferred to retain the 'flaccid obscurantism' of set intellectual forms which had survived from the fifteenth-century 'golden age' of thought. Like the Portuguese *Academias,* including John V's 1720 Royal Academy of History, or the British Academy, these were elite clubs with funds and presses rather than colleges on the French or German model (Chojnacki 1974:537–40; Carrato 1977:359). The term 'academy' could cover a wide range of institutions: in England, an academy was the rough equivalent of a grammar school.

Academies and colleges which concentrated on the classics were only to a limited extent vocational training centres with specific careers in mind for their pupils in the church, the law, the army or civil service. Even in the specialist military or other colleges, vocational aspects could blend with socialisation in the ways of the gentleman or the haut bourgeois, diluting the purely technical training. This was less the case in certain specialist vocational establishments, and especially in places which taught the skills of buying and selling. Sixteenth-century Florence had its abacus schools in which future merchants learned how to trade cloth, how to convert one currency into another for exchange purposes and how to tackle the dozens of different weights and measures in use across Europe. One Venetian school which taught arithmetic and double-entry book-keeping boasted 143 pupils in 1587. In the seventeenth century this powerful, independent city-state had schools for civil lawyers and notaries, courses in Greek and Turkish for merchants' sons, colleges of naval architecture and design. *Scuoli d'Abbaco* (abacus schools) in Renaissance Florence were in fact elementary commercial schools offering courses in exchange rates, interest calculations, contract and partnership law, weights and measures (Goldthwaite 1972).

Indeed, the other valuable skill for international traders was linguistic. Sailors, skippers, merchants and dockers at great ports such as Antwerp, Genoa and London must have picked up foreign languages from visitors. Boys could also receive formal instruction. Francesco Scudieri of Cremona, son of a cloth merchant, gave his occupation as 'man of letters who teaches music and Italian language to Germans and other northeners' (MacKenney 1987:183). Along the Baltic coast, enterprising Dutchmen set up specialist language schools to cash in on the growing demand for command of foreign tongues which had been generated by the expansion of international trade. Jan van Deelen ran a French school at Danzig in the 1590s to teach boys practical skills in that language, such as how to count, prepare invoices, bargain, solve delivery problems, make out receipts and deal with the customs. Van Deelen drew on a long tradition of such schools in the Low Countries, and during the seventeenth century many more were set up in the Baltic cities: Toruń and Elblag, for instance (Grobelak 1979:176–80). Merchants needed arithmetic for accounts, currency transactions, weights and measures; geography to estimate distance and insurance; foreign languages to bypass the need for middle men; writing for orders and accounts.

The eighteenth century saw a proliferation of these vocational schools. A surprising number of eighteenth-century Dutch communities had 'evening-classes', running from 4pm to 7pm on winter evenings in the countryside, later in the towns, where working youths could attend when their duties as apprentice or servant were done. Boys were in the majority (de Booy 1980a:267). Peter the Great's garrison schools *(Garnizonnye Shkoly)* were part of his campaign for the modernisation of Russia, teaching officers' sons reading, writing and mathematics but with a military slant. He set up mining schools at Olonets (1716) and Ekaterinburg (1721) to train men for state armaments and later private industries (Kahan 1985:153; Keep 1985:201–4).

In Italy the eighteenth century witnessed an expansion and formalisation of technical education. Except for Venice, technical instruction had been handled by individual guilds but when these began to decline some of the more enterprising states of the north started to provide vocational training in geography, geometry, maths, navigation and modern languages as an alternative to the traditional classical curriculum (Ricuperati & Roggero 1977:255–8). Italy was a leader in this field. Technical education developed only slowly in France before the nineteenth century, two notable exceptions being the *Ecole des Ponts et Chaussées* (1744) and the *Ecole des Constructeurs de Navires* (1763). Most countries latched on to the idea of technical education from the later eighteenth century. Portugal's schools for nautical and commercial studies began to appear in earnest from the third quarter of the eighteenth century, though clearly building on three centuries during which a huge volume of practical experience had been built up (Marques 1972:414). Denmark's school laws of 1814 included a provision for classes in vocational skills at the urban *borgerskoler*. All these institutions had a hard, practical purpose. Not so the artistic school founded by the Lithuanian court treasurer Antonio Tyzenhauz, a philanthropist who took serf children aged eight to ten and employed foreign teachers to instruct them in dancing, music and the ballet. In the early 1780s, sixteen girls and eighteen boys spent half of the day in these endeavours, the rest of the time being devoted to more traditional scholastic areas such as needlework and French for the girls, writing and arithmetic for the boys (Mamontowicz-Łojek 1968).

The importance of the grammar schools and *collèges* lay in three areas. First, they provided a training in skills which could be directly useful in obtaining a job as an official of church or state. Humanist literary, non-vocational education opened up careers in diplomacy, government service, the clergy and education. The ability to speak eloquently and without rehearsal in classical Latin, and to read, write and teach it were viewed with approval by employers looking for obedient and self-disciplined accumulators, classifiers and regurgitators of material. Classical education had few explicit employment goals but it strongly presupposed certain destinations for its young men (Grafton & Jardine 1986:23–4). The more practical and non-classical institutions of the late seventeenth century onwards equipped boys to enter commerce or the military or the developing professions. Second, by concentrating on the classics, traditional grammar schools enabled young men to participate in international scholarship and, by assimilating a uniform set of values and information, to become members of a social and cultural elite. In fifteenth-century Italy and sixteenth-century England advanced education for what was a small minority of pupils was aimed at 'the production of a small, politically active minority who were heirs to a mature foreign culture, and who were thereby hallmarked as of the requisite moral and intellectual calibre to make substantial contributions to their own developing communities' (Grafton & Jardine 1986:220). Classical education was a seal of cultural approval and could be an end in itself as well as a means to an end. In Muscovy, training in Church Slavonic grammar and literature performed a similar function. Third, the schools afforded qualifications for entry into establishments of higher education. The systematic reorganisation and secularisation of education in the eighteenth century will be dealt with later.

WHERE WERE THE SCHOOLS?

Across Europe the early modern period saw an important shift from restricted to widespread, if not universal, literacy. Population increase, economic growth, social change, the development of the nation state, Reformation and Counter-Reformation, the intellectual currents of the Renaissance and the Enlightenment: all served to stimulate the demand for reading, writing and counting. Associated with this change was a marked increase in educational facilities. New schools were created and existing ones enlarged, the pool of educational resources expanding so widely as to merit the title 'educational revolution' conferred on England for the century *c*.1540–1640 by Lawrence Stone (Stone 1964). Stone's work on England has been emulated and extended in other countries to reveal a remarkable rise in documented schooling. Developments in Stone's century built on an existing medieval tradition of schooling and was therefore an acceleration of a trend rather than a completely new departure. Schooling at all levels had been present in the late medieval period but, under the impact of the dynamic forces of the sixteenth century, educational provision expanded rapidly. The pace of change, glacial in some parts of Europe (such as Muscovy), approached a torrent in others. Württemberg had 512 communities with just 50 schools in 1534 but 270 by 1581. At least 410 new schools, mostly endowed grammar, were established in England between 1480 and 1660, but in reality the figure is probably double this if we take into account the fee-paying schools which taught Latin among their subjects (Stone 1964:42–7). More than twenty new colleges were founded in Portugal's main towns in the 1530s and 1540s. Of 271 French *collèges* in existence in 1789, 53 per cent had been founded before 1600 and 74 per cent before 1650 (Marques 1972:195; Chartier *et al.* 1976:186). In some areas the trend began later or was continued longer. Bremen in 1638 had four parish schools and twenty-six *Winkelschulen* but by 1716 there were thirty-nine 'corner schools' and in 1788 about a hundred; the first *Armenschule* was founded in 1705 for poor children (Engelsing 1973:48). English universities too doubled their intake between *c*.1550 and *c*.1640 and the Inns of Court, legal training centres, also flourished. All but the very poorest classes were able to benefit.

Stone's arguments have proved highly influential in our under-standing of early modern schooling but there are a number of qualifications as well as amplifications to be made. Estimates of the availability of schooling in different parts of Europe are fraught with difficulties. The offical enquiries by church and state into the plantation of schools used specific but differing criteria of what a school actually was. Some investigations sought to identify the presence of a teacher, and might treat anyone at all qualified to instruct as such – minister or church assistant, for instance, in Norwegian dioceses; concern might be with the provision of a salary or the presence of a building which could be designated a school; a final category of investigation was interested only in schools which taught certain subjects, usually Latin. Surviving records certainly underestimate the number of schools which existed in some form or another, and discriminate against areas where traditions of informal, seasonal and peripatetic teaching were strong: the Dauphiné of France, for example. The French diocese of Tarbes on the eve of the French Revolution illustrates the potential for distortion which can occur. In lowland parts, 69 per cent of parishes had a fixed school, 5 per cent a peripatetic school and 26 per cent none at all. For valleys the figures are 40 per cent, 24 per cent and 36 per cent, while for mountain areas (the diocese was partly in the Pyrenees) they are 11 per cent, 5 per cent and 84 per cent (Chartier *et al.* 1976:25). Mountain areas would come out badly whichever criterion we adopted, but the valley/ lowland divide, substantial in terms of fixed schools, is much less obvious if we take travelling teachers into account.

Great care is therefore needed when comparing figures on the number of schools in different areas. One authority asserts that England around 1600 had one school for every 10,000 people whereas the German duchy of Württemberg, with 401 folk schools in 512 communities, had a ratio of one per 1,100 (Green 1979:93). This comparison is not valid since the English figures refer to grammar schools and the German ones to all types of (mainly vernacular) institution. What is more, the English figure is a substantial underestimate: a figure of 1 : 4,000 or better would be closer to the truth (Stone 1964:44). Despite this, it is possible to derive some idea of the relative availability of formal education in regions of Europe and to distinguish between the environments which helped and hindered schooling. Local and regional variations were substantial but, in general, towns were more favoured than rural areas and lowland more than upland zones; Protestant countries usually had more schools per head of population than Catholic; north-western Europe (except Scandinavia) was better endowed than the Mediterranean world and eastern Europe.

In all parts of Europe, urban environments boasted superior educational provision. Antwerp had 150 schools of all kinds in the mid-sixteenth century, Ghent had forty (twelve of them grammar schools), Flushing six and Veere (with a population of only 2,000) three. Breda could claim fourteen teachers, Tournai eleven and

Poperinghe seven (Parker 1979:21). Venice at the end of the sixteenth century had 250 teachers in a population of 135,000 and Milan, which was much smaller, 120 schools of various sorts. The Venetian figure of one teacher for every 135 males aged twenty or younger is superior to that of Lyon in the 1550s and 1560s where the ratio is 1 : 400, though the figure of thirty-eight masters excludes those at the Latin *Collège de la Trinité* (Davis 1975:209). The concentration of schools, especially secondary ones, in towns is illustrated by the case of Spain. By 1600 there were 4,000 grammar schools and most towns of more than 500 households had one. Rural areas languished not only in provision but also attendance. A census of Latin grammar schools in the 1760s revealed that villages of less than 100 residents *(vecinos)*, in which half of Castile's population lived, contributed only 10 per cent of the pupils; 44 per cent came from towns of 1,000 *vecinos* or more (Kagan 1974:42, 47–8).

Schooling was more widely available in towns and cities than in the countryside. In three Polish dioceses during the mid-seventeenth century, two-thirds of urban parishes had schools, compared with half of rural communities. A century later the bishop of Cracow's visitation of 753 parishes in Little Poland revealed figures of 61 per cent and 27 per cent respectively (Olczak 1974:325; Litak 1973:47–8). A more extreme profile exists for Scandinavian countries. Denmark's church ordinance on education of 1539 makes no mention of rural schools, asking parents to instruct in the home instead (Dixon 1958:13). In Finland, virtually all schools of any consequence were in towns. The same is true of Sweden, where an enquiry of 1768, prompted by the clergyman Schlüter's private scheme for parish schools, showed the imbalance. Sweden had 2,216 parishes at this time, almost all firmly rural. Excluding Stockholm and the island of Gotland (on which all 92 parishes had schools), there were 165 settled rural schools (75 privately endowed, the rest parish-funded) plus a further 100 ambulatory schools where the master went from farm to farm and hamlet to hamlet staying for two or three weeks in each. All sixty of the main towns had schools, some two, but only an eighth of rural parishes could claim one (Barton 1977:529, 536). Prussia in 1800 had 11,000 village schoolteachers, Paris in the 1780s had 500 primary schools for half a million people (Engelsing 1973:74).

Differences also existed between rural areas, notably between upland and lowland regions. In 1814, 92 per cent of the 400 parishes in the densely settled diocese of Lund in southern Sweden had schools whereas there were hardly any in the thinly-peopled northern diocese of Härnösand (Barton 1977:536). The problems faced by upland communities are neatly summarised in James McParlan's 1802 *Statistical Survey of the County of Donegal* in Ireland.

> The state of education in the mountain regions is much more backward than in any other part of Ireland that I am acquainted with; in the remote and sequestered glens, the inhabitants, being only few and scattered, and unable to employ teachers, are indeed in a very degrading state of ignorance.

Poverty and dispersed population militated against the extensive provision of fixed schools, though the example of the Hautes Alpes of south-eastern France shows that these drawbacks did not necessarily mean an ignorant population since literacy there was higher than in neighbouring lowland zones (Vovelle 1975). Just a half of villages in some western parts of Brandenburg (1801-3) had a sexton or other person who could act as a teacher - Arendsee and Salzwedel, for instance - while some central provinces reported that every parish had such a man (Neugebauer 1985:270).

One of the great themes which runs through historical writing on education is that Protestantism and schooling are connected. Luther, Calvin and the other revolutionaries who broke the mould of medieval Christendom after 1517 shared the belief that the Bible was the sole source of truth and that each individual Christian should have access to the Word of God through the Scriptures. Luther changed his views on education during the 1520s. He ceased to believe that private Bible reading was the best way of spreading the Reformation to individual believers in the way he wanted and instead advocated the expert guidance which could be provided by pastors and the central role of the catechism in promoting religious understanding (Gawthrop & Strauss 1984:34-5). However, for many reformers the way to a godly life and indeed salvation itself was by reading. Protestant communities would therfore be more likely to wish to educate their children than traditional Catholic ones, and would create schools to do so. A correlation would therefore exist between the confessional leanings of a region, country or community and the availability of schooling.

There is a considerable measure of truth in this argument. The advent of the Reformed faith had a direct (if delayed) impact on the expansion of education in Protestant countries such as Scotland and Sweden; the influence of the Pietists coupled with state action catapulted Prussian society into mass literacy during the eighteenth century; and in regions where Catholics and Protestants were in competition for the hearts and minds of the people, the dynamism of Protestant educational provision enervated Catholic schooling.

Examples of the stimulus provided by Protestantism are not far to seek. By the end of the seventeenth century, the largest concentration of Protestants in France was to be found in the south-east: Rhone, Privas, Vernoux, Cévennes, Causses. In the upland parts of this region, Protestant communities almost always had a school whereas these were much thinner on the ground in Catholic towns and villages. Protestants were apparently more successful than Catholics in overcoming constraints of distance and poverty. The lowland areas were uniformly better provided with schools though, interestingly, in all parts Catholic communities adjacent to Protestant ones had better educational provision and higher literacy. A similar 'emulation effect' is evident in eastern Europe. The first Protestant school in Poland was established at Pincòw near Cracow in 1551, and most of the early foundations were Calvinist. Dioceses such as Poznań, which had a number of Protestant schools, enjoyed superior Catholic schooling thanks to the force of competition: some Catholics were prepared to send their sons to Protestant schools, despite official opposition. Further east still, the challenge of Catholicism stimulated reorganisation of Russian Orthodox education in the same way (Laget 1971:1416–17; Vovelle 1975:135; Martel 1938:214–17; Litak 1973:50, 57).

Before being carried away by the educational dynamism of the Protestants, we should recognise that the developments we have outlined were not irreversible and could be matched by the powerful forces which carried the Catholic or Counter-Reformation to the states of Europe. Protestant schools in Poland and the Ukraine were commonly sited near the castles of their protectors rather than in the important centres of population where the Jesuits placed their colleges. Indeed, the Protestant schools suffered damaging competition from Jesuit foundations at Vilna, Polotsk, Niasviz, Orsa, Pinsk, Vitebsk and Brest after 1569. The dynamic Jesuits had fourteen colleges in the province of Poland in 1608 and a further eleven in Lithuania; by 1756 these figures had risen to thirty-nine and twenty-eight respectively (Litak 1978:126). Nor was the effect of the Reformation always immediate and dynamic. In Prussia and Denmark it was not the Lutheran Reformation of the early sixteenth century which brought about widespread literacy but the Pietist campaign of the early eighteenth century (Dixon 1958:14, 18; Gawthrop & Strauss 1984).

The crucial question here is what would have happened if

Protestantism had *not* been present? The answer to this is less simple than we might at first suppose. First of all, educational provision in some Catholic parts of Europe was at least as good as Protestant, notably north-eastern France and the towns of northern Italy. The Jesuit schools of Pomerania were as good as Protestant ones in the area at the end of the sixteenth century and it is clear that the religious complexion of a region was not the only factor influencing schooling. In Protestant parts of south-eastern France, school provision and attendance were far inferior to Catholic areas of mainly Protestant Baden in Germany (Maynes 1979:614). Second, the Reformation did not suddenly create schools in places where none had existed before. In Scotland, England and Poland, a strong tradition of schooling had existed well before the Reformation. It took the Scottish Calvinists the best part of a century to get their parish school system going. Literacy might be low in fifteenth and early sixteenth-century Europe, but schools were far from absent. Third, the power of Protestantism could be a mixed blessing and competition between faiths could damage education. After the rising of 1641, Irish Catholic schools were persecuted by the Protestant, English establishment. Catholic parents could only send their sons to Protestant schools where they were treated as second-class citizens and evangelised by teachers who subscribed to an alien faith. As early as 1596 Bishop Lyon of Cork reported that while parents were happy to have their boys taught English, a Protestant education was not acceptable. He also recorded suspicious circumstances concerning grammar books, pages of which announcing the Elizabethan supremacy had been ripped out 'although they came new from the merchants' shops' (Moody 1976:137–40). The impact of Protestantism in such an environment was negative, making Catholics less literate than they might otherwise have been. The same is true of Catholics who lived in the Protestant province of Utrecht, subject as their schools were to proscription by dogmatic Calvinist authorities. Faced with a choice between a Protestant education and none at all, some parents chose the latter course (de Booy 1977:353–4).

The ratio of school places to the numbers of eligible children varied enormously between different parts of Europe, between town and country, and according to the gender of the child. Eastern and southern Europe were less favoured than the north and west, but even within these broad distinctions there were differences between, for example, the north and south of Spain, or between upland and lowland parts of Languedoc. Except for Denmark and southern Sweden, the Scandinavian countries had virtually no formal schools until the nineteenth century. One child in five of those aged seven to fourteen received schooling at Copenhagen in 1791 but the rural position was far worse (Dixon 1958:32).

We can illustrate the range of experience of educational growth by contrasting England during the sixteenth and seventeenth centuries with some of the states of eastern and central Europe in the eighteenth. England experienced two main phases of school creation. The first was during the reigns of Elizabeth I and James I and was principally a phenomenon of the southern and eastern counties which at that time were the richest and most economically developed. The second period of expansion came at the end of the seventeenth century and beginning of the eighteenth. Between 1698 and 1723 some 1,329 charity schools were set up, and in the four decades before 1740 one third of all the schools not providing a classical education in 1818 were created (Tompson 1977:74). In Russia, initiatives by the state during the 1780s produced the first significant increase in schooling: 8 public schools in 1782, 269 in 1790 and 315 by 1800, the number of teachers rising from 26 to 790 during the same period (Black 1979:149). One community in ten had a school in late seventeenth-century Moravia and in the province of Upper Austria in the Habsburg monarchy were to be found 303 schools with 12,900 pupils in 1774 but 410 and 19,300 just a decade later. In Sweden only 10–15 per cent of rural parishes had a school in 1768 but by 1814 at least 45 per cent possessed one (Okey 1986:25; O'Brien 1970:561; Barton 1977:536).

Just as the timing and rate of expansion were uneven across Europe, so too were the fortunes of different types of school. Most obvious is the fact that advances in education for boys had almost invariably to precede those for girls. The German duchy of Brandenburg is a case in point. From 1500–39 its 102 towns had fifty-five boys' schools in all, but only four for girls. Between 1540 and 1572 the number of boys' schools had risen to seventy-eight, the girls' to just nine. The steady expansion of educational provision for male children continued to the end of the century when there were 100 schools. But it was between 1573 and 1600 that a huge leap in the number of girls' schools took place: up five-fold to forty-five (Green 1979:106). At the same time, expansion of education for girls was not usually accompanied by improvements in the quality and scope of their learning. Specialist Russian institutes such as the *Smol'nyi* were set up only to create a better class of traditional noble woman. Girls might receive training in French, but it was to make them appear socially more accomplished rather than to fit them for a career, unless that of wife. Fathers were enjoined to keep a close watch on what their daughters read, some eighteenth-century German periodicals listing special *Frauenzimmerbibliotheken.*

The process of educational advance was cumulative in most cases. Halting, uneven and slow it might be, but one generation was usually able to build on the achievements of its predecessors. However, progress was not uniform, and it was not irreversible. Schools opened by the Jesuits in the towns of south-west Ireland in the 1560s had closed down by the 1580s thanks to religious and political opposition to their presence. Warfare and disease were the most common causes of disclocation. Mostly the reverses were temporary, as was the case in the Netherlands during the duke of Alva's attempt to suppress the Dutch revolt between 1567 and 1573 or during the Russian occupation of Finland in 1717 when many buildings were burned down and one teacher resorted to carving an ABC book into the trunk of a tree so that he could continue lessons in the forest out of sight (Whittaker1984:16). Fighting between Russia, Poland and Sweden, which raged through parts of Byelorussia in the years 1654 to 1667, seriously damaged the few schools which existed in the region, a setback from which they never recovered. Civil war and plague in Transylvania (1657–60) decimated schooling: some buildings were destroyed, others had their libraries dispersed. One of the two Icelandic grammar schools, that at Skálholt, was destroyed by an earthquake in 1784.

Less spectacular, but potentially much more damaging, was a creeping erosion of educational advances by poverty and apathy. Industrial development and population increase in the towns of north-east France, England, Scotland and northern Germany from the end of the eighteenth century strained educational resources and in some cases caused them to contract. The number of petty schools at Bremen fell from around 100 in 1788 to sixty in 1810 because children were working in tobacco processing and could not attend day schools. A rise in evening and Sunday classes could only partly compensate for the social and educational problems caused by early industrialisation (Engelsing 1973:70). Ecclesiastical visitation records show that most Polish parishes had a school of some sort in the late sixteenth and early seventeenth centuries, but that by the third quarter of the eighteenth century clerical disinterest, wars and economic depression had produced substantial deterioration in some areas, notably the outlying parts of Little Poland. If we compare the dioceses of Poznań, Pszczew and Srem in the mid-seventeenth century with the period of the national education commission (1777–84), we see that in Poznań the number of parishes with schools stagnated at 49 per cent, in Pszczew it fell from 70 to 62 per cent and in Srem there was a modest rise from 51 to 60 per cent (Wiśniowski & Litak 1974:321-2; Olczak 1974:325-6). Poland had enjoyed an expansion of education contemporaneous with that in much of England between *c.*1575 and *c.*1625 but had been unable to sustain it on a national level. Developments in schooling tended to be episodic. Jesuit schools in Poland saw their most dynamic phase between *c.*1560 and 1648 but, after the peace of Westphalia, military, economic and social changes combined with the problems of recruitment to the order to usher in a period of stagnation. This lasted until the 1740s when Stanislaw Konarski's Piarist reformers stimulated the Jesuits to renewed efforts which were prematurely terminated by the dissolution of the order in 1773. At their lowest point, in 1710 during the Great Northern War, the number of Jesuit teachers in Lithuania fell from the 1700 level of 126 to 91 (Litak 1978).

NATIONAL LITERACY CAMPAIGNS

The expansion of schooling during the early modern period was attributable mainly to piecemeal measures taken by individuals or by small groups such as village communes. Charles Démia's work in the Lyon area during the seventeenth century is a well-known example. This is not to say that there was no attempt at regulation by national bodies. On the contrary, the early modern period witnessed many initiatives by the church and, increasingly, the state to control, extend and structure the provision of education. Efforts to supervise the training of children were made throughout the centuries from the Renaissance to the Industrial Revolution, and can be categorised both by period and intention. During the sixteenth century the principal drive came from a desire for religious conformity whether in the bounds of a nation state or within a principality or even a single town. During the eighteenth century the overwhelming aim was to assert state control over education, provide resources for it and, in Catholic countries, to fill the gap created by the suppression of the Jesuits. All parts of Europe were touched by developments during these two centuries, but the seventeenth century was a period of comparative stagnation except in Scotland and some of the Scandinavian countries. The methods used were diverse but the goals were surprisingly homogeneous. Running through all these efforts was a strongly authoritarian attitude to learning which was intolerant of diversity and which viewed education principally as a tool of order and improvement at a societal level rather than as a force for enhancing individual development.

Early attempts to structure education and to extend its provision as widely as possible in society were initiated largely by the church. Driven by the religious changes of the sixteenth century, Protestant and Catholic hierarchies alike sought to regulate what was taught in schools and to ensure that their message reached the ears of impressionable youth. Church constitutions of the Protestant principalities of Germany required each pastor to possess a Bible and to ensure that children were taught the elements of religious knowledge. Ecclesiastical authorities envisaged that the parish clergy would educate boys and girls, and thus took a keen interest in what was being taught and by whom. As early as 1480 the synod of Alcalá in Spain ordered priests to possess a parchment *cartilla* on which were to be written the articles of faith, the Ten Commandments and a list of sacraments, vices and virtues. This was to be posted in a prominent place and read out to the people on Sunday. Worried about the defective religious knowledge of the people, the synod also advised priests to employ a deputy who could hold a school (Dedieu 1979:263). The word *Børnelærdom* (religious education for children) runs through all Danish educational regulations from 1539 onwards. The church always had a say in who was to be appointed as a schoolteacher, and in some cases had the right of nomination. Many teachers were, in any case, secular or regular clergy. The authorities also kept a close watch on the content of education. Formal visitations were conducted on an annual basis in seventeenth-century Scotland, while the clergy and parish elders in the Dutch areas of Waal and Holland were ordered to visit their schools quarterly during the 1620s. Visitations were less frequent at Amsterdam in the early seventeenth century, but might last up to two weeks (van Deursen 1978:60).

The church's right to vet educators had long been established and was consolidated in the century of the Reformation. It did not, however, work alone. The backing of secular authorities was essential if ecclesiastical injunctions were to be obeyed, as Scottish and German reformers discovered. Indeed, reformers and governments worked together to draft the regulations which governed education in the towns and villages of Protestant Europe. More than 100 *Schulordnungen* were promulgated in the German principalities between 1518 and 1600, most of them religious in content but supported by the power of the civil magistrates (Strauss 1978). Day-to-day supervision of Danish schools after 1739 was left to the parish clergy and officials though ultimate control rested with the bishop and county sheriff.

The reasons behind the interest of the lay authorities are not far to seek. Some writers believed that the state had a positive duty to educate its people, following the Renaissance ideal that learning, progress and the overall quality of a nation were interdependent. The sixteenth-century Spanish jurist Diego de Simancas wrote: 'One of the most important functions of the state must be that children and youths are correctly educated and perfectly taught, since subjects who are poorly trained as children grow up to be the worst enemies of the homeland.' (Kagan 1974:12) To some extent, rulers felt that providing education, and grammar schools in particular, was a mark of their standing as enlightened, Christian monarchs. The efforts of Christian III of Denmark in his Icelandic territory in the 1540s offer one example. Some were clearly committed to the Protestant faith, including the Calvinist duke of Zweibrücken and the Lutheran count of Sponheim, both with lands on the Rhine. Hard, practical reasons also existed. Most sixteenth-century states suffered from a lack of literate administrators, and a commitment to extend education was often associated with a desire to select the most gifted children as possible trainees for official posts (Vogler 1976:350–2; Dixon 1958:10–11). A more destructive aim was the eradication of a faith, one of the goals of seventeenth-century French monarchs being to extirpate Protestantism by insisting on education by Catholic teachers.

Co-operation between ecclesiastical and secular authorities in the creation of national educational systems and the fostering of literacy was central to the success of initiatives before the eighteenth century. Examples of very different approaches taken in Scotland and Sweden provide informative case studies. Scotland had the first educational campaign which was truly national in its conception. At the time of the Calvinist Reformation in 1560, John Knox and his followers had set out their ambition for training a nation of believers in their manifesto, the *Book of Discipline*. However, it was not until 1616 that the Scottish Parliament (independent from that of England until 1707) passed the first statute which specified that every parish was to have a school and a teacher whose salary was to be paid by the local landowners in rural areas, and by the town council in urban communities. Further legislation in 1633, 1646 and finally 1696 strengthened these provisions, making them enforceable at law. The results were impressive. By the beginning of the eighteenth century, virtually all parishes in the most densely settled and economically developed central lowlands of Scotland had a parish school, some more than one. These schools provided basic literacy for the youngest children and usually instruction in both English and Latin grammar. Scholastic education was to be supplemented by the learning of the catechisms and Creeds at home, an ambitious programme which produced a population with remarkable, if not total, literacy by the mid-eighteenth century (Houston 1985). Similar attempts were made to subsidise education in other countries. Denmark's school law of 1739 envisaged that parents would pay fees, but a diocesan fund was also to be created to spread the burden of cost for poorer communities, income being derived from the poll, church and land taxes (Dixon 1958:25).

Sweden's experience was very different, though the goals of religious orthodoxy, social order and national development were much the same. Instead of Calvinism, it was the Lutheran church which provided the drive towards mass reading ability in Sweden. Poverty and dispersed settlement made the extensive creation of schools impossible except in some of the southern provinces, and the church strove instead to ensure that men, women and children acquired a basic knowledge of religion and reading, to be taught by parish priests and by literates to illiterates in the home rather than in schools. One important figure, C. G. Nordin, who later became a bishop, argued against the establishment of schools in 1785 in terms which show what could be achieved without them.

> Through the attention of the authorities and the efforts of the clergy during the past forty years, the public has ... acquired the ability to read in a book in such numbers that in general parents can themselves, without expense, give their children necessary Christian instruction in their own homes. And if certain parents should not be capable of this or should lack time or opportunity, there are generally old soldiers, widows, maidservants, cripples or others in every village who can occupy themselves with giving instruction ... That instruction in such cases might be less than perfect ... is something that has to be accepted, especially since it makes little difference whether a manservant or maid spells badly. (Barton 1977:539)

Compared with Scotland, this was a more limited campaign but one which seems to have created universal reading ability by the late eighteenth century.

More extensive efforts to regulate education were instigated in the states of continental Europe during the eighteenth century: Poland, the Habsburg monarchy, Prussia, Denmark, Spain and Portugal. The essence of the eighteenth-century reforms was the provision of a national, secular educational programme suited to the needs of the state. They were implemented by secular authorities for largely utilitarian ends, in contrast with the earlier church-inspired programmes which stressed religious learning and orthodoxy. And most were the product of individuals or groups of intellectuals stimulated by the ideas of the Enlightenment and able to catch the ear of the government. In eighteenth-century Portugal the *estrangeirados* (literally 'imitative of foreigners'), an elite of widely travelled intellectuals, formed an important pressure group while in the Netherlands the *Maatschappij tot Nut van het algemeen* (Society for the Common Good) performed a similar function, presenting in the 1780s schemes for a national education system covering all classes, regulated by the government, offering a standardised curriculum and non-doctrinal religious instruction. Danish initiatives from 1784 (building on schemes first set out as early as 1539 and further developed in 1739) grew out of a change of government and arose from social reforms introduced by the nobility to improve their economic standing relative to that of the peasantry. The net effect was to reduce paternalist ties with tenants and to loosen the bonds of communal life. In order to fit the peasants to be good citizens in their newly independent condition, it was felt necessary to improve education and a commission was set up in 1789 (Gold 1977:51–2). Attempts at secularisation and state control began in the early eighteenth century – the Austrian authorities tried to curb the Jesuit domination of education as early as the 1710s and in 1723 the Hungarian Diet brought public education under the nominal control of the government. But it was not until after the middle of the century that reforms were implemented in earnest (Carrato 1977:361; van der Laan 1977:294–6).

Examples from the *comté* of Nice, Poland and the Austrian territories show what was afoot. Victor Amadeus II of Savoy mounted one of the first eighteenth-century state takeovers of education. Central to his efforts was state control over teaching. Formerly vested in municipalities, bishops and, principally, the Jesuit order, a law of 1729 transferred control by specifying that all masters were to possess a royal diploma from Turin university (a step partly aimed at reviving the flagging fortunes of that institution). Administration of the reforms was in the hands of the Reform Ministry based in Turin and was delegated to local officials or *riformatori* who were in charge of licensing teachers, supervising exams and checking that education was directed at ensuring loyalty to the crown and the laws of the kingdom rather than to any supra-national religious ideal. These reforms epitomised the secular emphasis in eighteenth-century educational change, since Victor Amadeus's measures were part of a programme of social, economic and governmental reorganisation associated with a change in the nature of the Savoyard state from a duchy to an autonomous monarchy after the end of the War of Spanish Succession (Bordes 1979; Féliciangéli 1980). In areas of northern Italy under Habsburg control, further reforms of the 1760s and 1770s were designed to train bureaucrats and produce obedient subjects: university teachers were chosen for their political soundness and practical training rather than on intellectual merit, and government-vetted textbooks were substituted for lectures. Maria Theresa went as far as establishing a school of public administrators at Padua (Woolf 1979:103, 127).

The state initiative in Poland was one of the most successful in Europe. It was set up after the expulsion of the Jesuits in 1773 to organise schooling in such a way as to create a hard-working, well-trained and enlightened population which would serve the economic and political needs of the state. Building on a long tradition of educational provision and on earlier reforms by individuals such as Stanislaw Konarski (who founded a noble college in 1741) the commissioners sought to reform teaching methods and to create a formal educational hierarchy staffed by trained teachers. Poland's National Education Commission even involved itself with the production of schoolbooks. By commissioning authors to produce texts of the appropriate level for different classes or selecting them by open competition, the Polish body was able to avail itself of the best pedagogic writers in Europe. The Elementary Book Society, founded in 1775 by the National Commission, produced twenty-nine texts between 1777 and 1792. Reforms were not, however, implemented overnight and the Commission's main contribution during the eighteenth century was less to increase the number of schools than to outline new educational goals and fresh teaching methods (Majorek 1973; Bartnicka 1973; Seidler 1977; Litak 1973:63).

The blueprint for change in Hungary was the *Ratio Educationis*. Part one of this programme covered the organisation and funding of schools, part two the syllabus and teaching methods, part three defined scholastic discipline. Other areas of the empire such as Transylvania had their own ordinances. The reform programme of Maria Theresa and Joseph II did help to expand education in their territories as well as formalising control of schools and colleges by the

secular authorities. As with other educational reorganisation programmes, the effect of the Austrian one was to demote the church to
the status of an adviser on religious education, though in reality the
church remained important for teaching and everyday administration
of ordinary schools. The empress Maria Theresa spoke for all the
rulers of contemporary Europe when she said that 'school affairs are
and will forever remain a realm of politics' (Adler 1974; Bajkó 1977;
O'Brien 1970).

On paper, the national literacy campaigns of the early modern
period appear extremely impressive. Educational provision was
expanded and subjected to an unprecedented measure of control.
Funding was increased, curricula improved and more children than
ever passed through schools: in 1717, Frederick William I ordered
compulsory attendance for all children aged five to twelve in Prussia.
In terms of expanding and improving education, the overall
achievements were, in an early modern context, considerable even if
they were subject to compromise and geographically patchy. In
central Europe the reforms probably did expand schooling to an
appreciable extent, and the new methods of teaching formulated by
Felbiger were to become important during the nineteenth century.
Over the rest of Europe the story was either of outright failure or of a
consolidation and codification of existing provision, though given
the limited power of many states over their subjects we should not
underestimate even these achievements. Some states made hardly any
changes. England never had anything but the vaguest central
government policy on education at any stage during the early modern
period, and in its satellite states of Scotland, Wales and Ireland the
eighteenth century did not involve any significant developments in
state control. Despite the ferment of writing on education and the
national campaigns elsewhere, the eighteenth century saw little
activity in Sweden. Of the major continental states, France did not
attempt a systematic reorganisation, though there were royal
ordinances promulgated in 1698, 1700 and 1724 to establish teachers
in all French parishes and to allow local taxation of inhabitants to
pay for education. Schools of some kind were already present in most
French communities by the end of the sixteenth century, and the main
development in the seventeenth was the church hierarchy's systematic
backing for educational provision. Despite the limited role of the
French state in education before 1789, every parish in north-east
France is said to have had a school by 1704 (Chartier *et al.* 1976:27;
Croix 1981:1202; Graff 1987:149).

The principal problem faced by all European states, even in the later eighteenth century, was a lack of funds to pay for impressive schemes and of coercive power without which it often proved impossible to implement even the most basic reforms. National educational programmes exemplified the weaknesses of early modern state power. The difficulties involved in realising schemes of educational provision envisioned by intellectuals and codified by legislatures is neatly illustrated in the case of Portugal. In 1772 the School Board issued a report on education which formed the basis for a royal decree. The addendum to the decree, called the *Mapa dos professores e mestres das escolas menores* ... ordered, among other things, that 479 primary schools should be set up in the most densely populated communities. The problems of establishing this educational network were huge. Nothing like an adequate pool of qualified teachers existed to staff the new foundations. Furthermore, the proposed system of financing was difficult to operate. A new tax, the *subsídio literário,* was to be levied on the consumption of meat and alcohol in order to place education on a stronger and more independent financial footing. The 100,000,000 *reales* which this tax was soon realising each year were supposed to fund the public educational system but were siphoned off to pay for the school of commerce, the noble college, the Lisbon academy of science and various other elite institutions. In Spain too the royal reforms of a decayed system did little more than halt further educational decline (Carrato 1977:378–9).

The obstacles were endless. Authorities might insist on compulsory education for all children between certain ages, as Duke Ernest the Devout of Saxe-Gotha did in 1642, but they had no systematic way of ensuring attendance. Laws might be passed but administrators omitted to institute formal means of control, a problem in early seventeenth-century Scotland and in many German principalities during the sixteenth and seventeenth centuries. Town councils might proscribe clandestine schools but find them impossible to eradicate, as in eighteenth-century Cracow. Russian efforts to introduce the lessons learned from Prussia in the later eighteenth century foundered on the shortage of qualified teachers and the absence of a tradition of institutionalised learning in Muscovy. The ambitious Danish–Norwegian school law of 1739, implementation of which was delegated to local landowners, was deliberately sabotaged by those who would have had to pay its cost, in order to save money (Dixon 1958:26). And divisions in states such as Germany and Italy made any uniform, 'national' educational change very unlikely. Eighteenth-century campaigns, at best, laid the foundation for the major advances in literacy which took place during the nineteenth century and they marked an important step in the extension of state control over society.

Historians have tended to emphasise the significance of national literacy campaigns because they are, in some senses, the precursors of the regulated and integrated systems which developed in the nineteenth and twentieth centuries and because they mark one facet of the state's desire to tighten its control over its subjects. The immediate effect on literacy was usually slight since the laws tended either simply to codify existing practice or failed to provide adequate machinery to implement change. A good example is the state of Brandenburg-Prussia, frequently held up by advocates of educational reorganisation in the early nineteenth century as an early and successful example of what could be achieved by central control. Elementary education was theoretically compulsory after 1717 but the state, more interested in money and warfare than education, did little to realise this in practice. Children were to attend for two days a week even in summer but not every parish in the early eighteenth century had a school or a teacher. Popular education continued to depend, as it had done in the middle ages, on local clergy, town and village authorities and on local landowners and their officials. Numerically, *Winkelschulen* were more significant than official schools even at the end of the eighteenth century and most impetus behind educational innovation came from the localities rather than from central government (Neugebauer 1985). A similar pattern prevailed in Britain. More than two-thirds of England's school-children were educated in schools wholly financed by fees in 1750, and even in Scotland, which had a much more active campaign, the figure was still 43 per cent in 1818.

WHO WENT TO SCHOOL?

Advances in schooling took place all the way across Europe during the early modern period, from Iceland to Hungary and from Finland to Spain. More school places were available than ever before both at the elementary and the more advanced levels. Historians have waxed lyrical about the dramatic effect of the 'educational revolution' in producing widespread literacy. It would be churlish to deny the enormous achievements of individual charity, religious orders, town councils, parish vestries, church and state. However, we should be equally mistaken in assuming that the creation of schools everywhere made education available to all the children of school age: roughly six to twelve years old. We must examine the proportion of eligible children who attended schools and also their social background since the opportunity for education was determined by economic and, to a lesser extent, geographical accessibility.

In some countries of Europe, the overall percentage of children who were able to attend school at some stage during their youth was high. There are no absolute standards here but, during the eighteenth century, areas where half or more of the school-age children received instruction at some stage during the year were educationally advanced. A fifth to a third represents an average achievement; less than 10 per cent can be seen as the bottom of the range with figures close to 1 per cent by no means unknown even in 1800. Among the favoured zones was Brandenburg-Prussia where attendance in the second half of the eighteenth century ran at 50 per cent or more depending on the local area. Investigations conducted in the 1830s showed that some communities could boast figures as high as 93 per cent (Gawthrop & Strauss 1984:53–4). The northern provinces of the Low Countries, England, Lowland Scotland and much of north-eastern France enjoyed similar levels. A survey of the diocese of Reims near Paris in 1774 showed that virtually all parishes had a school and that 14 per cent of the total population were being schooled, roughly four-fifths of eligibles. Further to the south, the city of Lyon had approximately 24,000 children of school age during the eighteenth century of whom roughly 7,000 attended school (Chartier, *et al.* 1976:42; Perrel 1980:81:). Southern Germany too could boast extensive school attendance in the eighteenth century. In the towns of Mannheim and Heidelberg at the end of the eighteenth century, enrolment levels exceeded 80 per cent (Graff 1987:289). Of Vienna's 19,314 eligibles in 1770, 4,665 attended public schools, 6,632 went to Sunday schools or were taught privately, leaving only 42 per cent who received no education at all. The number of schools increased in Bohemia between 1780 and 1809 but population growth kept the attendance level at about two-thirds (O'Brien 1970:545–6, 562). Conceivably, some communities had reached these levels long before the eighteenth century: Renaissance Florence may have put nearly half of its children through elementary school, though only 13 per cent of boys were educated in Latin grammar (Graff 1987:78).

These figures represent the best achievements in eighteenth-century Europe. Drawn from a cluster of northern European nations, they lump together all sorts of schooling and do not distinguish between places available to boys and those to girls. These distinctions are important when we turn to the vast tracts of Europe in which attendance at school was a rarity rather than a normal part of growing up. Southern parts of France offer one example. One-third of eligibles received schooling in the diocese of Tarbes in 1783 but this figure breaks down into two-thirds of all the boys compared with just one girl in fifty (Chartier, *et al.* 1976:43). This is a grand achievement compared with much of eastern and central Europe. Even after reforms had led to a major expansion of schools in the last two decades of the eighteenth century, Russia had less than half of 1 per cent of its school-age population under instruction in 1807. Around 53,000 Russians received elementary education and approximately 9,000 were taught beyond the most basic level. Girls made up just 9 per cent of pupils in the public schools. The province of Galicia in the Habsburg monarchy could claim a meagre 20,000 attenders out of roughly half a million eligibles in 1789 (Alston 1969:19; Kahan 1985:153–4; Krupa 1981:82). And the best estimate for Poland in the early eighteenth century, given the sparse facilities and small size of schools, is less than 1 per cent (Litak 1973:53–5).

The German states, north-eastern France, Holland and most of mainland Britain, along with certain (mainly urbanised) areas of Italy, were the most favoured from the point of view of educational provision. Rural Spain, southern and western France, most of rural Italy, the southern Netherlands and parts of the Habsburg monarchy form an intermediate group. At the bottom come eastern Europe, Scandinavia, Ireland and certain areas such as Highland Scotland and the deep south of Italy. However, even this outline does not cover all the dimensions of education. The other aspect about which we need information is the social distribution of pupils and students in the establishments of Europe. After all, the mere existence of school places does not necessarily mean that all ranks in society had an equal opportunity to use them.

Indeed, the most obvious fact about the social origins of pupils is that it was, in general, only in the most elementary schools that we find anything like a representative cross-section of early modern communities. Only in the humblest classes of the educational hierarchy did the children of labourers and journeymen sit with those of merchants and artisans in numbers roughly proportional to their share in society as a whole. These were the classes which taught reading and religious knowledge, usually by rote. For many children they were the beginning and end of their educational career. At the more advanced levels, the grammar schools and the *collèges*, the imbalance in the social distribution of the boys was marked and the domination of places by the gentry and the bourgeoisie striking. There were only three pupils of peasant stock among 112 at the Jesuit *collège* at Nice in 1726; twenty-four were artisans but the rest were the sons of nobles, merchants and professional men. The *école royale*, which replaced the Jesuit school after the secularisation of education by Victor Amadeus II in 1729, was only slightly more socially balanced: four peasants and twenty-eight artisans among ninety pupils (Bordes 1979:419-20). Avallon in southern France had 20 per cent artisans and 7 per cent farmers in its intake between 1711 and 1779. Among the elite who could afford to enter as *pensionnaires* to the *collège* of Grenoble, 1786-92, less than 1 per cent were farmers. Some of the smaller provincial *collèges* of France, which depended on the social and occupational make-up of their immediate hinterland for pupils, could claim a more even social spread. That of Auch, 1598-1607, could manage 44 per cent artisans and 35 per cent farmers (Chartier, *et al.* 1976:193; Frijhoff & Julia 1976:117). Most students at the important French schools were bourgeois in origins; the same was probably true of Spain (Kagan 1974:53). Their parents could see the benefits of secondary education for social mobility and could pay the living expenses and fees required. Artisans and peasants who did attend a *collège* went to one of the lesser ones which were little better than grammar schools, while the traditional nobility (the *noblesse d'épée* as opposed to the legal and administrative nobility or *noblesse de robe*) preferred to educate their sons at home. A similar profile existed in the better grammar schools of seventeenth-century England. Bury St Edmunds (1656) was made up of boys more than half of whom came from aristocratic backgrounds: 17 per cent were the sons of clergy and professionals, 16 per cent tradesmen, 15 per cent yeomen and none at all from the ranks of husbandmen or labourers; the social bias is pronounced (O'Day 1982:36). Some mixing did take place, but it was not extensive. Interestingly, in the public schools of Russia in 1801 a third of pupils were peasants. A survey of thirty-eight major schools in the province of Novgorod meanwhile revealed that 11 per cent of children were from serf backgrounds (Black 1979:148; Alston 1969:19).

Institutions of secondary and higher education were very much the preserve of the gentry and the bourgeoisie. Nor were the better-off classes above poaching places which were intended for the children of the poor. Well-off middle-class parents might feel it beneath them to send their offspring to public schools, as they did in the Habsburg monarchy under Maria Theresa, but they were usually assiduous in placing their sons in schools which had any reputation at all for excellence. Dublin's City School was supposed to be for the sons of impoverished freemen, but many places were taken up by members of the prosperous middling and upper classes, including in the seventeenth century the future Duke of Marlborough. Charitable resources earmarked to educate children of the poor at the grammar school in Nördlingen were diverted for the use of boys whose parents appear from taxation records to have been far from the breadline (O'Brien 1970:545; MacLysaght 1969:206; Friedrichs 1979:227). Some teachers were even reluctant to take poor children because they lowered the tone of the school and might drive away children of the better sort (Dixon 1958:17).

Free schools were important because cost was the most serious obstacle to educating a child. In a sense there was no 'free' schooling because a poor family would have to forgo the contribution which even a youngster could make to its communal budget, but if the community or a charitable body could bear the money cost of an education or even provide a subsidy it could make basic literacy available to poor boys and girls who would otherwise have been left ignorant. Most countries provided some free learning to the children of the indigent poor (England more than Italy, for example) but the numbers in receipt were small and confined in practice to a very few privileged poor. Members of the teaching guilds in Spanish, German and French towns were supposed to take on a few poor children free of charge. A handful of Spanish boys were taken on charity, *de limosna*, in Madrid's schools, and religious bodies such as the Franciscans and the *Béates* provided very basic literacy for some poor children in Catholic countries. Few were lucky enough to get this far. If parents or guardians wanted to educate a child, they had to pay.

The cost of schooling depended on length of attendance, whether a boy had to board (as was common at the prestige grammar schools) and curriculum. Payment was based on the selections which parents made from the pedagogic menu provided by the teacher. The simpler the skill, the cheaper it was to learn. The charges set by the Madrid schoolmasters' guild in the seventeenth century were two *reals* a month for reading, four for reading with writing and six for all three. In contemporary Rotterdam, three months' instruction in reading commanded a fee of twenty *stuivers*, reading and writing thirty while fifty were charged for the three Rs (Larquié 1981:156; van Deursen 1978:61). These graded fees meant that for poorer families, only basic instruction in reading and the ubiquitous religious knowledge would be affordable, if that.

For the comfortably-off middle and upper classes, the decision to educate was only partly related to cost; for the lower orders it was often the only consideration. Those who lived in abject poverty comprised between 10 and 20 per cent of the early modern population. They had no surplus income and could not hope to educate their children unless someone else paid. Many more, perhaps the majority of the population of most countries, lived on the margin of poverty, generating a modest surplus in good years but falling into debt in bad times. The categories are seen in the rather extreme case of southern Spain. A 1575 survey of New Castile counted 70 per cent of adult males as *jornaleros* (landless agricultural labourers) who were chronically poor. The peasantry were scarcely better off, needing half their gross annual produce to pay taxes and dues, and nearly all the rest for rent. Small wonder that the inhabitants of a village near Toledo complained in 1580 that 'after paying the rent, nothing was left to them'. The marginality of many families is shown by the marked contraction in the numbers attending elementary schools in France during years of bad harvest and high food prices such as 1589–94, 1693–5 and 1711–13. Children were taken away from school or never sent in order to save the few pennies which might make the difference between survival and starvation for a family. For these sorts of people, the cost of post-elementary education would be an unthinkable burden. A good secondary education in early seventeenth-century Amsterdam could cost anything from 45 to 300 guilders a year; the latter sum was half as much again as the most that a wage earner could expect to make in a year (Kamen 1984:154; Chartier, *et al.* 1976:52; Vogler 1976:341; van Deursen 1978:72–3).

The importance of the net cost of education to parents is evident if we compare a part of Europe where the burden was largely borne by parents with one where schooling was heavily subsidised by the better-off or by the community. Communities in the Vaucluse region of southern France paid their teachers a salary and fixed fees of five to ten *sous* a month which parents were required to contribute. Nearly 90 per cent of the teacher's income came from fees around 1800. In contrast, towns and villages in the Baden area of Germany, which possessed a similar, mainly agricultural, economy, were able to pay a much higher proportion of the teacher's income as a salary; the average master derived only 25 per cent of his earnings from fees. Baden communities could do this because they had substantial amounts of communal property and could thus earmark resources for the teacher's stipend: *Schulpfründe*. As a result, the real cost of education was nine times as high in the Vaucluse as it was in Baden, and the deterrent to educate which existed in southern France did not inhibit parents to anything like the same degree in Baden. In the former area, only 20–30 per cent of children aged six to thirteen attended school *c*.1800 compared with Baden's 70–90 per cent (Maynes 1979).

Cost was an important determinant of the length of time a child might spend in a school. Education for most children was sporadic and discontinuous, especially in the lower levels of the hierarchy. The majority of boys and girls who attended any school could expect to receive between one and three years of education. In the Serbian and Rumanian provinces of the Habsburg monarchy, only boys destined for holy orders were educated for more than three years in the rural schools. Those lucky enough to attend any school in southern Norway in the eighteenth century spent five years there on average. Boys who reached grammar-school level could look forward to a longer and more intensive course: three to five years at the Latin school of Hornbach in the Rhineland, for instance. The Latin school at Lannepax, south of Condom in Gascony, was said to offer a six-year course as early as 1500 (Adler 1974:25, 43; Vogler 1975:287; Loubès 1983:317). Significantly, a year at an elementary school meant in reality just a few months. Rural schools in the southern Norwegian diocese of Akershus ran for an average of ten weeks in the year during the 1740s and even the 1827 school law laid down a very modest three-month 'year'. Absenteeism of about one-third was the norm at any point in time. In the Low Countries during the seventeenth century, it was usual for children to spend between five and ten weeks a year in rural elementary school (Tveit 1981; 1985; De Booy 1980a:265).

School regulations could be used to reinforce this pattern. Those governing St Etienne du Mont in 1730 prescribed a maximum of two years for any pupil, and charity schools for the poor had few aspirations beyond a year or two of catechism and reading. However, authorities might also try to increase the duration of learning. Eighteenth-century ordinances for the Austrian provinces specified that learning should start at age six and last for six or seven years; parents were obliged to send their offspring and local baptism records were to be consulted to make sure that all eligibles were dispatched to a school (O'Brien 1970:557). Methods of compulsion were, however, weak and in any case schooling was subject to interruptions caused by season, warfare and disease. At the same time, the incentive to educate a boy for any length of time was manifestly lacking in certain parts of Europe. Of 1,432 youths who enrolled in secondary schools in the

Russian province of Archangel between 1786 and 1803, only fifty-two received a graduation certificate. All schools and even the universities had a high drop-out rate (Alston 1969:19).

The implications of a brief and basic education for the literacy of the early modern masses are clear and important. Optimists believed that a child could be taught to read, by which they meant read aloud from a set text, in the space of a year, but in the province of Utrecht in the sixteenth century a more realistic three years was postulated (van Deursen 1978:68). Given that most children spent three years or less in a school, formal education could only have produced a commonality possessed of the most rudimentary literacy. The level of facility in reading must have been low, that of writing less still. Quality of understanding cannot have been high either. Even if basic literacy was increasing, many would have been wholly unable to participate in the scientific and literary advances of the early modern period.

Education depended principally on financial resources. Money made an education available and there is clear evidence from countries as diverse as Spain, Scotland and Germany that the children of parents who were paying the highest fees tended to receive more of the teacher's time. And masters in control of large classes of mixed age and ability had an understandable inclination to neglect ordinary plodders in favour of the potential high-fliers who were learning Latin and who might progress to an academy or university. Discrimination worked against the poorer classes both in access to schooling and in the quality of education they achieved. Any democratising effect which schooling might have had was strictly tempered by social prejudice and inequalities of wealth.

CHAPTER THREE
Ways of teaching

One of the most valued goals of twentieth-century education is to inculcate a capacity to think independently. The pupil should assimilate an existing body of information and then exercise critical understanding upon it. If such a thing happened in the early modern period, it came about largely by accident. Teaching methods in the sixteenth, seventeenth and much of the eighteenth centuries were explicitly designed to instil a fixed set of ideas and facts into the pupil. The aim was not to expand imaginative understanding but to guide the mind along certain set paths. At both elementary and advanced educational levels, the emphasis was on the reception of a particular viewpoint, usually dictated by the dominant ecclesiastical and secular authorities; orthodoxy was prized much more than originality. As Lawrence Stone (1977: 166) has written, the classical education of post-Renaissance Europe, seen by many as the jewel in the pedagogic crown, 'demanded effective repression of the will, the imagination, the emotions, and even intellectual curiosity'. The means by which pupils learned to read and write were central to the meaning which their skills took on and had an important bearing on the uses to which they could be put.

TEACHING MATERIALS

This stress on order and conformity ensured that memorising or learning by rote played an enormous role in the educational process. In most elementary schools it was the only means of learning offered to the children. Writers on education argued that constant repetition would instil a habit of learning in pupils, a view extended by the sixteenth-century Strasbourg educationalist Jean Sturm who stressed that repetition would help develop the memory (Trenard 1977:437). Religious education across Europe was founded on rote learning of the essentials of faith. The aspirations of Protestant and Catholic churches alike were humble, requiring little more from their flocks than an ability to memorise set forms of words which were regurgitated at intervals to teacher or priest. The Creed, the Lord's Prayer, the Ten Commandments, a basic catechism and perhaps some psalms: for many children this was as far as their education went. What passed for reading was often not what twentieth-century observers would understand by the word. The literacy campaign in Scandinavia was based on known texts, the definition of under-standing predicated on specific responses to particular questions. Even in 'advanced' countries such as the Netherlands, where the church did try to promote extensive Bible reading, the emphasis on rote learning was every bit as strong (Luttinen 1985; Strauss 1978; van Deursen 1978:59).

The authorities' aspiration to produce uniformity, order and godliness by education could be realised most effectively through the medium of the catechism. A catechism was a list of questions about the central tenets of the Christian faith and with these came a series of set answers. Some cathechisms were brief and featured one-word answers such as yes, no, God, Christ; others were more substantial and called for a fuller knowledge. All were to be learned by heart. Across Europe from Greenland to Galicia, the catechism was the key to religious education. Even the eastern Orthodox church, to which the catechismic form had been unknown in the medieval period, produced one in Polish and Church Slavonic in 1645 (Martel 1938:109). Secular and ecclesiastical figures were united in their advocacy of this powerful pedagogic tool. It was, after all, ideal for their purpose of passing on simple knowledge and agreed concepts to a (hopefully) passive audience. Basic religious precepts were set out unambiguously to be learned by the children, explained, if necessary, by the pastor and repeated frequently. Elementary religious education was based exclusively on this medium: school regulations for the German duchy of Württemberg in 1559 make no mention of the use of the Bible until the fifth or sixth form. Catechism was at the leading edge of any early modern christianisation or conversion campaign. From the 1470s in Spain the catechism was the main tool in the hands wielded by the church hierarchy in their drive to instruct the people in religion, an emphasis reinforced but not initiated by the Council of

Trent (1545–63). A Dominican called Villanova set up catechism schools at Milan in 1536 as part of the early Catholic response to the challenge of the Protestant reformers: the catechism there was known as an *interrogatio*. Luther's shorter, small or lesser catechism was the main weapon in the hands of Hans Egede, an evangelical preacher who worked to convert and educate the Eskimo subjects of the Danish crown in Greenland after 1721 (Gawthrop & Strauss 1984:35–9; Dedieu 1979:263–5; Poutet 1971:93; Gadd 1981:84).

The whole point of the catechism was that it was *safe*. Repeating set phrases rooted the basic religious tenets in the minds of the masses, and by stressing the religious basis of civic obligation its use strengthened the social order. The potentially disruptive influence of reading the Bible and of independent thought were substantially reduced, and it was not until the end of the seventeenth century that significant religious groups such as the Pietists began to advocate and practise the teaching of mass reading and critical understanding of the Bible. Small wonder that from Luther to Condorcet there was substantial agreement that the purpose of religious education should be to encourage submission to the dictates of the faith and that for this purpose the catechism was unequalled. Critical understanding played no part in this and, since education for the masses usually did not progress far beyond basic instruction of this kind, millions were consigned to a mind-numbing educational regimen.

Apart from religious works, most school books were either ABCs, primers, grammars or classical texts depending on the level of education. Except in some monastic, Jesuit or elite grammar schools, it was normal for pupils to use any text they could lay hand on and as a result not all children were using the same book. Teaching of reading began with an alphabet which the pupil learned by heart as a sequential whole. The next step was to recognise individual letters out of order, then to identify syllables, whole words and phrases. What the boy or girl was learning was less how to read than how to decipher set forms. Pupils were asked to name single letters, spell out syllables and words, pronounce words and finally to read aloud in class. In France the pupil pronounced a flat vowel before consonants so that 'letters did not link together phonetically in combinations that could be recognised by the ear as syllables of a word' (Darnton 1986:18). This mode of teaching changed hardly at all during our period and was used in all types of elementary school in slavish emulation of past practice. Printed ABCs were generally of pamphlet size, set out alphabetically and sometimes with verses to help memorisation. The official 1695 Swedish psalm book – which went through more than 250 editions and 1.5 million copies before 1819 – had 413 psalms, number 260 of which was called 'The Golden ABC' since each of its twenty-four verses began with a different letter of the alphabet (Claeyssen 1980; Lucchi 1978; Johansson 1981:162). The sixteenth-century Italian *Babuino* provided word practice for elementary classes in the form of lists of names and adjectives for regions, countries, cities and inhabitants (Schutte 1986:10, 12).

More substantial were grammatical primers, ranging in content from the very simple to the fairly demanding. The Dutch *Trap der Jeugd* (Stages of Youth) was made up of a list of increasingly difficult words to test spelling and recognition, and only in chapter seven was the child introduced to reading through the medium of family trees from the Bible. Slightly more advanced was Russian *Bukvar* published by Ivan Fedorov in Lvov in 1574. It came in two parts. The first was an ABC *(Azbuka)* to give command of the alphabet and some of the basics of grammar and orthography, including guides to conjugation, declension and derivation. The second consisted of texts for reading and memorising, beginning with a set of prayers from the Book of Hours. This was a much simpler work than the Church Slavonic *Grammatiki Sflavénskiia Právilnoe Síntagma* published in Ev'ye in 1619. The first fully analytical Russian (as distinct from Church Slavonic) grammar was not produced until 1696 and then by a Dutchman in Oxford since most educated Russians would study high-status Church Slavonic rather than the vernacular. The first specific English grammar was published in 1586, but the most significant expansion in production of vernacular dictionaries and grammars came during the seventeenth century and again after the 1730s. The religious and moral content of all school books was high. The 1770 Russian *Detskaia kniga* (Children's book) comprised forty question and answer couplets, each with a moral, political or social lesson, making it 'a catechism of autocracy and service in the Russian Empire'. *Spiegel der Jeugd* (Mirror of Youth), used as reading practice, contained a litany of the cruelties inflicted by the Spaniards and French on the Dutch Protestants (Jakobson 1955:12–25; de Booy 1980a:266–7; Black 1977:445; Tompson 1977:66–70).

ABCs, primers, grammars and classical texts were all produced specifically as school books from the sixteenth century, disproving the claim that there were no special books for children until the eighteenth century when the concept of childhood as a singular phase of life is said to have originated (Moore 1985). In many of the petty schools, however, teaching materials were much less grand. *Le Répertoire des Ouvrages Pédagogiques au XVIe Siècle* lists nearly

3,000 separate books preserved in French libraries which were used in schools, though not all were 'school books' in the strict sense (Choppin 1980:8). Teachers might use almost anything as a basis for instruction, and often had to in parts of Europe where texts were sparse or parents too poor to buy them. A chronic shortage of texts hampered education in central Europe during the early eighteenth century since the few primers available were printed in a Russian version of Church Slavonic barely comprehensible to speakers of the local vernacular. In Iceland, children might learn their writing by copying out old manuscripts or the exercises of older boys as a way of easing the pressure on texts. Even at the prestige grammar schools on the island, boys might have to copy out their own version of a textbook from the sole example or take it down by dictation from the teacher. Interestingly, evidence from areas as diverse as Russia, Italy and Germany in the seventeenth century suggests that the Bible was not extensively used except for teaching the more advanced classes, while in Sweden it was too expensive to figure extensively among household contents until the nineteenth century (Adler 1974:25; Hermannsson 1958:xxi; Johansson 1981:162). As late as 1817 it was reported that at one village school near Bremen in northern Germany, the sole Bible was shared in rotation by four children at a time (Engelsing 1973:87–8). Biblical texts such as psalters were, however, extensively used.

A child who received any formal education probably stopped at reading, especially if that child was poor and female. Writing cost more and might be regarded as superfluous. Taking one school, that at Marbais in Brabant (Low Countries), at one point in time, 1730, forty boys and twenty-six girls are recorded in receipt of reading instruction compared with just seventeen boys and four girls taking writing lessons (Ruwet & Wellemans 1978:71). One in ten of all pupils in the small towns of Larvik and Drammen near Oslo received writing instruction *c.*1800 though in the larger cities more than half were taught it (Tveit 1985). In the classroom, a board with printed examples of letters and writing styles, called a *cartilla* in Spain, was placed at the front of the class for copying by those pupils whose parents had paid for them to learn writing. Writing was indeed a quite separate skill from reading, and was taught at a relatively advanced stage in the school career: usually in the third or fourth year. It was a delicate task requiring the use of fragile quill pens and expensive materials unsuited, so some commentators believed, to the coarse hands of lower-class children. The notion of teaching reading and writing simultaneously was not widely adopted until the nineteenth century. Writing materials were expensive, and in poor countries such as Finland children used either a sandbox and their fingers or a stick, then a slate and chalk or a wax tablet and stylus before graduating to a pen and paper (Luttinen 1985:38).

Learning to write was similarly a question of copying rather than creating. Finnish schools of the early modern period never taught composition to those children who were learning writing. Instead, they copied letters, accounts and memos of the kind which they might encounter in later life or took dictated passages to show that they could write legibly and spell tolerably. Some Low Countries schools drew a distinction between copying classes and the more exalted Latin, arithmetic and composition classes (Luttinen 1985:34-8; Ruwet & Wellemans 1978:33). Such a process cannot have developed understanding of the possibilities created by writing, though it did clearly train children in skills which could be turned to other ends when they grew up. But this was not necessarily the case even for professional scribes. Many Russian manuscripts of the sixteenth century contain serious errors which can only have resulted from mechanical copying by clerks who treated the original document as a series of characters rather than as an integral and intelligible text, a familiar problem in copied documents throughout medieval Europe. Phonetic spelling of book titles by Parisian appraisers' clerks at the same time suggests lack of thought and unfamiliarity with the volume in question: Marot's *L'Adolescence* became *La Dolescence*, for example (Schutz 1955:7). In fairness, spelling was not fixed until the use of dictionaries became widespread in the eighteenth century, and anyone who has ever checked the addition in early modern account books will vouch for the hit-or-miss accuracy of counting even by 'professional' book-keepers.

TEACHING METHODS

According to certain authorities, notably Philippe Aries, corporal punishment was becoming an everyday part of growing up and an integral part of the educational process for early modern children. Educational theorists were prone to argue that beating was a way of curbing a child's independent urges and of regulating his or her socialisation. The pious San Antonio of Florence opined in the fifteenth century that children needed 'both bread and blows', the Dominican friar Dominici pronounced that 'frequent yet not severe whippings do them good', and there was an English saying of this period which ran: 'As a sharp spur makes a horse run, so a rod makes a child learn' (Ross 1976:200, 214; Dunn 1976:396–7; Tucker 1976:246). In practice, corporal punishment does not seem to have been a central feature of learning, and excessive correction was frowned upon by both parents and the authorities, resulting in dismissal in some cases and, in 1699, a charge for murder being levelled against the schoolmaster of Moffat in Scotland for beating a boy to death with a fencepost in front of his classmates. The other major approach was that popularised by writers such as the Englishman John Brinsley in his *Ludus literarius or the grammar school* of 1612. Brinsley treated learning as a competitive game and believed in advance through emulation and competition among the peer group. Unusually, he also advocated the inculcation of more critical understanding into the pupil rather than stuffing him with memorised facts and responses (O'Day 1982:49–53; Chartier *et al.* 1976:121–3).

Early modern classrooms bore little resemblance to the experience of readers of this book. A school normally consisted of just one room into which children of all ages would be crammed. The age at which schooling began varied according to the type of education available. The crèches held by women for those aged three and above can be called schools at a pinch, but elementary education usually began at roughly six or seven years, more advanced training at nine or ten and most university students fell into the age group fourteen to twenty. Among schoolchildren of known age at La Rochelle in 1689, 86 per cent were aged seven to fourteen, while legislation from the German principality of Baden in the late eighteenth century said that education should begin at six or seven and last until thirteen or fourteen (Chartier *et al.* 1976:53; Graff 1987:289). Danish regulations of 1539 envisaged attendance to age twelve, after which time only boys of proven aptitude for learning would be kept on until sixteen (Dixon 1958:11). Most pupils sat on benches, though those who were learning to write might be placed at desks. The teacher sat at his desk which children approached individually in order to have their lessons heard, reading or reciting from memory. Regulations from the Dutch town of Haastrecht in 1723 specified that each pupil should be heard at least four times a day (van der Laan 1977:309; Chartier *et al.* 1976:114–26).

The concept of teaching groups rather than individuals and in classes divided according to age and ability was an eighteenth-century departure, associated with theorists such as Felbiger in the Austrian empire or with practical educational reformers such as the Brethren of the Christian Schools in France (O'Brien, 1970:558; Furet & Ozouf 1982:78-80, 115). The only concession to differing ages and standards of attainment was to put those learning, say, arithmetic on different benches or on different sides of the room from those doing reading or writing. Furthermore, it was accepted that in practice children of the 'better sort' of parents, what one French educational manual called *les personnes de condition,* would sit apart from the poor who were likely to be 'verminous and foul both in their clothes and speech' (Chartier *et al.* 1976:119). Artistic depictions of seventeenth-century classrooms give the impression of controlled anarchy, those children not at the master's feet being left to work or play apparently as they wished. Elite institutions had more than one master and several classrooms: Edinburgh's Royal High School had five teachers, compared with two at most grammar schools in lesser Scottish burghs (one teaching Latin, the other English) and just one in ordinary rural parishes during the early eighteenth century (Camic 1985:144). Sometimes the master went from house to house in sparsely populated areas teaching the children of a family in a barn, kitchen or yard: Norway and parts of France or Denmark *(omganslærer),* for instance (Furet & Ozouf 1982:70).

The hours during which school was taught were similar to those obtaining in the twentieth century. In the Dutch town of Haastrecht, class hours were 9-12am and 1-4pm with Saturday afternoon, the market day and all day Sunday off. At Dalkeith in Scotland, children arrived much earlier and were sent home at 9am for an hour to breakfast with their families. At the lower reaches of the educational hierarchy the hours in school were devoted to a mix of religion, reading and other literate skills, and practical training. During a five-hour day at a French cloister school in the seventeenth century, one hour was spent on religion, one and a half on sewing and weaving, two and a half on reading and writing (Chartier, *et al.* 1976:237). Religion was extremely important but it rarely took up the majority of the day, and during the eighteenth century it became less and less significant as parents began to demand a more secular emphasis in schooling and as the power of the state waxed at the expense of the church.

Classes were large and of mixed age: thirty to sixty pupils aged approximately five to fourteen. At one elementary school in the German town of Mannheim (1755), 400 pupils were taught by two masters, though this extreme example may have been the result of rapid urban population growth. Schools, however, were generally small by twentieth-century standards. A survey of Madrid's schools in

1642 showed that they ranged in size from 38 to 140 pupils. Average attendance at seven of the thirty-nine *Winkelschulen* of the north German town of Braunschweig in 1673 was just fifteen. The vast majority of rural schools in the Polish diocese of Cracow around the middle of the eighteenth century had less than ten pupils, in towns less than twenty. These numbers were low compared with the early seventeenth-century average for towns in southern Austria of 33 or the very high Dutch figure of 70 to 130 (Kagan 1974:13; Friedrichs 1982:373; Litak 1973:56–7). The sexes were segregated except in the simplest village schools as a result of an apparently obsessive interest in sexual morality on the part of the authorities. The concern with morality extended to regulations ensuring that every minute of the day would be filled in an orderly and profitable way, though in practice even the strictest pedagogues recognised that young minds needed at least some variety and a little free time.

It is important to recognise that this regime was purveyed by schools at all levels of the hierarchy. The programme of Latin grammar, rhetoric and literature was rigorous, methodical and precise, drilling the pupil in difficult literary and linguistic skills and drumming a large volume of facts into him. Even the famous schools such as that run by Guarino Guarini at Verona in the fifteenth century never bridged the gap between, on the one hand, the zealous and idealist rhetoric that literary studies would transform men into paragons of virtue and, on the other, the plain reality that what they offered was a training in routine competence. Creative achievement, moral training and the formation of a 'Renaissance man' were quite different and incidental to the learning process (Grafton & Jardine 1986).

Methods of teaching and the organisation of the classroom changed hardly at all throughout the period from the Renaissance to the Industrial Revolution. Schools at all levels emphasised set forms and the transmission of a fixed body of knowledge through an established pedagogic regime. The standard of teaching varied from school to school and it is incontrovertible that new ideas were floating around. Under Maria Theresa, the theorist Felbiger proposed teaching methods closer to what would be recognisable to the twentieth century, most important among which were that pupils would be taught in groups organised by age and ability, and that a Socratic or questioning method of instruction would replace rhetoric and repetition (O'Brien 1970:558). From the late seventeenth century in Lutheran Germany and Denmark, the Pietists began to promulgate an important message about learning. Originally a movement for purer Christianity and for moral reform among the clergy, Pietism in the eighteenth century became the purveyor of a state-supported campaign of education operating through schools. The Pietists argued that people should be taught to read the Bible critically, the teacher explaining and discussing meaning rather than simply handing it down (Gawthrop & Strauss 1984:44-9). Mechanical spelling and rote learning were increasingly under fire in the late eighteenth century, notably by the German Samuel Heinicke, who was one of the pioneers of the phonetic method of teaching reading, and in Denmark Christian Cramer spoke out against the prevalent one-class, one-teacher layout in schools (Engelsing 1973:65-6, 77; Dixon 1958:32). However, these ideas made little headway before the nineteenth century. Instead, as Mary Wollstonecraft wrote of the best London boys' academies, 'the memory is loaded with unintelligible words . . . without the understanding's acquiring any distinct ideas', a comment as applicable to the great Jesuit colleges as it was to the humblest *Winkelschulen* (Houston 1985:229). The number of schools expanded enormously in the early modern period, but the quality of instruction altered little.

SCHOOLMASTERS

In modern developed nations it is conventional to describe teaching as a profession, almost a vocation. Men and women who become teachers are usually university graduates and generally undergo further instruction in specialist training colleges. With variations, schoolmasters and schoolmistresses enjoy a respectable status in the community, and concern over their morality, competence and remuneration is often deeply felt. In early modern Europe the situation was rather different. Few people entered teaching in the expectation that they would end their days in such an occupation, except perhaps at the top of the educational hierarchy. Except when grouped into guilds, it is unlikely that teachers saw themselves as a 'profession' with a sense of group identity before the major national literacy campaigns of the late eighteenth century. It was only in the more advanced schools that significant numbers had either a university degree or experience of formal training in a seminary of some kind. Financial remuneration was frequently poor and the social standing of educators tended to be low. Differences in pay, qualifications and status were considerable, and rather than condemn the teaching 'profession' out of hand, we should think in terms of a 'mixed-ability staff'. Some teachers were decent, capable and conscientious people who were respected by the parents of the children they taught; others were negligent, incompetent and disdained.

The standards demanded by communities which hired elementary teachers were not especially stringent. In some cases this amounted to little better than an expectation that the candidate would be God-fearing and respectable with some basic competence in the subjects he proposed to teach. The town council of Seville in southern Spain began paying the salaries of some teachers in the late 1540s and an ordinance of 1561 about licensing stressed above all the need for men 'of good life and custom' (Perry 1980:178). Concerned by the spread of religious heterodoxy after the Reformation, secular and ecclesiastical authorities all over Spain displayed a keen interest in the strict orthodoxy of teachers.

Elsewhere in Europe, similar general standards were set. A Piarist priest called Hueber appointed the local gravedigger to teach some poor children for free in the rapidly growing Viennese suburb of Lerchenfeld in 1737, because he had 'good handwriting and some knowledge of arithmetic' (O'Brien 1970:546). For some central European church authorities, a good voice and the ability to read music were paramount considerations so that the teacher could lead religious services. Dutch magistrates' procedures were more formal and more rigorous. The schoolmasters in the town of Haastrecht were appointed by the town council after a public examination held in the church or, sometimes, in an inn. Candidates had to provide ample proof of their 'manner of living', and to display ability in reading, writing, arithmetic and singing (van der Laan 1977:308-9). More formal tests and more demanding examinations were introduced in many parts of Europe during the eighteenth century under the influence of Englightenment ideas and the growing desire of the state to control many areas of life. The Habsburg general school ordinance of 1774 (*Allgemeine Schul-Ordnung*) specified that teachers should pass a state exam, and as part of Victor Amadeus II's reform of the educational system in Nice (1729) all secondary school teachers were required to possess a royal diploma from the University of Turin (Féliciangéli 1980:87). A Danish law of 1739 set a minimum age of twenty-two for secondary teachers who should, in addition, have been either a student at a Latin school or already have taught in a vernacular school (Dixon 1958:24).

Teachers' formal qualifications can be quantified in the case of those who had been to a college or university. The English parish clergy, charged with catechising, contained a majority of university graduates by 1600 and, between 1627 and 1641, 154 of 261 licensed schoolmasters in the diocese of London were graduates (Wide & Morris 1967:397). Many more teachers were, of course, outside the licensing system. Levels of commitment are difficult to assess, but for those who did graduate, teaching could be a way of filling in time until a parish living and the attractive job of clergyman became available. Urban teaching guilds in Spain, France and the Netherlands did not demand very rigorous standards of their members. Teacher-training colleges before the eighteenth century were run almost exclusively by the Jesuits and other regular clergy. The first secular college of this kind in Denmark was the one at Blågård outside Copenhagen, begun in 1791 with two masters, a singing teacher and fourteen students. Graduates of this institution needed no further proof of their qualifications to secure a post, but others had to show they could read, explain the Lutheran catechism intelligently, count, write legibly and grammatically in Danish, and sing the psalms clearly and correctly (Gold 1977:61–3). It is useful to consider those who had matriculated as well as graduated, since many who went into teaching had failed to complete their university courses.

At the lower levels of the educational hierarchy, even basic literacy could be questionable. For many teachers, the only qualification seems to have been a willingness to tolerate the miserable salaries they were paid. Some made frankly outrageous claims about their pedagogic skills, the range of topics they could offer and the results which they could achieve. Writing masters were notorious for this, but in eighteenth-century Lyon, the worst charlatans were the Italian language teachers who, in order to enhance prestige and fees, claimed that they could produce accent, grammar and vocabulary of a high standard almost overnight. Séraphin Maglione arrived there in 1767 full of promises and not even the fact that he was forced to open an *épicerie* in 1771 to keep body and soul together could stop his stream of patter (Garden 1976:150). The *leccionistas* who came to Madrid from other Castilian towns during the second quarter of the seventeenth century to try their hand at teaching in competition with the licensed masters of the guild had a reputation for extravagant claims and modest standards (Kagan 1974:15–17).

These sorts of claims are rare and so far-fetched as to be beyond belief. Having said this, establishing the 'average' standard of teachers is difficult, partly because of the lack of quantifiable evidence and partly through problems of assessing typicality in qualitative material. Surviving documentation dealing with the quality of schooling most commonly refers to low standards, though we must be careful about extrapolating too much from these adverse comments. When authorities visited a school, they dwelt long on any shortcomings which were uncovered, but devoted to a competent teacher only a terse statement of his acceptability or no comment at all. Villages unhappy with a teacher might refuse to pay him or even sack him; contented communities might never refer to their master. The voice of children is very rarely heard in early modern sources except retrospectively when adults recalled unpleasant experiences such as beatings and favouritism, or good teaching and acts of kindness. In 1591 a Dutchman called Valcooch published a handbook written in rhyme in the hope of improving the standards of what he described, in terms hardly calculated to endear him to his readers, as the 'deeply ignorant parish schoolmasters'. Complaints about bad teaching are, because of the nature of the documentation which survives, much more frequent than remarks in praise. Indeed, we should not write off the humbler schools and their teachers out of hand. True, many taught in them only as a temporary expedient, but this does not mean that they were wholly without value. Sebastiano Vongeschi, a Pistoian monk convalescing in the small village of Cutigliano in the spring, summer and autumn of 1513, taught counting for five *soldi* a month, grammar for ten, primer, catechism and psalms for seven. He records in his diary that he did a roaring trade: had he been useless, he would probably have starved (de Booy 1980a:264; Lucchi 1978:597).

This Italian example illustrates a further point about teachers: most were outsiders and many did not stay very long in a community. The grammar school at Ribe in Denmark had twenty-five *rektors* between 1536 and 1660, only one of whom stayed more than ten years (Dixon 1958:14). Virtually all the teachers who worked in the French commune of Vallorbe were strangers until the end of the seventeenth century when the Glardon family began to establish itself as a sort of teaching dynasty in the village. Men from mountainous areas of south-eastern France and northern Italy commonly migrated to the plains during winter to hire themselves as teachers and notaries. The southern Alpine valley of Safien was known in the eighteenth century as the 'valley of the schoolteachers' (Viazzo 1983:162). These movements were usually seasonal, but in the Netherlands the political and military disruptions of the 1560s and 1570s produced a substantial and permanent migration of teachers from south to north:

442 teachers migrated between 1575 and 1630 and, indeed two-thirds of all the educators in Leiden during this period had come from the southern provinces (Parker 1979:250).

Teachers could be paid by two means. Either they received a salary from the community in which they worked or the parents of the children they taught paid them fees which depended on the length of time they were in school and the sort of lessons they were being given: reading, writing or arithmetic, for instance. The normal practice was to blend the two sources of funding into a composite income, sometimes with the addition of approved, linked jobs. Suligny in the Aube region of France paid its teacher 455 francs for the year 1813, made up as follows: 90 francs of salary, 90 francs for singing, 100 francs from wine donations, 150 from school fees, and the right to cut firewood was assessed at a further 25 francs (Furet & Ozouf 1982:110). No standard balance existed between the different components. In schools for the poor where fees were either non-existent or very low, basic salaries tended to be higher than in other establishments.

Teachers' incomes were very varied. In the province of Utrecht, salaries ranged from 24 guilders per year at Kudelstaart (1624) through 48 at Kamerik (1631) to as high as 120 at Jutphaas in 1635. Communities in upland areas of eighteenth-century Languedoc tended to employ teachers on short contracts for sums of 30–60 livres whereas in the low-lying regions 100–150 livres was the norm, suggesting year-round employment. At the end of the eighteenth century most Prussian teachers were earning between 100 and 250 talers a year though some received less than 100 and a handful more than 350. The *rektor* or headmaster of the school at Frankfurt-am-Oder was getting more than 400 talers a year, or roughly twice the remuneration of his five staff (Neugebauer 1985:310–11). In Spain, good pedagogues were in short supply and could earn much more by moving around from month to month or season to season (van Deursen 1978:61; Laget 1971:1404–5; Kagan 1974:41). Forms of payment varied too. In rural Austria and Poland, salaries might be paid partly in cash, partly in grain and firewood, partly in pasture rights for grazing cattle (Adler 1974:39; Wiśniowski 1973:42–3). The level of salary provided by the community in which a teacher lived and worked depended on the available resources. Communes such as those in Baden (Germany) which owned substantial amounts of communal property could afford to pay salaries high enough to allow the teacher to live by charging only very low fees. Around 1800 roughly 25 per cent of a teacher's income would come from fees, compared with nearly 90 per cent in regions such as the Vaucluse in south-eastern France where the cost of education could not be subsidised by communal funds (Maynes 1979).

Even allowing for variations and income supplements, there is no escaping the fact that as an occupational group, early modern teachers were poorly paid. Take the case of the Hjerm area of west Jutland at the end of the eighteenth century. In this poor, rural part of Denmark, teachers' salaries varied from just eight *rigsdaler* a year to eighty-two. At this time, the daily wage paid to an unskilled Copenhagen labourer was twenty-eight *skilling*. Assuming that the labourers worked five days a week throughout the year, this would place their total annual income at roughly seventy-six *rigsdaler*. The cost of living was slightly cheaper in rural Jutland, but there is no escaping the fact that the bulk of teachers there were getting less than common labourers (Gold 1977:50). In seventeenth-century Paris, teachers are always found in the lowest taxation brackets and across the Habsburg monarchy the average income was well below that of a minor state official. This was not true of Turin where, in 1608, an elementary teacher received a salary in line with the better-paid public officials, nor of the teachers at the Calvinist school of Gyulafehérvár, paid by prince Gábor Bethlen of Transylvania, who received a handsome salary. Yet other central European pedagogues were paid only a half of the income of a humble parish priest and it would be fair to generalise that teachers as a group were poorly remunerated (Cipolla 1969:30; Adler 1974:39). Low pay often meant low prestige. One of the carrots held out to the teachers by the Polish National Education Commission in the 1770s was to form them into a hierarchical guild and thereby enhance their social standing, yet the most dynamic men continued to use teaching as a springboard to a career in the clergy, bureaucracy or as a notary. Again, public respect for teachers could be high, as it was for some pedagogues in seventeenth-century Germany and Ireland, but this depended very much on individual qualities and on the level at which education was offered.

Given their highly variable backgrounds and qualifications, it would not be unduly cynical to state that teachers frequently deserved their low rates of pay. But we must allow that the poor remuneration rendered the profession unattractive to the most gifted individuals. Teaching could attract those too weak or sickly to hold down a manual occupation. As the clergy of Ribe in Denmark petitioned in 1789, what teachers 'have to live on is nothing more than hunger and poverty, which is why none want to be school teachers and we have to make do with poor, miserable, infirm wretches' (Gold 1977:50).

Especially at the lower levels of the 'profession', many had only the most general qualifications and most treated teaching as simply a stop-gap measure to make money. For some it was their main source of income, but there were few who depended solely on teaching for a living. Indeed, the catalogue of educators' by-employments covers almost the full occupational spectrum of early modern societies. In countries like Scotland, Denmark and the Netherlands it was usual for the official parish schoolmaster to double as deacon, sexton, clerk and precentor for the church; in some cases he also held the office of gravedigger (de Booy 1977:352). We have information about the background or by-employments of 432 sextons and village school-masters from Brandenburg (1668–1806): 71 per cent of them were connected with tailoring or other areas of textile working. This was perfectly acceptable to the local authorities and was not held to be incompatible with his teaching job. The same cannot be said of other additional occupations. Some teachers held classes in the kitchen or brewhouse while the normal functions of those rooms were being exercised. London schoolmasters might be scriveners, cobblers, tailors, fishmongers, pawnbrokers. Some in eighteenth-century Vienna moonlighted as beer-hall musicians and one even ran a bar in the very room where the children were reciting their catechism. A Dutchman called van Barendrecht used his classroom to organise a lottery contest (Anglin 1980:68; O'Brien 1970:546; van Deursen 1978:60). We should not be surprised by the rapid turnover of teaching staff. In the duchy of Zweibrücken in the Rhineland (1556–1619), half of all town teachers stayed less than two years in the same school, 57 per cent of village teachers and 76 per cent of assistant masters in the towns. Poor and irregularly-paid salaries, mediocre lodgings, conflict with the head teacher or the clergy or the parents, and outright dismissal for incompetence or moral transgressions account for the footloose character of many teachers (Vogler 1976:333–4).

There was no general commitment among those who provided education to widespread schooling simply for the sake of it. Secular and ecclesiastical authorities wanted to create a godly, obedient and productive population. For this purpose, schools had to be closely regulated. On their part, the teachers concurred with these aims. Appealing to the laudable end of maintaining educational standards, the schoolmasters of Europe were in fact concerned principally with maintaining their salaries and fees against the competition of those who sought to infringe their privileges. Teachers and authorities in Scotland did not even bother with this pretence, stating that unlicensed (or what they sometimes called 'unfree') schools in the towns were prejudicial to the financial interests of the official parish master or 'dominie'. Teachers were not well paid, and in addition those who obtained a licence might have to pay for it out of their own pocket. A certificate from the Parisian authorities cost thirty-two livres a year in Louis XIV's reign, roughly a tenth of the annual income of the average teacher. The *petits écoles* of the French capital were controlled by the Grand Chantre of the Cathedral Chapter of Notre Dame, a guild which policed other types of school such as the charity ones to ensure that their privileges were not infringed (Bernard 1970:261–2, 279). Antwerp had a flourishing schoolmasters' guild in the sixteenth century which dated from the 1460s, and in Madrid the teachers formed a confraternity, *La Hermandad de San Casiano* (1666) in an effort to freeze out competition from unlicensed teachers. Eighteenth-century Lyon had a separate writing-masters' association (Parker 1979:21; Larquié 1981:157; Garden 1976:136–8).

It is hard to see how the guilds could prove beneficial to education in the early modern towns. They probably did not improve the quality of recruits to the profession and in some parts of Europe, notably the southern Netherlands, they formed an archaic organisational barrier to changes in school curriculum until well into the nineteenth century. In Germany, the guild of Frankfurt-am-Main had, during the seventeenth century, secured the right for members of the *Gesellschaft der Deutschen Schulhalter* to pass on the privilege of holding a school to their sons, irrespective of their aptitude or ability (Van der Woude 1980:258; Friedrichs 1982:374). The farcical posturing which could result from disputes between licensed and unlicensed teachers is beautifully illustrated by a case from seventeenth-century Braunschweig in northern Germany. Braunschweig in the middle of the seventeenth century was a substantial town of some 15,000 people with three elite Latin schools, two franchised municipal German schools and thirty to forty *Winkelschulen* or 'corner schools' which were deeply hated by the two franchised vernacular teachers.

In 1648 the monopoly of teaching reading and writing in German held by the municipal schools was challenged by the arrival of a wild young man called Melchior Schurdan. His challenge was all the more galling as he had once been taught by one of those with whom he sought to compete. Schurdan's methods were unorthodox. At one stage he employed his mother to accost boys in the street and encourage them to leave one or other of the franchised schools in favour of the one run by her son. The official teachers, Pöpping and

Overheide, were livid and mounted a campaign against the young upstart. They alleged four reasons why the illegal school would have to be shut down which are instructive not only about their own priorities but also those of parents and the town council. First, Schurdan taught only reading, writing and arithmetic, neglecting instruction in religious knowledge. Second, Pöpping and Overheide were encountering growing problems with discipline in their own schools, so any attempt to adopt a strict stance over infringements of the rules would only drive scholars to the illicit school. Third, their earnings were suffering. Fourth, schoolboy taunts about the quality of the respective schools were spilling over into adult conversation and therefore threatening to disrupt the peace of the town. Schurdan's school was duly closed, but the problem of the *Winkelschulen* persisted: there were thirty-nine in the city in 1673, their numbers a testimony to the demand for elementary, secular instruction. Licensed teachers shared the perceptions of the authorities and their priorities were geared less to the heedless expansion of education and more to the preservation of their pockets and privileges (Friedrichs 1982:371-4).

SCHOOLMISTRESSES

When we speak of schoolteachers in the early modern period, we must devote most space to schoolmasters. Men dominated the 'teaching profession', if we can call it that, both numerically and in the educational hierarchy. Women teachers were probably fewer in number than men and the sort of education which they provided was generally of a more elementary kind than that of the masters. The contrast in numbers is stark. Records relating to the town of Lyon in south-eastern France reveal the presence of eighty-seven school-masters at some stage between 1490 and 1570; only five female teachers turn up in the same documents (Davis 1975:73). A more glaring gender imbalance is apparent in a survey of Venetian schools conducted by the authorities in 1587: 258 male teachers alongside a sole female, though it is likely that the investigation under-recorded women educators. Rome in 1695 had only sixteen registered schoolmistresses among a population of more than 130,000 people. The only educational institutions which were dominated by women were the schools attached to nunneries, on the one hand, and the specialist reformatories, on the other: places such as the *Zitelle*, the

73

Venetian home for the daughters of prostitutes, in which twelve sober and moral ladies were employed to prevent the coming generation from learning the errors of their mothers. At the other end of the spectrum, in the eyes of contemporary moralists, were the religious orders, prominent among whom were *Les Béates*. Founded in the countryside of Puy (France) during the seventeenth century by one Anne-Marie Martin, this order worked in sparsely populated rural areas such as the Massif Central. The sisters worked in everyday clothes, generally alone, and lived with the families of the poor, to whose children they taught reading and catechism. About 150 were at work in the diocese of Metz in eastern France at the beginning of the French Revolution in 1789 (Cholvy 1980; Furet & Ozouf 1982:177–9). In Catholic countries, schoolmistresses were commonly members of religious orders (Laget 1971:1409).

The eighteenth century saw a marked increase in numbers and improvement in status of female teachers in some parts of Europe. Lyon, where licensed masters outnumbered mistresses seventeen to one in the first half of the sixteenth century, could boast fifty male and fifty female teachers by the middle of the eighteenth century (Garden 1976:139). Yet the sort of education which women could provide was deliberately restricted. The norm was to allow them either to conduct the lowest classes and the youngest pupils, who would be learning simple skills such as the catechism or the elements of reading, or to teach only girls, who had a different curriculum to boys, or to offer only the most elementary instruction. The town of Namur in the Low Countries expressly forbade women to teach writing. In practice, this meant that schoolmistresses taught religious knowledge by rote, sewing and spinning, housewifery, a little reading and possibly the rudiments of counting.

Discovering the scholastic background and qualifications of women teachers is harder than for men. The only fact of which we can be certain is that none of them had been to university. Most were single: of 121 who we know worked in Lyon during the eighteenth century, only fifteen were widows and twenty-two were married. Possibly women used schoolteaching as a way to fill the time between leaving home and getting married, which was usually in their mid-twenties in France at this date, or as a supplement to family income once they had married. Alternatively, keeping a school was one of the few opportunities open to a woman of making an independent living if she wished to remain single, as roughly one in ten did in eighteenth-century France. Certainly, women tended to spend longer in a post than men, an unexpected finding since females were more geographically mobile than males in the early modern period. At Lyon between 1732 and 1792, only 9 per cent of 121 mistresses stayed in teaching in the town for four years or less compared with 19 per cent of 149 men. Of women teachers, 32 per cent remained to teach in Lyon for more than twenty-five years but only 19 per cent of men. Their social background is similarly obscure. In the duchy of Zweibrücken in the Rhineland, the women whose backgrounds we can trace were often the wives or widows of teachers or clergymen (Garden 1976:142; Vogler 1976:356).

If we rely on official records, the role of women in education seems at best marginal. Confined to elementary teaching, their numbers were few and their function was at times little better than that of child-minder. With exceptions, the evidence we have is consistent with a picture of their involvement in very basic book-learning, practical skills, religious instruction and moral guidance. Women were generally confined to the lower echelons of the educational hierarchy and are never found teaching in grammar schools, colleges or universities. In terms of the quality of the learning instilled, their situation as a group was inferior to that of schoolmasters. There was, of course, overlap at the bottom of the profession, and we must also recognise that there were many more female teachers than the records show. The French commune of Vallorbe first formally employed a schoolmistress to teach girls up to the age of ten as late as 1778, though girls' schools and women teachers had clearly been in existence long before this date. Secular and religious authorities liked schools to be licensed, and attempts to suppress those without a certificate of religious acceptability and political soundness shed partial light on the shadowy world of petty schoolteachers, many of them women. Five women teachers were licensed in their own right by the bishop of London during the reign of Elizabeth I (1558–1603), four in partnership with their husbands; a further thirty were prosecuted for keeping unlicensed schools (Anglin 1980:69). Beneath the officially recognised establishments were many which served local needs, perhaps just one street, and which were run by women. Exactly how numerous they were we can never know.

CHAPTER FOUR
Higher education

UNIVERSITIES

The early modern period saw an unprecedented increase in both the number of universities and in the proportion of the population who attended them. Many universities had flourished during the high Renaissance, *c*.1450–*c*.1520, and many continued to expand during the rest of the sixteenth century. Growth in higher education was achieved both by increasing the number of universities and by adding new colleges or by expanding the number of students at existing colleges. In England there were no new universities but a creation of new colleges within Oxford and Cambridge and an increased intake into existing ones. The latter institution had nearly 1,300 students in 1564 and 3,000 by 1622. At the other extreme were countries which had never had a university before the start of the early modern period: Ireland secured its first university (Trinity College, Dublin) in 1591, and Finland in 1640 (at Turku, now Åbo). Spain too relied principally on new foundations. There were six universities in Spain in 1450 but thirty-three by 1600 and further establishments were set up in Spain's New World colonies. The state was particularly important in new foundations (in Italy, for example) and began to increase its power over the universities. From the 1530s the rector of Coimbra in Portugal ceased to be elected from within the university and became a crown nominee (Marques 1972:197). In most countries a combination of all three modes of expanding were used, including Scotland, Italy, France and Germany, the latter having 3,200 students in 1500 compared with nearly 8,000 in 1600 (Engelsing 1973:33).

Uniform patterns of expansion, albeit at different periods, disguise important variations in the areas of study which were attracting students. The expansion of Oxford and Cambridge was based on intakes into the arts faculty, essentially theology and philosophy, and students could indeed take no other course since the London Inns of Court produced the nation's common lawyers. And unlike France's *collèges,* English grammar schools existed not as competition for the arts faculties but as necessary providers of preliminary training for university entrance. Spain's new students, on the other hand, sought out places in law faculties expanded to fill the need for trained officials. Scotland's late-sixteenth- and early-seventeenth-century growth in university numbers was fuelled by demand for training in Protestant theology while its eighteenth-century expansion was principally associated with legal and medical education.

Nor was growth universal and contemporaneous in all parts of Europe. Lisbon university was shut down in 1536 and not re-opened until just before the First World War. The universities of central Europe went through a period of contraction and crisis between the time of the Reformation and the Thirty Years War (1618–48). Matriculations at Cracow peaked around 1520, following a hundred years of fairly steady increase, then fell and stagnated for much of the rest of the century (Kaniewska 1986a:117–18, 128–31). Prague was badly affected by its associations with the Hussite heretics and by the political unrest in the region: its 'golden age' ended in about 1420 and the sixteenth and seventeenth centuries saw stagnation. Like Vienna and Cracow, failure to embrace Protestant theology had a seriously detrimental effect on its matriculations, the proportion of foreigners at Cracow falling from 23 per cent in 1510–60 to less than 1 per cent in the eighteenth century (Kaniewska 1986a:119–20; 1986b:141). Fewer foreign students (*ultramontani*) attended post-Tridentine Italian universities than in the fifteenth and early sixteenth centuries. Confessional divisions stimulated the creation of new universities in the sixteenth century but also reduced foreign matriculations in many. Across Europe, princes tried to keep their subjects at home as much as possible for political reasons (Kagan 1986:167, 169; Šmahel 1986:84).

Steps were taken to halt the rot. During the 1570s, bishop Vilém Prusinovský called in the Jesuits, the storm-troopers of the Counter-Reformation, to found a gymnasium and academy at Olmütz in Moravia, which was quickly given university status by the pope (Evans 1974:1–6). Over most of northern Italy, university populations rose during the sixteenth century, a notable success story being Padua with some 300 matriculations a year in the 1550s rising to around 1,000 by 1610. Others peaked in the late fifteenth century, Perugia and

Siena for example, and had a thin time in the following two centuries; Ferrara had *c*.550 students enrolled in the 1550s compared with some seventy around 1700 (Kagan 1986:157, 160–1, 166). At the same time, some of the growth was illusory. Of twenty-two new German universities set up between 1540 and 1700, only seven survived into the nineteenth century and some never attracted more than a hundred students at a time. The university of Évora in eastern Portugal (1550) offered a limited curriculum which was little different from that in a contemporary French *collège* until it was remodelled in the 1770s. Finally, the university of Paris hardly grew at all during the sixteenth century and nine of its forty-three colleges in 1600 had been closed by 1700. All French academies and universities were abolished in 1792, though soon re-established (Kamen 1984:221; Bernard 1970:260; Marques 1972:299; 414; Kagan 1986). The successes and failures of early modern universities reflect their dependence on political and social developments, and in particular their responsiveness to fashion and to demand by church and state for clergy and bureaucrats.

Indeed, the process of growth was far from irreversible and most universities experienced severe difficulties in keeping up their student numbers after the middle of the seventeenth century. The reasons behind this lay in three areas: the causes of the original expansion, the nature of the curricula on offer, and changes in the social, economic and political context in which the universities had to operate.

To a limited degree, the growth of higher education in the Renaissance was a product of a new desire for learning in itself, a humanist belief in the power of knowledge to improve individual and society. We cannot know how many students went to university fired by this ideal, how many went simply to have a good time and come out as fuller human beings, and how many looked only to the career opportunities which a university training would open up. Comments about students, which are less useful but more common than those by them, concentrate on the careerist aspects of the search for office. Doctor Juan Queippo de Llano, president of the *chancilleria* at Valladolid, remarked with sadness that 'the love of letters brings only a few to the colleges' (Kagan 1974:78). It is also true that some fathers intended their sons' university careers to finish them as gentlemen. One Richard Holdsworth, a former member of the college, wrote in 1635 to the master of Emmanuel, Cambridge, on behalf of a friend's son that 'his father means not to have him a scholar by profession but only to be seasoned with the varnish of learning and piety which is remarkable in many under your government' (O'Day 1982:125).

University attendance came to be part of the making of the early modern upper classes but, as we shall see, their attendance was sometimes rather transient and temporary.

Some graduates could become self-employed doctors or lawyers; some could work as teachers or urban administrators. Study of the job destinations of 782 graduates of Prague university who wrote books, tracts or poems in Latin between the fifteenth and seventeenth centuries shows that 1 per cent died before obtaining work, 72 per cent initially took employment as schoolmasters, 14 per cent went straight into professional posts, and the careers of 13 per cent are unknown. Most of those who went into teaching as a first job did not end their days there (just 12 per cent of the original 563), and the majority went on to become clergy, academics, merchants, municipal administrators and members of the liberal professions (Šmahel 1986:77–81). Ultimately, there were really only two major employers of university graduates at this time: church and state. Both demanded more and better-trained officials to cope with the competition for souls between Catholic and Protestant, and the drive for uniformity and order in the secular world. Thus, the university of Marburg in Germany was founded in 1527 explicitly to produce state servants while that at Leiden (1575) was a Protestant foundation to rival Catholic Douai and Louvain. This was all well and good, but when the demand for officials stabilised and when alternative paths to lucrative employment became available – attendance at specialist academies in Germany or French *collèges* for example – the universities began to suffer. The orientation of Italian universities towards legal studies is part of the reason for their decline in the seventeenth century since they had little to offer when new studies in science and the liberal arts became fashionable. They were sidetracked by new generations of students looking for 'education' rather than 'certification'. Italian *collegi dei nobili*, of which there were more than forty by 1700, attracted elites away from universities; the one at Parma drew in *c.*300 students a year at this date. Jesuit colleges offered particularly stiff competition since they were sometimes able to win over the official patronage of both secular and ecclesiastical authorities from universities in the same town (Kagan 1986:163, 165, 174, 176, 178). As higher education became more expensive and as the elites were increasingly able to buy offices for their offspring, as job opportunities contracted and as fears about the overproduction of highly educated men grew, as the upper class came to monopolise the paths to better jobs and as the bourgeoisie found alternative outlets in commerce, so the universities lost their primary role.

This development was far from inevitable. Had the universities been able to move with the times they would, as happened in Germany and Scotland, have been able to accommodate social, economic and political change. As it was, their archaic organisational structures and ossified curricula condemned them to stagnation and decay. The largest universities contained four faculties: arts, theology, medicine and law. Some had only one or two of these: Olmütz in Moravia, for instance, possessed only theology and philosophy classes; England's two universities had no common law departments. In others, some faculties were particularly strong, some especially weak: most Spanish universities were top-heavy with law students in the sixteenth century, as were Padua, Pisa and Naples in Italy with 75 per cent of all students from this group, but Paris' legal faculty stagnated until Louis XIV's reign (Brockliss 1978; Kagan 1986:163).

All suffered from similar problems of intellectual inertia, for an increase in student numbers did not necessarily mean developments in teaching methods or curricula. Medical faculties were among the most traditional. In early eighteenth-century Germany, anatomical lecture theatres were almost unknown and students had only an indirect knowledge of anatomy. One disenchanted Hanoverian official of the time believed that medical schools existed only to 'create ten or fifteen young angels of death so that the people may be buried methodically' (McClelland 1980:30). Throughout the university system, the problem was one of unchanging standards and rigid curricula. The 'new learning' of the humanists, which became fashionable in the early sixteenth century, was simply grafted on to the existing scholastic framework and traditional professionally-oriented courses. Rather than the leaders of intellectual development during the sixteenth and seventeenth centuries, universities were bastions of orthodoxy: in sixteenth-century France the defenders of Catholicism against all Protestant heresies and most new ideas, in the seventeenth and eighteenth centuries the developers and promoters of the intellectual underpinning of absolutism. In Portugal, intellectual developments during the sixteenth century took place largely outside a university environment. What Marques (1972:204, 300-1) calls the 'revolution of experience' associated with geographical discoveries tended speedily to outdate certain areas of scholarship in that country. Curricular developments rarely amounted to modernisation of what was taught since the universities continued to see their role as imparting a given body of knowledge rather than expanding or altering it. And in the eighteenth century the new academies in which the ideas of the Enlightenment were hatched and dispatched left most universities as backwaters of conservatism (Morgan 1978; Kagan 1974; McClelland 1980).

We must not be too critical of the universities since there were developments taking place within them. In France, for example, they transmitted and popularised new scientific and philosophical ideas which played an important part in the intellectual ferment of the Revolutionary period (Brockliss 1987). Padua, the leader in medical studies in the seventeenth century, was responsible for educating the great English physician Harvey. At the same time, some universities reformed teaching and curricula, and there are some signs of a European-wide recovery in university attendance in the later eighteenth century. In Spain, for example, numbers attending eleven universities for which good statistics survive stagnated at about 60 per cent of their 1800 level until the 1760s, then rose (Kamen 1984:222; Peset & Mancebo 1986:192).

Official curricula were, of course, only a part of the university experience. Hidebound university courses did not necessarily mean that students were subject only to the prescribed intellectual influences. Enlightened tutors or the large body of printed material which became available during our period could counterbalance archaic curricula. Poorly and irregularly paid professors in some Italian universities offered private tuition for fees – several at Naples were gaoled for this illegal practice in the 1620s – and students are said to have found these *lettori privati* much more useful than in-house university courses (Kagan 1986:171–2). Cosmopolitan ideas and life-styles, of the kind which confronted provincials at Madrid, Paris or Rome, could widen horizons and create a network of friends and patrons far more important than paper qualifications in a world where contacts were all. This is why some members of the upper classes treated their varsity careers as a sort of finishing school. Some parents complained at the lack of supervision of their sons at university and, indeed, fighting, drinking and whoring were notorious in student areas of a town. Riots between Italian and Spanish students at Pavia in 1594 left several dead, and in one parish close to the university of Salamanca, 60 per cent of all the children baptised in 1558 were illegitimate (Kagan 1974:203; 1986:175).

The difficulties faced by universities after the crises of the mid-seventeenth century are plainly demonstrated by the example of two countries whose institutions of higher learning effectively solved them. First of all Scotland, a small, poor and relatively unimportant country which nevertheless possessed some of Europe's most prestigious universities. Student numbers rose from just over 1,000 to 4,400 between 1700 and 1820, at a time when population less than doubled, attracted to Scotland's institutions of higher learning by important changes in teaching methods and curricula. Until 1708 at Edinburgh, 1727 at Glasgow and 1747 at St Andrews, students were taken through all the years of their university career by 'regents'. These non-specialist teachers watched over student life and morals, offering instruction by dictating chunks of text to large, passive classes. The pursuit of knowledge and independent thought were restricted by this stress on expounding set texts. The abolition of regenting was followed by the creation of a number of new specialist professorships, notably at Edinburgh, filled by gifted teachers and original thinkers such as William Robertson, Adam Ferguson and Dugald Stewart. The curriculum too began to be modernised from the end of the seventeenth century. Newtonian ideas were incorporated into science teaching and there were developments in theology within an Aristotelian framework. Francis Hutcheson, professor of philosophy at Glasgow, began lecturing in English rather than Latin from 1729. Medicine and the law were famous throughout eighteenth-century Europe for their advanced teaching methods and courses, and were important in changing Scotland's universities from glorified seminaries to much broader institutions which nurtured the distinctive ideas of the Scottish Enlightenment (Camic 1985:165–84; O'Day 1982:231–6, 273–9). Not all Scotland's universities participated in these developments for St Andrews languished during the eighteenth century.

The development of Germany's universities was similarly patchy but the system as a whole flourished during the eighteenth century. These had recovered fairly easily after the holocaust of the Thirty Years War. Some then began to reform their curricula and teaching methods and there were, unusually, new foundations at the end of the seventeenth century, notably Halle in Saxony (1694). Their real development took place during the eighteenth century as, under the stimulus of competition from the new *Ritterakademien* (Knights' academies) and of quickening interest from governments and elites, they began to change the subjects they offered and the way they taught.

The fortunes of institutions of higher learning in eighteenth-century Germany were much better than those of France, which had attracted so much criticism and so many enemies that they were swept away in their entirety during the French Revolution. In the 1600s there were twenty universities in the German lands with around 8,000 students, twenty-eight in 1700 and some 9,000 young men, and thirty-one by the 1760s, though with a reduced number of students (about 7,000 in all); by 1820 this number had been thinned down to twenty, giving Germany the leanest and fittest higher education system in continental Europe. German universities succeeded where others had failed for a variety of reasons. First, they had all been subject to state control from an early date. Second, they had a monopoly of the training of the higher bureaucracy in a state where that bureaucracy was a powerful force. Third, they legitimised the status of existing elites and offered a route by which other social groups could attain standing. Because there was less competition from alternative bodies like the French *collèges* or the English Inns of Court, the middling and upper ranks in German society took a close interest in curricula, admissions standards and employment openings. Local circumstances dictated how successful the adjustment would be, specifically: political fragmentation, the ability of rulers directly to influence their universities, the need for trained bureaucrats and the rise of cameralism (the new science of government). Catholic universities remained traditional in the main and Protestant ones were the pacemakers: Catholic nobles might even send sons destined for state service to Protestant universities. Those German universities which survived and flourished during the eighteenth and early nineteenth centuries were those which responded to the new needs of state and society. Those in Germany and elsewhere which did not went to the wall. The fortunes of higher education, as of elementary schooling, depended crucially on the social and political context and on the responsiveness of institutions of learning to it.

WHO WENT TO UNIVERSITY?

Patterns of attendance at institutions of higher learning were, not surprisingly, dictated by the same social and economic forces which determined who might go to school. University attendance was largely the province of the middling and upper classes while the nature of the course studied and the general experience of university were dictated by social origins.

Universities varied enormously in size, curriculum and quality. During the sixteenth century the Spanish university of Salamanca took in between 5,000 and 7,000 matriculands a year, dwarfing institutions like Seville, Granada or Baeza. More modest and much more typical of European universities was Pisa with a hundred new students a year and a total size of 600–700 in the middle of the sixteenth century. Prague at this time had suffered from political and religious wrangles, possessing only a philosophy faculty and a mere hundred students. The range of size in neatly illustrated in the case of German universities. Around 1600, Greifswald in Pomerania could claim approximately 100 students compared with the 900 at Leipzig in Saxony. Total attendance at the Scottish universities in 1700 was just over 1,000 (Kagan 1974:197–8; Schmitt 1974:8; Evans 1974:1–2; 1981:189; Emerson 1977:473).

Universities were numerous but they usually housed few students. Despite this, the proportion of the eligible population who were able to attend was, while small in absolute terms, impressive in a historical context. The expansion of universities in the age of the Renaissance meant that as many as 2–3 per cent of young men were able to enrol in university faculties during the early seventeenth century, a figure not equalled again until the early twentieth century. Estimates of attendance must remain tentative for two reasons. First, matriculation records do not always survive and those which do may be registers of oaths of loyalty which could be taken at any stage in a university career. As many as a third of those admitted to three Oxford colleges 1612–31 never matriculated (Stone 1969:49–50). The position is further complicated by the tradition of wandering from one university to another. Andrea Alciato, a noted jurist born in 1494, began his studies at Pavia in 1507, enrolled at Bologna in 1511 and graduated from Ferrara in 1517 (Kagan 1986:156). Graduation records are better but do not offer a perfect indication of attendance since throughout most of the middle ages and well into the sixteenth century taking a BA was simply a qualification to read in a higher faculty. Rituals of the kind modern graduates experience came when one took a doctorate. The drop-out rate was high. At the university of Alcalá in Spain between 1550 and 1702, between two-fifths and two-thirds of students left before the end of their second year of studies and a third of those at Pisa before the end of their third year. Of matriculands at the six elite *Colegios Mayores* during Philip II's reign, 9 per cent died before completing their course, and 16 per cent in that of Carlos II. Half of those who enrolled at Cambridge (1590–1640) did not finish, 15 per cent of matriculands graduated BA from Cracow 1510–60 (4 per cent MA) and only one student in twenty ever graduated from Heidelberg (1550–1620). What is more, the graduation rate fluctuated making it difficult to generalise about attendance. At the university of Toulouse the proportion of students taking degrees rose in hard times and fell when the economy prospered (Kagan 1974:132, 178; 1986:156; Ferté 1980:319–20; Kaniewska 1986a:127; Kamen 1984:225).

Second, the concept of an eligible population, which can be defined quite closely in the late twentieth century, was much more vague in the early modern world, the reason being that the age at which boys went to university varied considerably. The average age at matriculation to Spanish universities in the sixteenth century was eighteen, compared with sixteen two centuries later. In contrast, the average age at first registration in the university of Paris was just ten in the first half of the sixteenth century, rising to the late teens by the end of the seventeenth as students increasingly trained at provincial *collèges* before matriculating in the arts faculty. These averages disguise a substantial range of ages among the student population, many of whom were full-grown adults. Paris' arts faculty included men and boys more than a generation apart in the age of the Reformation, but by the eighteenth century the age-spread was narrower: roughly fifteen to thirty (Kagan 1974:17; Brockliss 1978:519). This is also true of Oxford and Cambridge in the 1630s when nearly all entrants were aged fifteen to nineteen (Stone 1964:57).

A third problem exists in estimating the proportion of eligibles in a given country, that of the high numbers of foreign students. For all their faults, early modern universities remained cosmopolitan institutions: 242 German students matriculated at Bologna university 1600–1 and 2,555 at Siena 1590–1609. Between 1433 and 1509, 44 per cent of Cracow's matriculands were foreigners, 23 per cent 1510–60 (Engelsing 1973:33; Kaniewska 1986a:119–20). Some universities attracted students because of their high reputation: Pisa for medicine, Leiden for law, Paris for philosophy. In 1527, king Manuel of Portugal endowed fifty scholarships at the *Collège de Saint Barbe* in Paris for his subjects (Marques 1972:194). Others depended on tradition: the universities of Scotland and Holland developed a special relationship from the early seventeenth century, for example. In some cases the lack of native alternatives drove young men to study abroad. The first university in Finland was founded at Turku in 1640. Until the Reformation, scholars went to Paris, after it to Erfurt, Leipzig and Stockholm. Irish Catholics had perforce to go to continental foundations such as Louvain throughout the early modern period; Norwegian, Icelandic and, occasionally, Greenland youths to Copenhagen. Staff too moved around Europe, including the famous sixteenth-century Scot George Buchanan who worked briefly in the university of Coimbra in Portugal before falling foul of the Inquisition.

In general, however, catchment areas were very regionalised: most Parisian students came from north-eastern France, those who went to Seville from west Andalucia, to Granada from the east of that province; the smaller and less significant the university, the more localised its geographical intake. This means that areas well-served by universities, such as northern Spain, would have higher than average percentages attending compared with less favoured regions, and towns like Madrid had nearly double the Castilian average in the middle of the eighteenth century (Kagan 1974). Central European universities recruited overwhelmingly from the towns: 91 per cent of Bohemian graduates of the university of Prague 1433–1618 came from towns, a figure which is almost the exact reverse of the proportions of the total population living in urban and rural areas (Šmahel 1986:76).

Taking all these problems into account, we can generalise about the proportion of eligibles who attended universities in early modern Europe. At the start of the sixteenth century, a figure of around 1 per cent prevailed over most of western Europe. With the expansion in university places during the century of the Reformation, the average rose to around 2.4 per cent in early seventeenth-century England, 2.8 per cent in the United Provinces of the Low Countries at the same time, and nearly 3 per cent of males aged fifteen to twenty-four in the province of Castile, which contained most of Spain's population. Proportions were roughly equal across western Europe at any one time and trends similar: a peak in the middle of the seventeenth century falling away to levels of 1 per cent or less by the time of the French Revolution. Levels stayed up to 1.5 per cent in Holland, and over 2 per cent in Castile and Scotland, but elsewhere the eighteenth century was a time of stagnation and decay in university attendance. Through the three centuries, numbers remained tiny. As late as 1775, Scotland's universities, among the major European success stories of the eighteenth century, were only enrolling 2,000 students a year despite their attractive new curricula and teaching methods, low entrance standards, low fees and bursaries to help poorer students. Germany's thirty-one universities took in under 7,000 and Russia's only proper university in Moscow drew approximately 100 under-graduates from an imperial population of 40,000,000 during the 1790s (Alston 1969:11; Kagan 1974; 1986; Frijhoff 1979).

Given the small proportion of the eligible population who attended, we should not be surprised to learn that the social distribution of students was restricted. One simple example illustrates the imbalances. At its height in the reign of Philip II, the university system of Castile drew in 20,000 students a year, or around 3 per cent of eligible youths in the society as a whole. However, somewhere between 25 and 35 per cent of boys from the gentry (*hidalgo*) class attended and virtually none from the ranks of ordinary peasants. Two-thirds of English society was made up of yeomen and husbandmen farmers, but these groups contributed only one in eight of the seventeenth-century student intake, and even the humbler provincial universities of France rarely took more than 5 per cent of their students from the peasantry. By contrast, 65 per cent of matriculands at Douai were sons of professionals or officials. Law faculties were particularly elitist. Of 126 young men who enrolled in the Faculty of Advocates of the University of Edinburgh in 1705, sixty-eight came from titled families and just seven were not from a landowning background. Half a century before or half a century later than this date, the complexion of the faculty was less gentrified, but the non-landed quarter of the intake came overwhelmingly from professional or mercantile stock. Two-thirds of the nobility in German universities of the eighteenth century were to be found in law departments. Young men from monied and titled backgrounds had a completely different experience of university to their humbler fellows. The sons of grandees and *titulos* at institutions such as Salamanca lived in style, dressed lavishly, had a degree course one year shorter than other students because of their supposedly superior preparation for university, enjoyed the services of additional tutors, employed servants to attend their lectures for them and normally did not take their degree (Kagan 1974:184–5, 199; Phillipson 1980:148; Kamen 1984:224; Chartier *et al.* 1976:277–8).

Universities became more rather than less elitist over time. In the late 1620s, 52 per cent of students at Oxford and Cambridge came from 'plebeian' stock but only 27 per cent in 1711, mostly because the universities had ceased to be a path for boys from humble backgrounds to make their way into the ranks of the clergy, who were becoming increasingly an hereditary caste (Morgan 1978:153–4). Indeed, it would be a mistake to associate the universities with substantial levels of social mobility at any period, and certainly not in the eighteenth century. The church took between 57 and 62 per cent of graduates from Oxford in the eighteenth century, and most graduates from theology faculties in Scottish and German universities at this time looked only to the comparative security and prestige of a clerical career. The ultimate careers of those who attended university depended closely on their social origins. There are indications of some broadening of the intake at Cracow in Poland and at some Spanish universities in the eighteenth century as the percentage of noble youths fell: at Cracow from about a quarter to a tenth over the century (Kaniewska 1986b:144; Peset & Mancebo 1986:192). This does not necessarily indicate that higher education as a whole was becoming more representative. The popularity of English universities for the sons of landowners fluctuated between the early sixteenth century and the end of the nineteenth. The percentage of gentlemen attending doubled in the century before 1625 before entering a slump from which enrolment levels did not recover until the end of the eighteenth century (Stone and Stone 1984). At the university of Paris in the eighteenth century, the humbler students looked only to the church, the wealthier to the law and artisans to a return to bourgeois life; medicine was considered a dubious profession for the well-born and only one man of noble status (Joseph Piton in 1696) graduated with a medical degree. The great nobles often did not bother with higher education, relying on travel to broaden their horizons. In eastern Europe they positively despised universities and academies until forced into them by state pressure. For the upper classes as a whole, university simply created alternative avenues to positions which the students would have enjoyed anyway (Brockliss 1978:533, 539).

The social distribution of students was determined partly by attitudes and perceived opportunities, partly by the sheer cost of attendance. Fees, board and lodging (if the student did not live at home) and the payment for taking a degree all added up to a formidable charge on the parental purse. Fees in the university of Paris arts faculty were fairly low at between twelve and thirty-six livres during the sixteenth and seventeenth centuries, and were abandoned in the eighteenth. However, boarding in a pension cost something like 300 livres a year in 1700 (double for a single room), an impossible sum for a day labourer whose annual total earnings were less than 100 livres. Still more fantastic were fees for taking a degree: 30 to 50 livres for arts and law in the sixteenth century but a massive 800 livres for medicine. At least the cost of attending university in France rose in pace with costs in general: it would have cost a provincial 75 livres a year to be a student in Paris around 1500 and 750 livres in 1800. In contrast, England was a land where prices remained fairly stable between the early seventeenth century and the middle of the eighteenth, but the charge for a year at Oxford or Cambridge more than doubled to more than eighty pounds. Only in Scotland did it become cheaper in real terms to attend university in the eighteenth century. The importance of cost is clearly shown by trends in enrolments to the provincial French university of Toulouse. During years of bad harvest or trade dislocation, the number of students who matriculated in the law faculty and who came from the diocese of Rodez was halved. Students of modest means preferred the cheaper provincial universities to Paris but their relatively marginal economic standing might push even these beyond their reach (Brockliss 1978:528-30; O'Day 1982:198; Ferté 1980:317-18).

To combat the inhibiting effect of cost on attendance, all universities had some kind of bursaries for poor but able students. Renaissance learning included the idea that talent would be equally divided among all ranks of people and that a state should encourage all able men to be useful to it in some way. Thus, sixteenth-century Spain had six *Colegios Mayores*, four at Salamanca and one each at Valladolid and Alcalá. These were self-governing institutions where 100-250 students could obtain scholarships and accommodation. By the beginning of the seventeenth century, wealthy students had increasingly infiltrated these institutions, admission to which became more and more dependent on patronage and money rather than poverty and ability. In the eighteenth century they were nothing more than elite colleges where the nobility and officials sent their sons to be trained as bureaucrats (Phillips 1977:348). The same thing happened to colleges for the poor but gifted at the university of Paris during this period and, indeed, the story is a depressingly familiar one all over Europe. Between 1543 and 1604, four new residential colleges were founded at the university of Pisa, two by the Grand Dukes, two by cardinals. However, abuses similar to those in Spain and France soon became apparent and in 1598 Grand Duke Ferdinando I noted with disgust that prospective students made a show of poverty to get into his college but once there showed off as though they had enough of everything and did very little work (Schmitt 1974:9). Across Europe, places were usurped by the elites who had more than enough money to pay the full rates. The university of Cologne included 743 'poor' students among its numbers in the years 1486-90 but only ten 1556-60.

The substantial expansion at all levels of the complex educational hierarchy fully merits the title 'an educational revolution'. More people than ever attended schools and universities while educational institutions were reorganised to reflect changing social needs and the new power and demands of the state. Continuities too were strong, notably in teaching methods and materials, and in the structure of the teaching 'profession'. At the same time, the impact of change was limited by existing attitudes and social structures, notably the way in which the wealth of parents and the gender of a child dictated access to post-elementary education. The variety of experience of educational change was enormously varied across Europe and the fortunes of the universities highlight the important fact that progress in education was not linear and that educational institutions depended intimately on the social and political environment in which they operated. Education's impact on society was dependent as much as it was independent. The universities of early modern Europe reflected and perpetuated inequalities of wealth and opportunity and the ideological assumptions which pervaded the upper reaches of society. Schooling certainly played a more central role in the process of growing up for most western European children in 1800 than in 1500, but we must recognise that demand for learning had to exist to fuel the drive towards education and literacy and also that the school was not the only place in which the acquisition of literacy might take place. An understanding of the nature of demand for literacy and the ways in which that wish could be satisfied are central to the way literacy developed and the uses to which it was ultimately put.

CHAPTER FIVE

Ways of learning

Schools were of enormous importance in raising the literacy of a broad spectrum of the early modern population. Schools were not, however, the only positive force behind developments in literacy. After all, even when schools are provided not all parents will wish (or even be able) to send their children to them: some form of compulsion must be exercised or, more significantly, *demand* for education must exist to encourage families to bear its cost. We shall deal with this issue later in the chapter, for the demand side is extremely important in determining advances or stagnation in literacy. Schools would only be effective when they were an integral part of family and community life rather than alien impositions of outside authorities or social groups. At the same time, we must recognise that the whole explanation for structures and trends in illiteracy does not lie with schools. Some type of instruction was probably essential to mastering basic skills such as deciphering letters and syllables even if only a little information could be transmitted to a child during the brief and intermittent schooling he or she received. Formal, scholastic learning was important since such knowledge would not be generated spontaneously, but it was only one way of acquiring the fuller skills of reading, writing and counting, while learning in adulthood could reinforce earlier instruction or even make up for its absence. Indeed, for many people, education in a school was only part of a much wider process of learning which encompassed the home, peer groups and work experience. For many from the lower classes who made up the bulk of the population, schools were only a small part of growing up. The process of learning was part of the wider experience of socialisation which shaped their consciousness and informed their everyday lives. We must examine the many forms of learning which supplemented schooling or in some cases substituted for it altogether.

OUTSIDE THE SCHOOL

Learning outside of formal schools could take place in all sorts of contexts, of which the most obvious was the home. The best known example of learning in the home is that of the Renaissance aristocracy. In countries as diverse as England and Spain, affluent families employed private tutors to teach their sons the skills of the gentleman. Private tutors remained central to the education of the children of nobles and gentry who did not follow the official religion of a country – English Catholics for example – since the only alternative for those who did not wish their offspring to be brought up in a different faith was to send them abroad. Where schools were in short supply anyway, as in sixteenth- and seventeenth-century Finland, this might be the only way of educating children for the rural gentry and nobility. Boys from this social class were taught the elements of literacy alongside more advanced skills such as Latin, modern foreign languages and perhaps accounting. The final gloss was provided by instruction in riding, fencing, dancing and the other trappings of gentility. At the time of Napoleon's invasion of Russia, to which the Renaissance came rather late, prince Barjatinskij's son was receiving this sort of wide-ranging, practical and mainly personal instruction which, as with many aristocratic youths, culminated in travel abroad (Eeckaute 1970; Engelsing 1973:50–2). For the lesser gentry and for the daughters of the nobility, a stay in another gentle household could provide a similar training at less cost. During the eighteenth and nineteenth centuries the use of governesses spread down from the upper classes into the homes of the prosperous bourgeoisie who used them to give their children a grounding in elementary learning and etiquette, and to train girls in the ways of the middle class spouse. The resort to private tutors declined after the sixteenth century as landowning families began increasingly to send their sons to urban grammar schools and then university, their daughters (if they were formally educated away from home) to the newly fashionable 'finishing schools'.

Education in the home was not the exclusive preserve of the upper classes. John Jones, a servant lad from near Birmingham in England who wrote an autobiography, tells of his brief stay at dame school around 1780 followed by two years of lessons from a retired stone-cutter in the winter evenings. Guillaume Masenx, born in southern France sometime during the 1490s, received a little basic instruction from an uncle who was a priest at Castelnau. Not that it did him much good, since we know that he spoke only the local dialect, knew no Latin or French and the documents on which his hand appears reveal poor writing and appalling spelling (Vincent 1981:94; Le Roy Ladurie 1974:125). In Russia and the Scandinavian countries, where properly constituted schools were rare before the nineteenth century, home learning was the norm. A Russian *Domostroi* or household guide of the sixteenth century shows that the family was conceived of as the basic social and political unit, dominated by a father who had a duty to raise his offspring to glorify God and the Czar, and that education would take place in the home and through the parents (Black 1979:15–16). The Lutheran literacy campaigns in Sweden and its dependencies relied solely on teaching by priest and parents in the home while in the sixteenth-century archbishopric of Milan, the reforming cardinal Borromeo recommended that while children should attend Schools of Christian Doctrine, fathers should also read aloud to their families from a devotional book after meals. Domenico Manzoni's *Libretto molto utile* (1546) was for fathers who took these religious exhortations seriously, though it offered no pedagogic advice on reading (Schutte 1986:15). Indeed, religious reformers of all churches recognised the power of learning in the home. Luther spoke of householders being 'bishops in their own homes' and specifically commended the ecclesiastical constitution of the town of Leisnig in Saxony which said that 'every householder and his wife shall be duty-bound to cause the wholesome, consoling Word of God to be preached to them, their children, and their domestic servants' (Strauss 1978:4).

These schemes required parents to teach children and masters to instruct servants. However, the younger generation might educate the older in situations where children were being taught outside the home and then brought their new-found skills into the household. After prescribing the way in which his donation for a charity school at Stratford-upon-Avon should be spent, John Smarte added that when the children 'can read in the Bibles that they may have them to church with them and that they read them at home before their parents at least 3 tymes in the weeke (for parents are oftymes taken more with their children's reading than with what they heare at church)' (Richardson & James 1983:149). The seventeenth-century Lancashire apprentice William Stout had attended grammar school but when his father died he took a three-week cramming course in writing and arithmetic before entering his apprenticeship. Once installed, his master used Stout's talents to educate his son. The young were similarly important in spreading the English language into Gaelic-speaking parts of Ireland and Scotland during the eighteenth century since English was taught in schools but most adults were Gaelic monoglots. Whichever way information flowed, the home was an important place for exchanging practical and intellectual skills.

Learning did not stop at the door of the school or the front step of the home. Peers were as important as parents in the process of socialisation. One observer remarked of the people of Sweden in 1631 that they were 'so fond of letters that although public schools are very few, nevertheless the literate instruct the others with such enthusiasm that the greatest part of the common people, and even the peasants, are literate' (Kamen 1984:210). Often these contacts were generated by personal friendships rather than by societal norms. A Protestant linen-weaver from Cambrai in France explained to a court in 1566 how he 'was led to knowledge of the Gospel by ... my neighbour, who had a Bible printed at Lyon and who taught me the psalms by heart ... The two of us used to go walking in the fields on Sundays and feast days, conversing about the Scriptures and the abuses of priests.' (Davis 1975:189). Within the large classes in most schools, older children helped younger with their lessons. Learning from friends and neighbours, classmates and playmates could take place informally, on a very personal basis. Under certain circumstances, these associations could become semi-formal. In south-western France there were coherent youth groups made up of young men and women in their teens and early twenties. These groups went beyond the boundaries of household and family to encompass all the youth in a village. In parts of Germany, groupings achieved a regular status in the form of the winter evening *Spinnstube* or spinning circle. The *Spinnstube* was a type of work sociability where unmarried girls in particular met to spin, knit and talk. Most of the interchange was of gossip and tales, but there were also opportunities to practise reading and to learn other practical skills (Medick 1984:317, 334–5).

All of these ways of learning could be a valuable addition to self-teaching. Schooling was brief for the majority of the population and anything which had been learned would have to be consolidated and expanded if full use was to be made of the elementary skills which had been taught at the age of six, seven or eight. Among lower-class writers of autobiographies, most had received very little formal education but had sought out reading and writing in their own way later in life. Writing of his late-eighteenth-century schooldays, the German autodidact Gottlieb Hiller recalled that he went to school in winter but had to work in the fields in spring, summer and autumn. Thus, he easily forgot what he had learned in childhood and had to make up the loss later in life through his own application (Engelsing

1973:70). Some ordinary people never attended a school and had to rely on their own efforts or the help of friends if they were to master the basics of literacy. The seventeenth-century Puritan Englishman Adam Martindale took his first steps in literacy with a primer and the help of a young man who came to court his sister. Small wonder that the sixteenth and seventeenth centuries saw a proliferation of do-it-yourself manuals. Strasbourg saw a spate of publishing of ABC primers as early as 1480–1520; from Venice in 1536 came Tagliente's *La Vera Arte de lo Excellente Scrivere* and from Lyon later in the century a *Brief Arithmetic* which promised to instruct a tradesman within fifteen days and offered mnemonic verses to help him learn. Italian ABC books of this period commonly used verses in alphabetic order to help memorisation in which the first word of the stanza gave an example of the letter (Davis 1975:213; Lucchi 1978:603–4; Chrisman 1982:121–2). Conceivably, the frequent publication of such books in northern Italy was a testament to the comparative significance of self-teaching in that part of Europe in the sixteenth century, though some of them were also used in schools.

A ready market for self-teaching aids is evident throughout the period. From 1776, newspapers available in Finland contained sections specifically set out to help people learn writing. Early nineteenth-century almanacs even detail the use of a stick in a sandbox or snow, or charcoal on a piece of bark, or even a finger on a steamed-up window-pane for those who could not get pen and paper but who wanted to practise; they advocated starting with capitals then progressing to cursive script, practising by taking dictation or copying chunks from the Bible (Luttinen 1985:44–5). Self-teaching had its limitations. For readers it could lead to misunderstandings; for writers to rough handwriting, uneven lines, irregular or phonetic spelling, poor punctuation and capitalisation, and erratic grammar. And, of course, one had to be able to read a little before one could understand the autodidactic literature. Tagliente's *Libro Maistrevole* (1524) was targeted at young people and adults who wanted to learn to read or to improve basic, possibly forgotten, skills but it required a volunteer instructor to guide the individual through the letters, syllables and words (Schutte 1986). It was not intended for the classroom nor for young children and possessed a secular, practical, vernacular emphasis rather different from what was practised in formal, scholastic education.

Self-teaching or learning from peers was probably of greater significance in some parts of Europe than others, notably in Scandinavia, Russia, southern Italy and the west of Ireland where schools were in short supply, though oral rather than written or printed forms of communication tended to predominate in these areas. It was also more important for the lower classes and for girls than for boys of the middling and upper ranks. Even if they went to a formal school it is unlikely that boys and girls would depend wholly on what they learned in the classroom for the acquisition of reading, writing and counting. The relative significance of the various inputs into literacy depended on the availability of education and its cost but also on cultural norms about learning and the desire for it.

DESIRE FOR LEARNING

All of this chapter and most of those on schooling depend for their force on the existence of some sort of demand for learning. Schools might be set up but there was no effective way of compelling parents to send their children to them. Church and state could provide educational facilities but they could not force the population to accept them or use them unless there was a desire for learning and a preparedness to pay for education. Literacy had to have a pay-off in order to make it attractive, and it is to the factors which created a demand for reading and writing that we must now turn. Literacy in the modern developed world is seen as a way the individual attains power over himself and his environment. Unfortunately, the surviving documentation does not allow a direct or systematic interrogation of the motives which encouraged an adult to seek command of literacy, or which decided a parent on a costly educational programme for a son. We can see that initiatives by church and state may build on an existing demand for education. For example, in Lorraine and Franche-Comté in the late sixteenth century, local communities were closely involved in the choice of school regents and displayed a keen interest in the quality of education, though exactly who was most vocal and how socially extensive concern was is difficult to quantify (Furet & Ozouf 1982:67). Nineteenth-century Russian peasants had some incentive to become literate since a cleaner and less exacting job might be the reward (Brooks 1985:12–13). There are no early modern questionnaires to tell us how large a percentage of the people felt that literacy would enhance their prestige, broaden their horizons or help them find a better job. We have instead to extrapolate from occasional, offhand remarks or infer motivation from changes in the economic, social, cultural and political environment.

Demand for literacy was determined by both positive and negative forces. On the positive side there was the pull of economic need, the desire for social mobility and the wish to attain qualifications required for certain (mainly bureaucratic) posts; prestige and the possibilities for enhanced social relationships; a richer spiritual life and the chance for vicarious experience leading to intellectual development. On the negative side there was a sense that literacy was needed to avoid exploitation, notably by the representatives of secular and ecclesiastical authorities or by landlords and employers. Running through all this are three principal themes. First, economic change which expanded the need for reading, writing and counting. Second, the growing influence and power of the state in everyday life, notably through armies and bureaucracies. Third, the development of religious pluralism from the Reformation onwards. No part of Europe was untouched by these developments and in their different ways they exerted a pervasive influence on the demand for literate skills.

At the end of the middle ages a 'European economy' did not exist. In its place there were hundreds of parcellised if overlapping local and regional economies. What trade there was took place overwhelmingly in foodstuffs and other agricultural products such as wine, skins and timber. However, only a tiny proportion of gross production ever found its way into the networks of overseas trade, and subsistence farming formed the focus of economic life for the vast majority of Europe's people. Transport was difficult and expensive, marketing poorly developed except in certain luxuries and bulk goods which could be transported by sea or river. Money was scarce and the patterns of transactions simple, dominated by face-to-face interactions in a marketplace or on a quay. The sixteenth, seventeenth and eighteenth centuries saw pronounced if gradual changes in this scenario. A much larger proportion of both agricultural and (expanding) industrial output found its way into the marketplace as economic relationships became more commercially oriented. Cash replaced barter and payments in kind while financial instruments such as bills of exchange and prolonged credit developed which allowed long-distance trade to expand. Trade became more diverse and accounted for a growing proportion of the wealth of European states as merchants opened up the New World and created fresh markets for new cloths and for products such as tobacco. Internal trade was fuelled by population growth – numbers roughly doubled in the sixteenth century alone – and by the growing concentration of people in the towns. Around 1500, just 3 per cent of

England's population lived in towns of more than 10,000 people but by 1800 the figure was 24 per cent. Half the population of sixteenth-century Holland lived in towns, an exceptional proportion by contemporary standards. Demographic and economic change took place only slowly in the early modern period but the social implications of commercialisation were considerable.

To cope with these developments, many more people would require the skills of reading, writing and counting. Farmers with an eye on profits had to keep account books and try to follow prices and developments in other regions. A sixteenth-century Friesland farmer stipulated in his will that of the three sons who were to share his legacy, 'he who turns out the most learned will have the major part of the property' (Parker 1979:21). Merchants and carriers in particular required far greater awareness of the market and a more sophisticated approach to dealing with it. One Stettin-based trading company ordered in 1756 that ships' captains should not take on sailors unless they could repeat the catechism while skippers themselves, except those close to retirement, had to display facility in writing, counting and keeping journals (Engelsing 1973:47).

Early newspapers were principally concerned with informing traders of political and economic circumstances in different parts of Europe which would be germane to their commercial dealings. There was, for example, little point in shipping goods to Marseille in 1720 if the port was in quarantine for plague. Indeed, one genre of early printed books was the practical guide for working traders, known variously as merchants' books, commercial dictionaries or *Gesprächbüchlein*. These were multi-lingual phrase books whose aim was to help traders to cope with the bewildering array of objects which were being traded, the diversity of legal systems and tariffs, and the huge variety of weights and measures in use. Sometimes presented in dialogue form, language and format were standardised and simplified to help the merchant find lodgings, describe his wares, negotiate terms, discuss the weather and political conditions, be polite and friendly, write a receipt. These pocket-sized books were published in England, France, Germany and the Low Countries from the end of the fifteenth century and usually covered two to four languages, though some ran to eight (Perrot 1981; Griffin 1637).

Merchants' books give examples of the new uses to which literacy could be put and the incentives which economic change created to learn literacy. Greater use of literacy for practical purposes established confidence in this way of doing things and thus generated further demand for practical literacy and numeracy. The volume of paper produced by commercial transactions was enormous even in the fourteenth and fifteenth centuries, especially by the most go-ahead merchants of the day from the city states of northern Italy. The business archive of Francesco Datini of Prato between 1384 and 1411 includes 125,549 commercial letters from 267 places of origin and the total correspondence runs to 600,000 pages, a passion for paper which extended to north-western Europe during the sixteenth and seventeenth centuries (Hyde 1979:114). As early as the fifteenth century, the use of written instruments in business permeated the lowest ranks among Florentine artisans, presupposing a knowledge of reading, writing and arithmetic alongside a certain habit of mind about keeping records (Goldthwaite 1980:312–13).

Economic change was a powerful force behind the spread of literacy. Significantly, those parts of Europe which enjoyed low levels of commercialisation and urbanisation were generally less literate than economically advanced regions. In seventeenth-century Russia, roughly 1 per cent of the population lived in towns and the peasantry treated money not as a universal means of exchange but as just another crop like rye or oats. Large tracts of eastern central and southern Europe were 're-feudalised' during the sixteenth and seventeenth centuries, reducing the legally-weakened peasantry to poverty but allowing their lords to participate in the expanding trade in foodstuffs. Of course, economic development did not necessarily produce literacy, and backwardness did not condemn a population to ignorance. The mountains of south-western France and northern Italy contained pockets of highly literate people who valued reading and writing as a way to escape the poverty of their homelands. A general connection exists between economic change and literacy but it is by no means automatic and invariable (Smith 1983:293).

The penetration of marketing and of production for exchange into the most remote areas of early modern Europe was paralleled by the growing intrusion of the state into everyday life. Medieval polity had effectively comprised a large number of separate political and legal units loosely bound together by monarchies. The history of the early modern period is dominated by the search for integration and domination of these quasi-independent localities by increasingly powerful central governments. Their weapons were armies, bureaucracies and the law, the expansion of which created a demand for literacy among both personnel and subjects. On the one hand, the state needed more servants with literate skills, on the other the people had to be able to cope with the demands which courts, administrators and soldiers placed upon them.

The early modern period witnessed substantial changes in military tactics and in the size of armies, changes termed a 'military revolution' by Michael Roberts (1967). A force of 30,000 men was counted large in the sixteenth century but Louis XIV fielded at least 300,000 at the end of the seventeenth century and Napoleon's armies numbered over half a million. Armies needed food, clothing, weapons and ammunition, and they had to be paid. They caused economic and social changes which touched virtually every person in Europe in some form or another. The new tactics which transformed the face of warfare in the seventeenth century needed more literate and numerate officers and soldiers. The Russian army came increasingly under central control and high-ranking officers complained of being swamped with paperwork. Officers had to understand written orders, sign for their pay and for supplies, write reports, requisitions and orders for others. Literate troops could read orders, understand firearms manuals and write home to their families, improving efficiency and morale. Literature on military matters proliferated in Italy and France from c.1550. Military academies first appeared in sixteenth-century Italy and by the eighteenth century had spread as far afield as Russia where they formed an important component of the slender educational resources of Peter the Great's empire. The military revolution could touch all ranks. Swiss troops in service abroad commonly had to sign a special register for their pay while those of the French *Compagnie des Indes* had their own enlistment book. A Venetian of the early seventeenth century argued that command of literacy was essential for naval gunners. In fact, however, military developments were restricted to officers and sergeants since most infantry had only to master a few basic techniques. A petition from thirty gunners and riflemen at Oudewater in the Low Countries in 1618 includes not a single signature (Stephens 1980; Corvisier 1979:105–6, 180–1; van Deursen 1978:70).

The vast continental armies of the later seventeenth and eighteenth centuries were ultimately controlled by central bureaucracies. Officials proliferated to deal with warfare and its materials – money, food and weapons – and to administer towns and villages across Europe since an orderly and well-run country was a strong one. Governments needed diplomats, tax collectors, clerks, judges, even inspectors who perambulated the towns of eighteenth-century Prussia sniffing out unlicensed coffee houses. All would require high levels of literacy. In the early days, such men were in short supply, and many of the innovations in secondary and further education during the early modern period were deliberately aimed at improving the supply of capable servants for the state. Gustav Vasa, king of Sweden 1523-60, was chronically embarrassed by the lack of trained secretaries at his disposal as he struggled to administer his country in the same way he would a huge estate. Boys had to be sent abroad for training and Vasa was sometimes driven to dealing with the German language correspondence himself, complaining bitterly of the 'drunkards and ale-hounds, debauched and beastly tosspots' who were thrown up by the defective educational system in his realm. Peter the Great summarised the need felt by many rulers for a cadre of men fitted to enter 'church service, civilian service, and ready to wage war, to practice engineering and medical art' (Roberts 1968:112-13, 170-1; Alston 1969:4).

The influence of the state extended not simply to aspirant professionals but touched the humblest local officials. Seventeenth-century Sweden had its *postbonde*, or 'postal peasant'. Located every hundred kilometres or so along the main highways, these men had to be able to read addresses on letters and packets in order to dispatch them in the correct direction to the next appropriate *postbonde* or to deliver them to recipients in their own area. The work of the state required literacy and encouraged its acquisition. Parish officials too tended to be more literate than average. Village counsellors at Aniane in the Hérault valley of southern France were only 10-20 per cent illiterate in the 1660s compared with perhaps 80 per cent of their male constituents. Reading and writing were required of those who wished to sit on the town council of Buchorn (later Friedrichshafen) in southern Germany (1752). Illiteracy did not prevent men from becoming local officials but its disadvantages were potentially serious. Jacob Jacobsz. of Nieuwport in the Netherlands, nominated as an alderman in the early seventeenth century, announced that he was honoured by the call and would be delighted to take it up if only he could read and write (Le Roy Ladurie 1974:305; Engelsing 1973:47; van Deursen 1978:70).

The growing power of the state was achieved partly through its armies, partly through its bureaucracies and partly through the law courts. The pursuit of order, conformity and integration was furthered through the mechanisms of justice. Again, some educational developments were geared to the needs of a legal career, others were aimed at helping those on the receiving end of the state's intrusions to defend their interests. Göttingen university began in 1746 to offer new courses in *Reichsprozess* or imperial trial law, tailored to be attractive to nobles who were fighting off the more arbitrary administrative innovations of the new absolutist state

(McClelland 1980:45). Magnates too found the law and written forms useful in establishing and protecting their privileges. In eastern Europe the lord's court remained more important than the central courts throughout our period. Estate papers of the seventeenth century are full of written papers to the lord's officials and of written receipts for sums disbursed; even for alms paid out in church in the Polish Zamoyski papers. Thus a demand for scribes and men with a legal training existed (Pospiech & Tygielski 1981).

Legal developments placed many demands on ordinary people. Since most privileges enjoyed by Europeans were enshrined in the law, rather than in custom, a knowledge of its basics was essential for anyone who had contact with the agents of the lord or the state. Written documents and the law certainly could be instruments of state or magnate power, but they also fixed and guaranteed the rights of ordinary people, meaning that there was a defensive as well as an offensive need for command of literacy and legal precepts. Nascent British trade unions of the later eighteenth and early nineteenth centuries appreciated the importance of education for their members and the fact that ignorance made exploitation by employers easier. In Ireland the growing popular demand for learning from the 1780s was intimately associated with the development of Irish Catholic nationalism and the reaction to the domination of education by landlords, state and established church. Pioneers of the feminist movement in England from Mary Astell onwards recognised the place of illiteracy in preserving male dominance over women. The drawbacks inherent in illiteracy were sometimes clearly perceived and sometimes felt as a vague sense of unease, an awareness that it was just another of the disadvantages suffered because of being poor and powerless. It was said that the increasing circulation of banknotes in early nineteenth-century Ireland embarrassed and disadvantaged illiterates. As early as the sixteenth century, a small Durham farmer called John Taylor suspected his half-brother of shady dealings in trying to take over his land by 'bringinge certain writeings to me which I could not certainly tell what they were' (Cullen 1981:236–8; Wrightson 1982:195).

Two final examples summarise the positive and negative aspects of the legal revolution. In France, the guardian of a minor had to be able to write, and if illiterate would be forced to the expense and inconvenience of employing a professional notary to deal with all legal acts relating to the child's inheritance. The German city of Nürnberg required all who died in its bounds to have their goods inventoried by a licensed appraiser or *Unterkeuflin*. These men and women had to be able to read book titles, assess the value of goods, add up the total wealth and write the inventory (Chisick 1981:80-1; Wood 1981:8).

New demands for servants of the state and practitioners of the law greatly expanded opportunities for employment in the early modern period. Alongside economic change, these offered an avenue to social mobility in a world where population growth had made advancement increasingly difficult. Sons commonly followed fathers as farmers or traders but this was not always possible and some parents clearly wished their children to improve their social and economic standing. A *Universal Treasure* of *c*.1530 was directed to Venetians, 'especially to the sons of every father who desires his son's welfare'. From the later sixteenth century, impoverished Polish gentry and ambitious members of the commonality took jobs as clerks, court messengers and baillies while some of the poorer townsfolk of Muscovy earned a modest living as scribes and clerks in the chancellery-secretary's office (Pospiech & Tygielski 1981:76). Literacy became increasingly important in the army too. After the reforms of Choiseul, sergeants of the French military had to be able to read and write, thus closing off promotion prospects to the illiterate. These opportunities existed mainly for the middling and upper classes who could afford the advanced education necessary to enter the expanding ranks of the professions. But there were also chances for the more lowly who could do something as simple as reading newspaper advertisements used to recruit apprentices in northern England during the eighteenth century.

If literacy at an advanced level was important in securing upward social mobility, basic reading and writing was becoming increasingly important in ordinary social and familial life. In medieval Europe, literacy had usually been acquired in order to obtain a job in the church or to conduct business, and the power of economic need remained strong throughout the early modern period. From the end of the fifteenth century the advent of printing made reading increasingly important to participation in the full range of cultural activities, and writing enhanced the breadth and complexity of social exchanges. One example is the family memorandum book cum diary, known in France as a *Livre de Raison* and in Italy as *Ricordanze*. These day books were kept mainly by patricians and bourgeois but also by ordinary folk such as a Milan carpenter and a builder from Bologna. They record marriage settlements, inheritances and business deals; births, marriages and deaths in the family; remarks on the weather, plagues and politics, Self-written on cheap materials, these dealt with everyday, ephemeral, mainly private matters and reflect a growing awareness of the utility and pleasure of reading and writing (Hyde 1979:116–17; Marvick 1976:261; Burke 1987).

The significance of economic, political and legal developments for increasing the demand for literacy and learning is very evident. Beginning in the sixteenth century, the changes we have outlined gathered pace in the seventeenth and became still more compelling during the century of Enlightenment and Absolutism. There were hard, practical, secular reasons to learn reading, writing and counting, and to advance beyond these to specialist training in navigation, accounting, law and military affairs. Indeed, when treated as avenues to social mobility, these developments created demand mostly for secondary and higher education. Basic literacy was only of limited value for the lower classes though in areas such as the Hautes Alpes of south-eastern France and certain valleys in northern Italy it might, for example, provide a would-be migrant with the chance of becoming a schoolteacher in the less literate lowland areas nearby. Some negative incentives existed which can be reduced to the avoidance of risk, and these really only required elementary learning. To interpret the groundswell of demand for basic education, we must also analyse the less tangible value placed on literacy by sections of the early modern population. For it seems that there was a certain prestige attached to reading, writing and religious knowledge which had at least some grounding in concrete motives but which also drew strength from a more generalised emotional commitment to learning.

This pride in literacy only becomes apparent in chance asides by those who shared it, or in the comments of educated contemporaries who sought to pinpoint how the areas they visited differed from those they knew. The desire for basic literacy among the Scottish Lowlanders at the end of the eighteenth century was forcefully contrasted with the indifference of the Highlanders, and contemporaries remarked that elementary education was deemed essential by the inhabitants of some of the remote valleys of northern Italy. At the same time, there was developing in Finland an attitude which related signing to social standing among the ordinary farming population. In some parts of central Europe this was linked to developing nationalist sentiment as it furthered a sense of self-confidence and independence among dominated peoples. Ukrainians are said to have prized education and literacy more than Muscovites and to have provided many of the Russian empire's most able thinkers and bureaucrats in the nineteenth century, though it is difficult to separate such judgements from nationalist or particularist sentiment (Houston 1985; Viazzo 1983:166; Luttinen 1985:43; Saunders 1985:43-4).

Groups of literate people could develop a sense of identity and an enhanced feeling of worth, rather like a learned club. One example was the 'literary' confraternity set up in the small Polish town of Koprzywnicy during the fifteenth century. A religious confraternity was an association of people who lived in the same neighbourhood, or who worshipped at the same church, or who belonged to the same occupational group. In this case members had to be able to read and write. Participants in the eighteenth century were drawn principally from the prosperous bourgeoisie and nearly all were men: this was a powerful and exclusive body, prestigious in town life and significant in economic and political affairs as well as religious. The pride in shared literacy which had initially distinguished them from their fellows in the fifteenth and sixteenth centuries was reinforced in later generations (Ruciński 1974).

For some of the aristocrats who went to university, the prestige of attendance was much more important than the qualification it brought, and similarly those sent to grammar schools and colleges were receiving not simply instruction but also a shared sense of identity in their upbringing. One did not have to be literate in order to appreciate its worth. Literate parents could promote learning among their children but ignorants could aspire to provide their children with the education they had never had. For example, only a minority of the parents who subscribed a 1653 petition to set up a school at Kudelstaart in the Low Countries could sign their names (Voss 1980:256).

This must have been the case all over Europe in the sixteenth century when literacy was still restricted to a small minority of men. At this stage, and again in the eighteenth century, there were intellectual and spiritual forces which promoted a desire to learn. The Renaissance of visual and literary arts in the fifteenth century was generated by highly-educated upper classes and flourished most notably in countries like Italy and Spain which had high mass illiteracy. Renaissance Humanism, with its stress on learning as a good thing and its advocacy of reading classical texts, created a revived interest in reading, writing and the classics among the elites whom it touched.

The ideals of the Renaissance did permeate eventually to the masses, but for ordinary men and women the coming of the Reformation was a more momentous event. Competition for souls gave a fresh urgency to campaigns begun in the late fifteenth century to educate, arguably to christianise, populations tainted by what the ecclesiastical hierarchy saw as heresy, ignorance and paganism. Protestants sought to win over converts, Catholics to prevent this or to win back those who had been seduced away. A new interest in religious matters was also evident among the laity from the end of the fifteenth century, shown positively, for example, in the spread of prophesying and in membership of religious confraternities and negatively in attacks on abuses within the established church. With Luther came a new emphasis on the individual's relationship with God mediated through the only source of truth, the Scriptures. Protestants across Europe advocated personal knowledge of the Word of God, and sought to provide members of the reformed faith with the means to achieve a new, personal relationship with God: a vernacular Bible and the skills of reading it. 'Luther made necessary what Gutenberg made possible: by placing the Scriptures at the centre of Christian eschatology, the Reformation turned a technical invention into a spiritual obligation.' (Furet & Ozouf 1982:59). The Swedish literacy campaigners of 1686 spoke of all being able to read in the Bible for themselves while in Calvinist Scotland Janet Home's 1702 renunciation of popery before the church authorities of Edinburgh included a statement which faithfully represents the views of the Kirk: 'I doe believe it is the duty of every Christian who can read to be diligent in reading the holy Scriptures and meditating upon them, and that it is sinfull and unlawfull to forbid the people the free use of the holy Scriptures in a language they understand.' The Protestants were particularly anxious to spread religious knowledge to the ordinary people and were arguably more successful, but Catholics too strove from an early date to promote certain forms of basic literacy while resisting the spread of the vernacular Bible. Those wishing to use church rites in Louis XIV's Brittany were obliged to be able to expound the principles of the faith and to recite prayers. As early as 1496 the bishop of Saint-Brieuc ordered his clergy to instruct their parishioners in the catechism and to examine them regularly (Croix 1981:1200, 1205). In Spain too the campaigns of reforming bishops which began around 1480 were reinforced and extended by the Council of Trent in the 1560s (Dedieu 1979).

In practice, the reformers of the sixteenth and seventeenth centuries had to adopt a more modest strategy of offering instruction in the catechism, psalms, Creed, Lord's Prayer and Ten Commandments but their stress on reading did begin to influence an increasingly wide range of people. Elementary teaching texts were mostly religious, and throughout most of our period a large percentage of those who owned books had mainly or exclusively religious titles. Zealously religious men and women of accomplished literacy used their skills to take shorthand notes of sermons, a method of teaching writing in countries such as Scotland and Holland. Many extant diaries were written for spiritual purposes, recording hopes and fears, prayers made and granted, feelings of unworthiness of God's grace. Later reform movements such as the German Pietists truly brought the Bible to the masses along with well-staffed and closely regulated schools which began to teach critical understanding rather than merely rote learning of religious precepts (Gawthrop & Strauss 1984). Indeed, it is important not to exaggerate the impact of the Lutheran Reformation on mass reading since enthusiasm died away within a few decades and, as we noted above, Luther himself became opposed to unsupervised book reading while church authorities wanted to maintain a monopoly of truth and prevent the spread of alternative views. Sixteenth-century religious campaigns had essentially negative and defensive goals. They wanted to provide basic literacy for the masses and, like the state, more advanced education to train clergy and administrators. The Calvinists were more important in fostering personal religiosity of a kind which made men and women search out reading material and write down their thoughts for private reflection or publication.

LIMITATIONS

The list of forces which drew people towards education and literacy is lengthy and impressive. Economic, political, religious, social and cultural imperatives created an apparently compelling demand for learning which nourished the growth of the school system in early modern Europe. Yet, we may legitimately wonder why more people did not achieve the ability to read and write. Why was universal literacy not secured? There are four reasons. First, the cost of education could be prohibitive. Second, the occasions on which people needed to be able to read and write *in person* were not numerous for many groups in society. Professional writers and vicarious literacy through the aid of friends, neighbours and relatives could be quite adequate. Third, attitudes to learning were not standard among all classes and were not uniform across Europe. Fourth, oral culture – learning by watching, listening and talking – remained vital.

Looked at more closely, the decision to educate was based on three factors: the direct and indirect cost of formal schooling, the perceived benefit likely to accrue from literacy, and the general climate of opinion on both education and on children's status in society. Even if the money cost of education was within the means of ordinary people, there were other factors to be taken into consideration. Most important of these was the loss of earnings by the child. For most poor families in early modern Europe, survival or prosperity depended on the labour of all members of the household. Women performed all but the heaviest tasks alongside their menfolk both in the fields and in the urban workshops. The notion that a married woman would enjoy the position of 'housewife' was a luxury too remote to contemplate for the majority of the population. Women were conventionally allocated a dominant economic role in the home, but they also participated in the wider labour force.

Children too were an important component of the workforce in the sixteenth, seventeenth and eighteenth centuries, making a small but significant contribution to the family budget. Their role was particularly extensive in agriculture where boys and girls were used for marginal jobs such as bird scaring or weeding, or for routine, time-consuming tasks in order to leave their parents free for more arduous and important jobs – gathering firewood, collecting dung for fertilizer, or shepherding, for instance. One girl from the village of Codesal in Castile told investigators in 1569 that she had herded her parents' cattle from the age of ten onwards, and legend has it that the adventurer Francisco Pizarro spent his boyhood herding pigs in the hills above his home village of Trujillo in the same part of Spain. Older children might hire themselves out as *mozos de soldada* (servants) (Vassberg 1983).

Children's contribution could grow in importance in times of labour shortage, as happened in Spain during the seventeenth century, or when landlords demanded an increased number of days of labour service from their serfs or tenants, as happened in Bohemia and Moravia during the eighteenth century. When a natural disaster afflicted their community, they were mobilised to help. Plagues of locusts were a common problem in southern Spain in the sixteenth century: children joined their elders to gather them by hand and burn them. Pests on the vines were another natural disaster: the village of Turégano in Segovia organised the youth for aphid hunts in 1589, 1590 and 1591 (Vassberg 1983:67–8). What evidence we have implies that children recognised that they would have to leave school early or to forgo an education entirely in order to contribute to the family budget.

There were always chores for children to perform, whatever the economic context. Use of child labour was not as universal in towns as it was in the countryside. True, children were employed in the silk industry of Lyon from the age of seven, sometimes earlier. Yet the difference between town and country is clear in the holidays allowed to pupils. The town of Namur in the Low Countries allowed children eighteen days off during the year, but most rural schools only opened their doors between October and April. Attendance was too poor at other times to warrant the teachers' presence. Of the 187 schools in the diocese of Reims in the eighteenth century, 108 operated only between November and March (Ruwet & Wellemans 1978:33; Julia 1970:406). Rural parts of sixteenth- and seventeenth-century Germany had specific *Winterschulen*, so called because of their highly seasonal nature. We cannot be certain of the impact of children's employment on their chances of being educated, but it seems incontrovertible that it was detrimental. The time which boys and girls could spend at school was necessarily curtailed by the family's need for their labour. In some cases it prevented them from receiving any schooling at all.

Those to whom an education had been denied, or who had suffered from its premature completion, were not completely divorced from the products of literacy. They could generally find a literate friend, relative or neighbour who could read or write for them. Learning was not essential, and it might well be cheaper in the long run to hire or beg the services of a lettered person on occasions when it was needed, rather than wasting time and money on learning a skill which would rarely be used and which was not, at the basic level which ordinary people might attain, of much help in moving upward socially. The abacus, counting stones or fingers were alternatives to written accounts and livestock or sacks of grain could be counted with a notched stick. The vitality and pervasiveness of oral culture and the significance of vicarious literacy is dealt with in a later chapter. For the present, let us examine the professional scribes and notaries who earned a living by writing and the role as mediators which they performed. Formal writers, usually called notaries public, were useful to society from two standpoints. First, they could write for those who through ignorance or incapacity were prevented from so doing. Second, their small numbers and distinctive signatures kept the pool of writers to proportions where it was simple to check on the authenticity of a document. By providing regular forms and by authenticating letters and contracts, they reduced the chances of error and fraud in written records. Notaries were familiar in the towns of continental Europe, carrying a box of inks and pens and a portable writing desk, working in shop doorways, marketplaces, clients' houses or in their own small shops: the smallest house in modern Salzburg is a former scrivener's shop, a *Schreibstube*. Some 'writers' were highly educated professional men with a legal training: in Scotland, for example. Others were humble clerks whose orthography and general knowledge was often highly suspect. Those employed by appraisers of goods left by a dead person to write out inventories sometimes employed a phonetic spelling of book titles which leads us to suspect that they did not recognise the titles dictated to them. Thus Boccaccio's *Decameron* became *Un Livre de Cameron* in one French inventory of the sixteenth century.

Professional writers played a larger part in everyday life in Mediterranean societies than they did in northern Europe and more in areas of Roman than of customary law since the former placed more stress on written procedures. There were approximately eight notaries for every thousand people in Florence as early as 1427 and at Verona in 1605. Savoy had 1,000 notaries to serve its 600 parishes in 1700, or one for every 320 inhabitants (Siddle 1987). Some societies showed an active preference for professional scribes, partly through exigency and partly through fashion. The aristocracy of fifteenth-century Spain were not noted for their literacy, opting to delegate reading and writing to lowly clerks or to merchants who had to indulge in the trade which was so despised by the nobles. One early seventeenth-century Genoese patrician, Andrea Spinola, chastised many of his fellow nobles for the shameful way in which they preferred to depend on scribes and clerks to write for them rather than learning accounting and a clear hand for themselves. Early modern Italy was, and probably had been since the eleventh century, a 'notarial culture' where writing was dominated by professional scribes. This was true of much of the Christian Mediterranean, distinguishing it from England where personal writing was the norm from the fourteenth century or earlier. Most surviving documents from sixteenth-century Muscovy were written by clerks, even private correspondence. The decision to write in person depended less on mere literacy than on the social status of the individual and the nature of the communication (Franklin 1985:8–9). Writing personally became more fashionable over time in both Russia and Italy, a development which, alongside the spread of the printing press, reduced the demand for certain types of scribe. Worst hit were those employed in the mechanical copying of texts, and the medieval writing masters who made the transition to the new world of print had to turn their hand to selling books or teaching writing. There was a positive side too, since the huge expansion of written records created new demand for scriveners and notaries, notably in cities such as Paris and Rome during the seventeenth century. Whatever their fortunes, professional writers rendered full literacy superfluous for some members of the population.

Many influences encouraged men and women to seek out reading, writing and counting during our period. From the catalogue of those which we have studied, the reasons would appear compelling. Education and literacy were undeniably useful, and the desire to attain them unquestionably widespread. From our position as observers in modern developed countries, we would expect nothing less. Literacy always has a pay-off, and illiteracy is associated with reduced job opportunities, cultural deficiencies and even social stigmatism. Such a consensus did not exist in the early modern world. The ferment of interest in education among Enlightenment intellectuals, the drive for basic literacy from the church, initiatives by the state and demand for literacy across the full spectrum of society should not disguise the fact that not everyone perceived the benefits of education and learning in the same way. At the height of debate on education during the Enlightenment came a sarcastically-titled article in the autumn 1785 number of the Danish journal *Minerva* which shows that even the liberal-minded intelligentsia could have too much of a good thing. The sarcastic title ran: 'The Crown prince of Denmark's marriage to the little Turk's daughter, or an example of the education of the peasants, since that could just as well have been the title, but we were afraid that the education of peasants interests so few people that the article would not have been read' (Gold 1977:49). Poverty was one reason why no European country became universally literate before the nineteenth century, but there were also important social and cultural restraints on widespread reading and writing.

Hostility or apathy towards schools had several causes which cannot simply be attributed to ignorance or obscurantism. For religious minorities in a region or a country, the schools controlled by the 'official' faith might be seen as an artificial imposition, quite correctly since their aim was invariably to consolidate the recognised religion and win adherents of competing faiths away from their errors. Protestant schools in the mainly Catholic Highlands of Scotland and Catholic ones in the Protestant zones of southern France in the later seventeenth and eighteenth centuries were alien agencies of religious evangelisation. A minority religion could set up its own schools, though these would usually be suppressed. In Roman Catholic areas of the province of Utrecht, sixteenth-century efforts to establish Catholic schools were quickly squashed. Well-off parents could hire a private tutor or send their children abroad to a Catholic country, but most were faced with a choice between a Protestant education or none at all. Some chose the former, a decision made easier in the later eighteenth century as Calvinist attitudes became less dogmatic in the village schools of Utrecht. Yet the low literacy of Catholics in some Protestant-dominated parts of Europe such as Scotland and the Low Countries suggests many took the latter course (de Booy 1977).

A comment by a Protestant writer on another dominated people, the Irish Catholics, reveals a further reason for less positive attitudes towards schooling. John Dunton, in a letter written in the middle of the seventeenth century, tried to explain why the standard of the Irish priesthood was so low by highlighting their humble social origins and poor native training facilities (most trained on the continent, if at all). Anti-Catholic as he was, Dunton made the perceptive remark that 'they who had such estates as capacitated their children for liberal education ... seeing the small prospect to be had of a future livelihood by it, bestowed them otherways' (MacLysaght 1969:348). In other words, even those with the resources to educate their children might view their future job opportunities so pessimistically as to forbear spending money on an education. For the peasants in areas of Italy or southern Spain or huge tracts of eastern Europe, the incentive of social mobility through education might be too remote a possibility to be taken seriously. 'The almost complete attachment of the peasant to the land, the increased villein exploitation and the general decline of cultural standards deprived even the educated peasants of any prospects of social advancement' in early modern Poland (Litak 1973:60). Literacy may have seemed irrelevant to everyday life, its benefits too improbable to warrant investment of time and money. Locked into traditional field systems and communal controls, peasants had little use for literature with advice on agricultural improvement.

Pessimism about whether time and money spent on education would pay off was also fuelled by demographic circumstances. In twentieth-century developed countries, the vast majority of deaths take place among the elderly. In the pre-industrial world, mortality was much more likely in childhood. Of every 1,000 children born alive in France during the seventeenth and early eighteenth centuries, only 502 survived to reach the age of 15. In view of this swingeing mortality, some authorities have concluded that parents did not trouble to educate their offspring: why bother if there was an even chance that they would never live to benefit from schooling? Plausible as this argument may appear, recent research on England suggests that parents were prepared to spend considerable sums on their children's upbringing, education and all, in the hope that it would be of some use to them if they reached adulthood (Pollock 1983). It is also clear that the worst mortality occurred among children below school age and that, if they survived until their first birthday, boys and girls had a much better chance of living to adulthood than they had at birth. Child and adolescent mortality in England was among the lowest in Europe at this time, and it may be that the harsh facts of life and death had more of an influence on decision-making in less fortunate countries such as France or, indeed, Russia where the scientist Lomonosov guessed that around 1760 half the children born alive would be dead by the age three (Dunn 1976:384).

Education was not something that everyone would eagerly seek. Its value was not always immediately apparent and, especially in eastern Europe, specific social groups had to be *persuaded* or even threatened into accepting that education and literacy were worth having. Take the case of the Polish National Education Commission, whose work on educational reorganisation we have already discussed. The aims of enlightenment and regeneration appear laudible and uncontentious to a twentieth-century observer, but provoked considerable resistance from the nobility and teachers. The latter were relatively easy to deal with: the authorities removed the most recalcitrant and bullied others into compliance. A carrot accompanied the stick in the form of a higher status designation for teachers and their organisation into an hierarchical guild. The nobles were more of a problem. The state had to use blackmail – denying public office to those without the school diploma – and persuasion – informing them about the new ideas and organisation while flattering their position as the leaders of society – in order to gain a grudging co-operation (Bartnicka 1973). Nobles and teachers alike recognised that the new schools were being imposed by the state for its own ideological purposes. They had to be taught that they too would have an interest in the new system.

Attitudes to the statute of 1786 proposing a school network for Russia were similarly ambivalent. One town council responded, in a blunt and irritated vein, 'Schools are not necessary for the children of merchants and craftsmen. Therefore, we do not intend to send our children to school. We have no desire to support the schools and we see no value in them for us.' (Alston 1969:18). This opposition was not confined to the peasantry or the urban middle classes. Seminaries for training priests in early eighteenth-century Russia had very low attendance figures and attempts in the 1730s to enforce training were met by stiff resistance from those clergy who were supposed to send their sons (Freeze 1974:652–3). Literacy might be considered useful, but far from essential.

Indeed, it might be viewed with apathy or even outright hostility. One writer on the charity school effort in eighteenth-century Shropshire (England) despaired: 'The grown-up People are mostly illiterate, and ... are willing their children should be so too.' Some families may have feared lest an education beyond the very basic of reading and religious knowledge should distance their children from them. Stephen Duck, an early eighteenth-century English thresher and poet, recalled that his mother had taken him away from school at the age of fourteen in case 'he became too fine a gentleman for the family that produced him' (Watt 1972:42–3). Literacy could be a mixed blessing, especially for the lower orders, since it could distance ordinary men and women from their peers by giving them views distinct from traditional folk knowledge and received wisdom. Some may have ended up ostracised by their fellows, for whom basic literacy was more than adequate but whose attitude to 'intellectuals' was decidedly hostile (Vincent 1981:177–95).

Variations in attitudes could be highly localised. In an area as small as the duchy of Zweibrücken in the Rhineland, some villages displayed a firm belief in education, shown in their petitions to the authorities to appoint teachers. But an equal number were indifferent or antagonistic either because they needed their children to work or because they were hostile to the local clergy or teacher. Conceivably, positive or negative attitudes to education were a function of the general level of relations between the local community on the one hand and the secular and ecclesiastical authorities on the other. In some Italian rural communities wealth and power were concentrated in a few, distant hands, collective petitions for relief from rent or tax payments may have seemed pointless and the desire for literacy therefore remained low. The low literacy of Brittany may have been an expression of resistance to the intrusion of French and of written forms which were viewed as instruments of central control over a region with fiercely particularist sentiments. By contrast, the villagers of Boissy-sous-Saint-Yon in France, fearful lest their esteemed schoolmaster should leave for a better-paid job elsewhere, clubbed together to offer him a larger salary and better lodgings. And the village council of Casteldelpiano in Tuscany expressed the opinion, when hiring a teacher in 1571, that it 'could hardly find any other reason or occasion in which so conveniently and honestly to spend the money of this community, having regard to the utility and well-being of both the community and its individual members' (Vogler 1976:343–7; McArdle 1978:203; Watts 1984:215; Cipolla 1969:27).

The importance of social and cultural attitudes to reading and writing for the levels of literacy in different parts of Europe is neatly encapsulated in the Netherlands. In the northern provinces, the Protestant tradition of education and personal religious involvement through the Bible produced signing ability one and a half times greater than in the Catholic southern areas where the visual culture of the Baroque enhanced the power of oral culture and made custom and collective memory more significant than the written forms which prevailed in the north (Van der Woude 1980:258). The significance of cultural factors, educational opportunity, social status and demand for learning is apparent in the profiles of literacy which obtained in early modern Europe.

CHAPTER SIX

Sources and measures of literacy

The ability to read, write and count was central to many areas of early modern life but this does not imply a consensus about how we should define literacy or about means of measuring it. Among historians and literary scholars there are, broadly speaking, two approaches. The first is an intuitive one which treats literacy as a backdrop to cultural change without analysing the problems of its true extent in any depth. Particularly common in studies of literature – Spain in the 'Golden Age', France during the Enlightenment, England at the time of the French Revolution – this outlook is frequently simplistic, assuming that an audience existed for the large volume of printed material which was being produced but pausing only briefly to consider its actual size and the social distribution of readership. This old style of social history is thankfully becoming obsolete but is still found in some disciplines which feel obliged to offer historical background, however vague. Perhaps the most extreme version of this impressionistic school is that espoused by art historians who relate the depiction of reading in paintings to its prevalence in everyday life, while admitting the convention that portrayals are often stylised and socially biased. Were the books symbols (religious or material), instrumental aids or actual objects of study? The second is more rigorous in its methodology. Recognising the difficulties inherent in studying reading, writing, counting, and, crucially, understanding scholars have begun to examine critically the sources for studying literacy in the past and have set about reconstructing the actual levels of literacy among different social groups across Europe and the changes in reading and writing ability which occurred. The distinction between these two approaches is best summarised as that between *indirect* and *direct* measurement of literacy. And the basis of their differences are the types of sources which are employed.

INDIRECT MEASURES

Three main types of source survive from the early modern period which furnish the historian with 'indirect' measures of literacy. The first is the number of schools. We know that educational provision expanded enormously between the Renaissance and the Industrial Revolution, and tend conventionally to assume that this was somehow associated with increasing literacy. The exact nature of the connection is left obscure. Whether a growing number of schools provided by church and state produced more literate people or whether a more literate and informed population demanded better education is rarely considered. There is usually a relationship between abundant schooling and widespread literacy but this link is neither precise nor consistent over time or between countries: Sweden offers the example of a country with high levels of reading ability and very few schools. Furthermore, we have seen that educational advances were not equally beneficial to all classes of people, lords and peasants, males and females alike. The number of school places might grow but they might be filled mainly by boys from the middling ranks of society, leaving the lower orders and girls little affected. A proper understanding of the complex relationship between education, literacy and society is crucial if we are to elevate a plausible connection into a proven one.

The second main criterion adopted is the production and sale of books. The body of literature on this subject is enormous and again the line of argument is familiar: more books mean more literate people. The problem of interpretation is similarly plain: who bought the books, who read them and how were they understood? A simple example highlights the difficulties. We can be fairly certain that during the 1660s in England approximately 400,000 copies of popular almanacs and chapbooks were sold every year. We know too that there were about one million families in England at this time. It is therefore possible that one family in every two or three could have bought one of these cheap pamphlets annually: some said that the Devil himself always possessed a current almanac. An alternative and equally plausible figure would be that one family in ten bought four chapbooks or almanacs in any given year. The first figure implies a large and diverse reading public, the second a far more restricted one, and the historian would be equally justified in believing either. Spanish publishing was in the doldrums in the eighteenth century but as we shall see the second half of the century was a period of rising literacy following the stagnation of the 'Golden Age'. A French example confirms our doubts. The peak of chapbook publishing there came in the seventeenth century, and the contraction in the numbers produced during the eighteenth is difficult to square with evidence from other sources of increasing literacy during that century (Capp 1979:23; Bollème 1969:23). Subscription lists provide another indicator of the extent of the reading public. In this case, people paid in advance to have a volume printed and their names were listed at the back, sometimes with addresses and other personal information. However, not all subscribers are included; others are mentioned who were patrons rather than readers and represent salesmanship rather than a cross-section of reading tastes (Darnton 1986:11).

Third in our list of indirect indicators of literacy are the inventories of possessions left by individuals at their death. These inventories were usually compiled in cases where the person's estate had to be settled. In England and Scotland, neighbours and friends were charged with producing a list of movable goods while in countries like France and Germany licensed appraisers did the job. Books are mentioned only occasionally in these inventories: 10 per cent of Parisian lists of the sixteenth century included books and 20 per cent of those from Amiens during this period. Conceivably, most Frenchmen could not afford books. But they might also escape mention because they were not valuable enough to trouble over or because they had been given away before the person's death. Books were listed for valuation and it is therefore possible that only the most costly and prized were recorded while ephemeral material was ignored. French inventories are more detailed than German on this topic, making comparative analysis difficult.

We are also faced with the issue of readership: that a man or woman did not own a book did not prevent them borrowing one, and the simple fact of possession does not prove that a volume was read or consulted very often. Books might be bought for show. Mathieu Lalemant died in the winter of 1519. As an Amiens lawyer, he was presumably literate but the ten books mentioned in his inventory cannot have been extensively used since the appraiser found them locked up in a chest in his attic (Labarre 1971:105, 393–4; Schutz 1955:2). Giovanni Zonca, an Italian mercer, pleaded to the Inquisition that he had not read his collection of heretical works and pointed to the layers of dust on the volumes by way of proof (MacKenney 1987:184). The ambiguities in these indirect sources are considerable and we must use them with great care.

Equally ambiguous as indicators of the distribution of reading and writing in a country or even within a specific social group are the comments made by contemporary observers. Whole nations have been condemned to general illiteracy in historical writing on the basis of chance remarks made by those who wrote down their thoughts. The commonly-held belief that Muscovite Russia was almost wholly illiterate before the coming of the Enlightened Despots in the eighteenth century was based on archbishop Gennady's comments, statements made by the ecclesiastical Stoglav Council, reports made by foreign visitors and the writings of Pososhkov. Muscovites were probably less literate than Ukrainians who were educationally and culturally closer to Poland, yet the comparison is imprecise. Contemporary observers were inclined either to condemn a whole society as illiterate, or to raise it to near universal literacy. Members of the social elites who travelled around Europe had a rich variety of experiences to record about the appearance of those they met, their social customs, their mode of government, their religion and even their climate. They tended to focus on differences between their own society and the one they encountered, to the extent of making sweeping generalisations on the basis of a frequently brief and superficial experience of other nations. Viscount Molesworth said of Danish society in 1692, 'the common people do generally write and read', but what level of literacy is meant by this implicitly quantitative statement? (Dixon 1958:16). Between April and September 1549, crown prince Philip, son Charles V and heir to the vast territories ruled by his father, visited his lands in the Low Countries. One of the future king's entourage, Vicente Alvarez, noted in his diary of the tour that 'almost everyone', men and women alike, knew how to read and write. This fleeting impression hardly commands respect. Weightier are the observations of the Florentine Lodovico Guicciardini who lived in Antwerp for a number of years and travelled extensively within the Netherlands. In his *Descrittione di tutte le Flandre* (1567), Guicciardini observed that there were not only a great number of well-educated leaders there, but also that most ordinary countryfolk could read and write. These sorts of comments give us some ideas about the extent of literacy, yet they suffer from being imprecise and based on both uncertain criteria and undefined comparisons – in the above examples, possibly between the Dutch town-dwellers and the rural populations of Italy and Spain who we know from sources such as the Spanish *Relaciones Topográficas* of 1575 and 1580 to have been highly illiterate. Finally, we can take the example of the German jurist Ahasverus Fritschius who asserted in 1676 that newspaper reading had affected the whole of English society, even the peasants who picked them up on visits to towns and read them aloud to their friends at home. We must ask ourselves bluntly how he obtained this knowledge, and if it was simply an unsubstantiated impression or a piece of rhetoric (Voss 1980:257; Parker 1979:21; Gibbs 1971:345).

To a large degree, the observations about literacy made by contemporaries depended on the level of their own skills, their status in society and the particular point they were trying to make when they wrote. James Lackington, eighteenth-century bookseller and religious evangelist, regretted that 'in giving away religious tracts I found that some of the farmers and their children, and also three-fourths of the poor could not read'. Writing of the same period in English history, Dr Johnson described them as a 'nation of readers'. Edmund Burke's estimate of the 'reading public' in late eighteenth-century England was 80,000: a figure presumably confined to those who read newspapers, periodicals and political pamphlets (Watt 1972:39–41). *Journal von und für Deutschland* estimated in 1785 that the number of readers in Germany had increased by a half in the previous generation but offered no opinion about absolute levels (Engelsing 1973:56). Contemporary comments can, of course, prove useful by suggesting broad differences between countries or between social groups. Unless they can be reinforced by less impressionistic sources, we should treat them with caution. Indirect measures and anecdotal information are useful but only when backed up by more substantial evidence.

DIRECT MEASURES

Luckily, we possess such corroborative evidence in the form of the subscriptions made on documents by everyone from princes to paupers. During the late medieval period, the keeping of written records became much more common for the state, the church and the individual. Archives throughout Europe bulge with voluminous bodies of paper produced mainly by professional scribes but also by ordinary men and women. Many of these documents had to be subscribed by the person involved, of which the most important are petitions, contracts, wills, testimonies of witnesses before secular and ecclesiastical courts, and marriage registers. In discussing the relative merits of these sources, it is important to recognise that our main requirement is for a set of documents where either a representative cross-section of the population is included or where we have enough evidence about the biases in the source to make allowances for possible distortions. For example, some sources only cover males; others embrace only the better-off members of a community; more provide evidence on only one occupational group. The volume of documentation for studying early modern literacy is huge, but we must be careful in our choice.

Potentially useful in providing a large body of signatures or marks are petitions, bonds and oaths. All across Europe, groups of people banded together to beg, cajole or threaten those in positions of power over them to grant favours, to agree on a particular course of action, or to assert their loyalty to a cause. One of these occasions was to request a school, as happened at Lifford in county Donegal (Ireland) when in 1682 eighteen 'burgesses and commons' banded together; fifteen were able to sign their names in full. A generation later, more than 300 Ulstermen petitioned the governor of Massachusetts for permission to migrate there. In this case, illiteracy was confined to some 5 per cent of subscribers. These petitions cover particular social groups and cannot be taken as representative of the whole population of Ireland. Desire for a school might be stronger among those already convinced of the need for reading and writing, while emigrants may have been drawn from the more literate and dynamic sections of Ulster society. Contrast the disclaimer of responsibility for a recent political upheaval signed by only ten out of a total of forty-three people of the name of Burke from upper Mayo in 1588.

Some petitions or bonds are extremely useful in providing a 'snapshot' picture of literacy. A well-known example is the Protestation Oath subscribed by all adult males in England during 1641 and 1642 to assert their loyalty to the nation and to the established Protestant religion. In this case we know exactly the section of society included and can treat the source with some confidence (Cressy 1980:65–8, 71–8). With most other sorts of document, the position is much less clear. The restricted field from which many petitioners were drawn is neatly illustrated in the instrument of election of a new chaplain at Alagna in northern Italy in May 1781. The document records the choice of the Sacramento confraternity, forty-seven of whose fifty-four members could sign their names in full, but tells us nothing about the less privileged in Alagna who did not belong to the confraternity (Viazzo 1983:165). More ambiguous still is the oath of loyalty entered into by a group of Dutch sailors in 1616. While serving on the vessel *West-Vrieslant* they hatched a plot to take it over by force and devote themselves to the lucrative trade of piracy. A written oath of loyalty they compiled to bind themselves to each other said on it that twenty-eight of them in a circle had signed it. However, we have no way of knowing how many had to resort to marks or initials (van Deursen 1978:70).

Sources which cover small groups or particular sections of society are legion. Oaths and petitions are two examples, others include leases, receipts and documents which might generically be termed contracts. Biases in these sources are usually obvious. A receipt for poor relief was signed by eight of eighteen men at Letterkenny, county Donegal (Ireland) during the early years of the eighteenth century: they are described as 'poor decayed Protestants'. More commonly, contracts were made by the other end of the social spectrum, those who had property to buy or sell. Land leases, abundant in all European countries, are biased towards men from the middling levels of society and only rarely include women or poor people. Dowry contracts entered into between families with cash or land to bestow on their offspring have been used to study literacy in and around Turin in northern Italy during the eighteenth century, but again the lower orders are under-represented. Between 1710 and 1790 only two-fifths of couples whose marriages are recorded in parish registers for the area entered into dowry contracts which were formally booked by notaries, these mostly from the middling and upper ranks of Piedmont society (Duglio 1971:486–8).

This bias against the lower classes is also true, if to a lesser extent, of wills. All across Europe, the sick, the dying or simply the careful, expressed hopes for their souls and wishes about the ways in which their goods and chattels should be distributed after their death. Geographical coverage is not even since in some areas will-making was not the custom while in others (notably eastern Europe) the concept of personal property which could be disposed of by an individual was much less developed than in the west. As with many early modern manuscripts, some have simply disappeared, been destroyed by damp or fire, used as wrapping paper or for scribbling, discarded as wasteful of space. These documents were sometimes written by the testator himself though it was more common to have the task carried out by a scribe or notary, amateur or professional. Those able to sign in person did so. In England, those prevented by illness or age had to make a mark but in countries such as Spain with a Roman legal system the notary would record illiteracy or incapacity. The problem with wills is two-fold. First, the poor are badly represented since they had few means worth a formal disposal. Second, people who in health would have been literate might be forced to make a mark or ask someone else to subscribe for them because of their condition. In some parts of Europe it was held to be unlucky to make a will except when death seemed imminent.

More comprehensive in their coverage are some military records. Russian paybooks of the seventeenth century include only officers, but many states during the later eighteenth and more extensively in the nineteenth began to conscript able-bodied young men into their armies. Eighteenth-century registers of national regiments in Habsburg service, *Musterlisten* (preserved in the military archives of Vienna), contain the subscriptions of recruits. For the Low Countries, conscription registers do not begin until 1843 (Ruwet & Wellemans 1978:15–16). But for their late starting date and the fact that conscripts were drawn disproportionately from certain regions and from the less favoured social classes, conscription records would be useful in providing us with information about young adult males.

The number of separate documents is a testament to the importance of literacy. From the list of sources we have encountered so far, it may appear that the problem for the historian is one of embarrassment of riches rather than paucity of documentation. In reality, we must choose sources with great care. Many sorts of document provide a partial or even distorted impression of the distribution of literacy among the people of early modern Europe. Some favour males over females, others rich over poor. A French act of April 1736 required witnesses to marriage ceremonies to be both godly and literate. In some cases, we can suspect a bias without being able to prove it. Baptism records in Spain and the Catholic southern Netherlands occasionally register the signature or mark of godparents but we know that fathers and mothers chose spiritual parents for their offspring from a particular sort of neighbour. Socially segregated sharecropping communities in northern Italy had a pattern of choosing godparents only from other peasants while, in contrast, parents in less polarised villages in northern France tried to select someone from a higher social group as a possible patron for their child in later life. One of the duties of a godfather was to educate the child in religion, meaning that he might be chosen for his literacy (Kagan 1974:26; Ruwet & Wellemans 1978:20, 22). If, as is usually the case, we have no additional information in the sources about why a certain person was selected, the results of our analyses could be seriously distorted.

No source is absolutely free of bias, though we can make allowances if we know precisely the section of the population who were involved in subscribing a particular document. What this means in practice is clear when we compare the literacy of males and females from the town of Anderlecht in the early nineteenth century who subscribed notarial acts with those authenticating marriage registers. Among males, 26 per cent signed notarial acts in full compared with 55 per cent of men who married. The female figures are 38 per cent and 64 per cent respectively (Ruwet & Wellemans 1978:63). It is immediately obvious that those men and women who subscribed legal instruments drawn up by a notary public, a professional scribe, were nearly twice as literate as those who put their names or marks to the marriage registers of this small town near Brussels. Why should we accept one literacy profile rather than the other? The answer lies in the nature of the source. Notarial acts tend to include the propertied sections of the community who would be more literate than average. In contrast, the vast majority of the population married at some time in their lives, and marriage registers can be accepted much more readily as a source which provides reliable information about the community as a whole.

Marriage registers are common to all European countries, beginning (nominally at least) over most of western Europe in the sixteenth century. Regrettably, few countries insisted on the bride and groom subscribing the register until the nineteenth century. The city of Amsterdam was unusual in requiring subscription of the betrothal register from 1578 (Van der Woude 1980:261). France did so from 1686, and extensive studies of Gallic literacy have been possible using this source. A national survey of the numbers of brides and grooms able to sign their names in selected periods of years was carried out by a retired schoolteacher called Louis Maggiolo at the end of the nineteenth century. Numerous articles and monographs have used these documents, the most comprehensive being Furet and Ozouf's *Lire et écrire* (1982 trans.). England's marriage registers record signatures and marks from 1754 but Scotland's not until the beginning of civil registration of all vital events in 1855. Subscription was not required on Italian marriage registers except during the Napoleonic occupation between 1806 and 1814 (Vigo 1972-3:129). Marriage registers are an excellent source because they cover some 90 per cent of the population at some stage in their lives (most in their mid-twenties in north-west Europe) and because they sometimes afford information about the occupation or social status of the couple which can be useful in presenting a more precise profile of the distribution of literacy.

Where we lack marriage registers, we are often fortunate in possessing a similarly trustworthy source: depositions of witnesses before secular and ecclesiastical courts. Civil and criminal courts alike normally kept records of testimonies relevant to the case in question. Men and women made statements ranging from a few words to tens of thousands about themselves, their neighbours or complete strangers. There were heretics like the Italian miller Domenico Scandella, known to his friends as Menocchio; Scottish fornicators like Elspeth Moodie, mother of three bastards each to a different father; rapists, murderers, thieves, drunkards. These were hardly typical of their peers, but those called upon to give evidence about their exploits were very probably a fair cross-section of local communities. True, men were preferred over women, children, the very poor and lunatics by the courts because their judgement was regarded as sounder. Yet representatives of these 'inferior' groups did find their way into the courts. At the same time, most deponents provided biographical summaries at the start of their testimonies, furnishing detail on their age, occupation or social status and residence. In order to authenticate their evidence, witnesses would be asked to sign or mark their testimony. This valuable information allows us to break down a group of deponents into different social groups, and thus to examine in detail the distribution of literacy. Some depositions are still more detailed. The Spanish Inquisition, in particular, examined accused persons most closely about their beliefs: what they thought, what they had read to develop their ideas, with whom they had discussed heretical concepts, whether they could write, how well they could read. One study of the Inquisitions of Toledo and Cordoba during the sixteenth, seventeenth and eighteenth centuries is able to distinguish eleven different levels of literacy from examinations. A Morisco (Moorish) healer called Ramirez told his interrogators that he possessed a number of books but that he could only read with difficulty and could not write a word (Rodriguez & Bennassar 1978:23-4; Bennassar 1982:269). Such finely detailed information is fascinating, and adds flesh to the bare skeleton of literacy skills which the depositions usually allow us to reconstruct. Yet not all accused persons were examined in the same way, and the lack of systematic evidence means that we cannot use these rich testimonies with any confidence for purposes other than illustration. Judges graded the religious knowledge of the accused from good through mediocre to bad (wholly ignorant) but there were at least seventy different judges at the Toledo tribunal 1540-1650: not all asked the same questions and not all exercised their subjective judgements on ability in the same way (Dedieu 1979:272-6).

The ability to sign a name on a document should not be taken as a wholly adequate indicator of literacy. After all, it tells us about just one point on the wide spectrum of skills, between stumbling through a few words and writing a diary or a theological text, which we call literacy. Most studies of literacy highlight the problems with signatures, often in order to dismiss them as a viable indicator. A person might write his or her name in full, but be able neither to read, nor to write more than their name. We know that in seventeenth- and eighteenth-century France, the writing teacher might copy out the pupil's name on a slip of paper so that it could be copied when the need arose: a *modèle*. One man from Becherel in what is now Belgium claimed that he could sign his name, but when put to the test he had to admit that he could not manage without his *modèle*. The practice was not universal, however, and one study of Falaise in Normandy during the years between 1670 and 1789 concludes that people did not learn to sign without also learning to write words and phrases other than their name (Ruwet & Wellemans 1978:73; Longuet 1978:222).

Regrettably, nearly all early modern sources give only one signature at one precise point in a person's life. Only by chance, or by the painstaking reconstruction of a local community, can we tell how facility in writing changed over time. Work by Belgian scholars on towns near Brussels at the start of the nineteenth century shows an encouraging consistency in signing among those married more than once. Marriage registers for Turnhout and Anderlecht confirm that for more than 80 per cent of males and females (and in 97 per cent of cases for the men of Anderlecht) the quality of signature was the same from one marriage to the next. At Turnhout, 84 per cent of women used the same sort of subscription, 6 per cent had improved their writing over time and for one in ten it had deteriorated. This example is drawn from a period when familiarity with writing was probably much greater than in earlier centuries, yet the consistency in subscriptions over time is encouraging and suggests that men and women had learned their writing well enough for it to be a robust skill (Ruwet & Wellemans 1978:77).

Other sources permit the historian glimpses of levels of writing ability far in excess of simple signatures. On some Russian legal documents it was not sufficient merely to sign one's name: a signature and an affirmation was required which would have been too difficult to fudge for someone who had only learned to write his name: these were called *rukoprikladstva*. Officers in the Russian army of the seventeenth century had to make out receipts for their salary. Either in person, or by proxy, they were required by the paymaster to write their names, and to specify in writing the amount of money or payment in kind they had received, and the period for which this was due

(Stephens 1980:116). In sixteenth-century London, the guild of ironmongers ordered that those who were bound apprentices to members of the company should write and sign an oath of obedience. Between 1520 and 1550, 72 per cent managed to do so, and during the second half of the century this figure had risen to 94 per cent (Rappaport 1983:116). These were formal requirements imposed by institutions, and they indicate that for those involved writing was more than just reproducing their name. The very demands placed upon them might have encouraged men to broaden their literacy. Less formal were the New Year's wishes which Dutch children of the eighteenth century gave to their parents or to other family members. Well-written on paper printed with historical or Biblical illustrations, these felicitations were usually copied from a book of examples and were sometimes written for the boys and girls by adults. Usually the children wrote them themselves, as was the case with Cornelis Jubaan, a twelve-year-old who lived and went to school in a poor area of Rotterdam. His greetings to his grandfather are clearly and competently written, and the corrections he made suggest a good command of language (Van der Laan 1977:310).

The division between signing a name in full and making a mark is to some extent an arbitrary one which disguises the remarkable range of subscriptions which men and women made on documents. Some marks were crude, little more than a scrawled line or cross or circle; sometimes they included inverted letters or other semi-dyslexic errors. But others were ingenious and must have required some level of manual dexterity. In sixteenth-century Languedoc an artisan might draw a rough hammer, a peasant a ploughshare or a rake, a stonemason a square or a trowel. Among signatures too, there are clear differences in quality. Metalworkers at Montpellier in southern France, notably the swordmakers or *espaziers*, usually signed with ease and fluency. Indeed, it is possible to make subjective judgements about differences in the quality of signatures are well as their quantity. The larger towns of Normandy, such as Rouen and Rennes, had higher proportions of clear and practised signatures than was the case in the smaller towns (Le Roy Ladurie 1974:161–4; Longuet 1978:223).

Only diaries and journals allow us to be sure about the extent of literacy. Commonly, these tell us about a sole individual or, at best, his immediate family. John Clare, son of a Northamptonshire labourer born towards the end of the eighteenth century, wrote a diary-cum-autobiography in which he told of his mother's total ignorance of letters and of his father, who could read parts of the Bible if necessary, but who preferred ballads, stories, prognostications, telling tales and singing songs over a mug of ale with his friends. Other journals afford a broader picture. Take the example of Adam Eyre, an English gentleman who wrote an account of life during the period of the Civil Wars in the late 1640s. He was fully conversant with writing, for otherwise he could not have set down his thoughts and deeds. He could read fluently, because illiterate friends and neighbours came to him to have written or printed material read to them. For others he wrote petitions, deeds of sale and apprentice indentures. He wrote and received letters himself, and records in his diary that at one point in the winter of 1647 he 'spent most of the day in reading'. At that period he was working his way through Foxe's *Book of Martyrs*, which he began in October and finished in December. Of course, the very fact that Eyre wrote a diary marks him out from the great majority of early modern people. Yet, he was not alone by any means: Sebastiano Arditi, a sixteenth-century Florentine tailor; Nehemiah Wallington, a seventeenth-century London turner; Pierre-Ignace Chavatte, a Lille weaver of the same period. During his course of studies at the university of Salamanca in Spain, a young Italian patrician called Girolamo da Sommaia kept what he liked to call *Ephemerides seu Diarii* included in which was a record of his sexual exploits written in Greek (Burke 1987). All these and more wrote diaries, but they were remarkable among their contemporaries.

Like most diarists, Adam Eyre recorded his thoughts and actions for his own interest. More unusual still were those who went so far as to write for publication. While it is impossible to estimate the number of authors in the early modern period, they were apparently distributed widely throughout society. In the early 1520s, ordinary townspeople in Germany were prepared to write and publish pamphlets attacking abuses in the established church, among them a student, two artists, a married woman, an artisan and a gardener. These men and women were part of a tradition of independent lay comment on the church which pre-dated Luther and which disproves the traditional view that only the clergy wrote such tracts at this time. Some ordinary people read the Bible, followed debates, formulated their own views, wrote them down and succeeded in having them printed (Chrisman 1980:51–2).

Direct evidence of reading is difficult to come by and often impossible to quantify. Reading may have been the most significant of the spectrum of skills we call literacy because it gave access to vicarious experience and may therefore have opened up new avenues of thought and action. Few documents offer any direct insight into this important capacity, though most authorities assume that a greater proportion of the population could read than could write. Because reading was taught before writing and schooling was brief, many children may have left with basic reading and nothing more. Library registers sometimes reveal who borrowed books and when, but like inventories give no certain and direct evidence of reading. Diaries show reading, as do court records: the Florentine Inquisition treated any intensive and private reading as highly indicative of heresy since in the sixteenth century vernacular Bibles were illegal. Only in the case of Sweden do we possess sources which record directly and systematically the extent of reading ability among the population at large. Following a church law of 1686, most parishes began to keep examination registers of reading and religious knowledge. Parishes were divided into examination districts by the priest and the registers are arranged by household. Individuals are named, and their age, status and relationship to the family head is recorded alongside their skills, typically split into ten categories such as prayers, Luther's explanation of the five articles and five reading levels from 'cannot' through 'begun to read' to 'can read'. These registers were principally intended for children and youths but cover all the population aged above six. The quality of reading ability is difficult to assess because the clergy who kept the records judged the candidates subjectively, but these registers, which are also found in other Scandinavian countries, are uniquely useful in affording a quantifiable measure of reading (Johansson 1981:168). Sweden was unusual in its stress on reading and because of the absence of schools. The only other region in which people learned *only* to read was in the more educationally-backward parts of southern France, but this was linked to a particular form of Counter-Reformation Catholicism and cannot be generalised. The *Béates*, the third order of the *Congrégation des Soeurs de l'instruction de l'Enfant Jesus* (founded in 1688), were in the forefront of this campaign to teach reading to girls (Furet & Ozouf 1982:178–9, 183). Many indirect measures of reading exist and these are dealt with more extensively in later chapters on the uses and significance of literacy. The following chapter relies mainly on signing ability to outline structures and trends in literacy.

CHAPTER SEVEN

Profiles of literacy

The ability to read and write was, broadly speaking, a function of access to schooling and of demand for basic learning coupled with prevailing social and cultural attitudes to literacy. Commercial, religious, administrative and intellectual 'revolutions' of the fifteenth century onwards enhanced the supply of education and fuelled a growing demand for instruction. This chapter deals with the net effect of these developments on structures and trends in illiteracy between the Renaissance and the Industrial Revolution.

Early modern education favoured some skills over others. Schools taught reading before writing and both before more esoteric training in geometry, languages or accounting. Reading took from one to three years to learn, writing the same again. The importance of a stratified learning process and of frequently brief periods of school attendance is fundamental to the way in which we understand the distribution of literacy among the people of early modern Europe. If we adopt a criterion which focuses on writing we shall probably discover that literacy was rather restricted in its scope; on reading a more even distribution will become apparent. Equally significant is the availability of education to different social classes. Access to schools was heavily dependent on the economic resources of a family and the shaping power of wealth and status on literacy is very apparent when we turn to the distribution of reading and writing.

In the western world today, basic literacy is treated almost as a birthright. All but a handful possess the simple skills of reading, writing and counting. Those who do not are regarded as not only socially disadvantaged but also, arguably, somehow socially pathological, personally inadequate and a disgrace to any society with aspirations to civilisation and humanity. The position in early modern Europe could not have been more different. Access to education was uneven and the need for literacy very variable. As a result, the social distribution of literacy was heavily skewed towards certain sections of the population. Put crudely, this meant those who could pay for an education or whose social, cultural and economic life required them to learn would be literate. What this amounted to in practice was a world in which command of writing was disproportionately in the hands of males from the middling and upper classes.

Despite its comparatively low level of economic development, early modern Europe was characterised by societies in which wealth was often extremely polarised. In southern Spain, Scotland and most of central and eastern Europe, landownership was concentrated in the hands of a few thousand lords. Over most of Europe more than half of the taxable wealth of a country belonged to less than 10 per cent of its inhabitants. Anywhere from a tenth to a third of the population lived below the poverty line and there were many more who existed above it but were always in danger of starvation and misery. The contrast between the splendid palaces of France and Italy, and the squalid, overcrowded conditions in which the urban poor lived is as striking as that between the lavish and varied diet of the rich and the meagre fare of the anonymous poor who died on the roads and in doorways when bread prices were high. Wealth and social status had a powerful bearing on something as basic as the difference between life and death. Small wonder that who and what a person was should have had such a pervasive influence on literacy.

RICH AND POOR

Across the whole of Europe between the Renaissance and the beginning of the nineteenth century, literacy was intimately related to social position. Take the case of Spain between 1580 and 1650. All clergymen could sign their names as could the *letrados* (qualified bureaucrats), merchant elite and most of the upper nobility, but not the poorer *hidalgos* or lesser nobles. Between one-third and one-half of artisans, shopkeepers and the better-off farmers could sign. Among employees, the nature of employment and the status of the employer were important. Servant retainers of noble households were usually literate but humble tavern staff or journeymen were largely illiterate, as were virtually all the day labourers (Bennassar 1982:270). At the other end of the continent, among the inhabitants of the Palatinate of Cracow (1564–5), 9 per cent of officials and bourgeois were illiterate compared with 22 per cent of the richer nobility and 78 per cent of the taxpaying peasantry (Wyczanski 1974:708). A similar profile existed in later sixteenth-century Languedoc. Urban merchants were almost all literate; two artisans out of every three could sign a lease or bond in full, one in ten farmers but only three out of every 100 labourers (Le Roy Ladurie 1974:161–4).

More than a century after this (1710), merchants from Turin were 47 per cent illiterate, artisans 89 per cent. And two centuries later, the profile was still apparent in the large silk-working and agricultural community of Vigevano in northern Italy. Men involved primarily in farming were 84 per cent illiterate compared with 46 per cent for craftsmen and tradesmen, and 32 per cent among those in the service sector (Duglio 1971:509; Vigo 1972–3:134). Position in the social hierarchy remained an important determinant of literacy throughout the early modern period. In north-western Europe these steep contours of illiteracy between the peaks of attainment reached by the elites and the modest achievements of the lower orders were moderated yet the same distinctions remained.

Occupation is usually a reliable indicator of social position in the early modern period. Wealth was commonly associated with occupation and status, and it is therefore unremarkable that literacy and wealth tend to be related to each other among local populations. For the Palatinate of Cracow, tax documents show that landowners paying the lowest assessment were 71 per cent illiterate; the next band in wealth showed illiteracy of 47 per cent but the richest nobles had only one in five illiterates in their ranks (Wyczanski 1974:708). In the hinterland of Turin at the time of the French Revolution, 65 per cent of those entering into dowry contracts where 700 lira or less was involved were unable to sign the papers compared with 20 per cent of those in the 800–6,000 lira bracket (Duglio 1971:508).

The distribution of reading skills is rather more generous than we have seen for writing. Indeed, some Scandinavian countries and possibly also Scotland had achieved nearly complete reading ability among their populations by 1800. This meant that the social distinctions in literacy which were so much a fact of life in other parts of Europe were extinguished. This is not always the case, and we should be extremely wary about attributing universal literacy to these societies. While Sweden was advancing to mass reading ability and ironing out distinctions attributable to social class and gender, these remained strong in Iceland. During the 1750s, male household heads in one area were 24 per cent illiterate, their sons were 32 per cent, the men servants they employed 49 per cent and parish paupers 75 per cent: a profile which would be very much in line with other countries not blessed with such a supposedly 'democratic' literacy campaign (Guttormsson 1981:148). And there is evidence to suggest that some Catholic areas of Europe had achieved basic 'reading' and religious knowledge by the first half of the seventeenth century (Dedieu 1979).

The extent of divisions between social groups varies over both space and time. In the sixteenth century when literacy was very restricted, virtually all those who could read and write came from the landlord, mercantile or professional classes. Beneath them lay a yawning chasm of illiteracy. This stark differentiation was tempered over time as more members of the middling and lower orders – artisans and farmers, for example – picked up the skills of the book and the pen. In some places this change had to wait until the nineteenth century. Greenland had virtually no fully literate people except landowners until the second half of the eighteenth century, though as in all Scandinavian countries simple reading and religious knowledge had advanced more rapidly. Poland and Russia too retained a restricted literacy regime deep into the nineteenth century. For England, lowland Scotland, the Netherlands, northern Germany and north-eastern France, sharp divisions in achievements between upper and lower orders had been tempered into a more evenly graded curve by the end of the seventeenth century.

Breaking down literacy attainments by social groups creates an impression of discrete categories. The occupations and status groupings used to structure the above analysis of literacy's relationship to the social hierarchy are based on the main divisions in economic function and wealth. Lords were wholly literate, peasants hardly at all; one in every three artisans could sign his name but only one labourer in fifteen. In reality, there were literates and illiterates in each class of society and the distribution of literacy is most accurately envisaged not as a set of clusters but as a spectrum. Take the example of the military. Officers in the Russian army of the seventeenth century had to write a receipt for their salary. A pay-book survives with the names and subscriptions of 243 officers from fourteen regiments stationed at Belgorod in 1669 and 1670. Among this cosmopolitan group, 44 per cent were illiterate, 23 per cent signed in Russian and the remaining 33 per cent in some foreign tongue such as German or English. Literacy followed rank: eighteen of twenty-one colonels were literate, forty-two of sixty-seven captains and thirty-five of ninety-two lieutenants. The 85 per cent literacy of those above the rank of captain, classed as staff officers in the 1647 Russian translation of a German military manual, came from their dealings with the central government as well as soldiers and their special need for reading and writing skills (Stephens 1980:116–23). Within occupational groups, there existed a finely-graded hierarchy of literacy.

The differences between 'degrees of people' were not simply those of wealth and status. Education for the poor was very different from that given to the elites as we saw in earlier chapters. Female education was also restricted both in quantity and quality, a fact which becomes very evident when we compare the literacy of men and women.

MEN AND WOMEN

The value of literacy as a social indicator is clear when we examine the differences in reading and writing abilities of men and women. One of the great constants of early modern literacy is that men were far superior to women. This gulf is particularly obvious in the ability to sign one's name on a document. Only 28 per cent of the women who subscribed contracts made in the French town of Lyon during the 1560s and 1570s did so with their full name. In the Spanish capital of Madrid at the middle of the seventeenth century, 31 per cent of all males who made wills or declarations of poverty were recorded as illiterate – *no podía firmar* – compared with 74 per cent of women (Davis 1975:72; Larquié 1981:140). This pattern is repeated in more or less extreme forms all across Europe in the centuries between the Renaissance and the Industrial Revolution. One man in three and two out of every three women could not sign the parish register when they married at Amsterdam in 1630; by 1730 the figures were 24 per cent and 49 per cent illiterate and by 1780 15 per cent and 36 per cent respectively. For rural France in the 1740s, just one woman in eight was literate compared with one male in three. What is more, the quality of women's signatures is generally much inferior to those of males even when they were able to sign in full (van Deursen 1978:68; van der Laan 1977:310; Houdaille 1977:68).

The evidence of a yawning chasm between the literacy of males and females is tempered to some degree when we turn to reading abilities. As we have seen, reading and writing were taught separately, the former before the latter. For girls, education was generally brief and often confined to subjects which would fit them for the roles of wife and mother conventionally allocated to them. Most female children who received a school education left it once they had been given the basics of religious knowledge and reading. For this reason it is likely that men and women enjoyed much closer levels of simple reading skills than writing. Indeed, it may be that in countries like Italy and France two or three women could read for every one who could write. In the Scandinavian countries with literacy campaigns directed solely towards reading, the genders were effectively equal in literacy by the second half of the eighteenth century. However, more advanced reading and understanding would have been the preserve of those with a longer education: middle and upper-class youths.

As a gender, women were less literate than men. Yet in all respects they were subject to the same environmental differences which stratified literacy among husbands, fathers and brothers. The influence of social status is particularly evident. During the sixteenth century most of the literate women came from social elites such as the nobility and upper bourgeoisie: wives and widows of merchants, goldsmiths, lawyers, printers and others. In late sixteenth-century Poland, more than 90 per cent of all literate women came from these groups (Urban 1977:257). During the seventeenth century, literacy began to percolate through to the lower layers of society, more peasant and artisan women joining their wealthier and more socially exalted sisters in possessing a command of reading and writing. The literacy of men advanced more rapidly and the social hierarchy of literacy for women therefore remained evident for longer. By the middle of the eighteenth century, only 20 per cent of bourgeois women at Lyon were illiterate, but 50 per cent of the wives, widows and daughters of artisans and more than 80 per cent of those from the poorest classes. This ranking is one of the most favourable anywhere in Europe. Many parts of southern and eastern Europe show far more extensive female illiteracy. As late as the 1800s, even at the highest social levels among women in the Italian town of Vigevano, four-fifths could not sign the marriage register (Garden 1976:135; Vigo 1972–3:134). In these areas of Europe the gap between men and women was more extreme than in the north-west. For every 100 literate men living in the hinterland of the northern French town of Rennes at the end of the seventeenth century, there were sixty-four literate females compared with just twenty-five in rural Provence (Chartier *et al.* 1976:94). Of Peter the Great's Russia, one authority concludes that 'to be a woman . . . was to be illiterate and a virtual slave to father and husband' (Black 1979:152). In some of the Scandinavian countries such as Iceland and probably Norway, the reading campaign failed to iron out differences between social classes or genders by the 1750s. In a group of nine Icelandic parishes between 1748 and 1763, 75 per cent of fathers could read well compared with 47 per cent of mothers; for male and female house servants the figures are 49 per cent and 36 per cent. The gap between reading among men and women is less than that for signing ability we have encountered above, but is still evident (Guttormsson 1981:148).

The fact that women as a group were less literate than men does not mean that all women were illiterate. Even the most disadvantaged groups had some literate members. Overlap existed between the literacy of women as a gender and the lower classes among men. At the same time, women from gentle, aristocratic and upper bourgeois origins enjoyed reading and writing abilities comparable with those of male categories such as richer peasant farmers and urban craftsmen and tradesmen. By the end of the eighteenth century the wives of town-dwelling Provençal notables had achieved the near total literacy of their husbands. The same was true of contemporary Koblenz. Men from the upper classes in this Rhineland town were universally literate and women from that section of society only 3 per cent illiterate. At the other end of the social spectrum, male day labourers were 33 per cent illiterate, their womenfolk 60 per cent. The differing importance of high social status to men and women is shown in the abilities of the middling ranks of the town: 8 per cent male illiteracy among crafts, trades and officials compared with 40 per cent for women. Below the elites, social position had a much weaker impact on the literacy of women than men (Vogler 1983:444).

Furthermore, some unusual females achieved standards of learning equal to those of men: no small accomplishment in a world where education for girls was severely circumscribed and where the prevailing male attitude to the literate female was summed up by the phrase 'learned beyond her sex'. One prodigy, Louise Sarrasin, the daughter of a Lyon physician, began to be taught Latin, Greek and Hebrew at the age of eight. Others mastered the male-dominated world of print and used it to attack the prejudices levelled against them. Susanna Parr criticised the reverend Lewis Stockley in 1659 for his blasts against what he saw as 'weake women (who are not able to speak for themselves in *Print . . .* so well as men)'. And there were prominent women who both wrote and patronised the arts: Marguerite of Navarre was an important patron for Protestant writers of both genders in sixteenth-century France. All this was an uphill task, for women writers operated in a negative, censorious and dismissive climate generated by men (and, not infrequently, other women). James I of England, presented with a 'learned maid' able to speak and write Latin, Greek and Hebrew remained ostentatiously unimpressed, enquiring drily, 'but can she spin?' (Davis 1975:72). The Humanist tradition which pervaded secondary education treated more advanced female education as an end in itself, not as a training for anything specific. Signs of cultivation denoted a leisured life, itself a way of adding lustre and prestige, and of acting as a social advertisement of rank and wealth (Grafton & Jardine 1986:56–7).

TOWN AND COUNTRY

The ability to read and write was not evenly distributed among all ranks of people in early modern Europe. Men were more literate than women and the higher social groups enjoyed far superior achievements to those of peasants, artisans and labourers. This uneven distribution of reading and writing skills is equally apparent when we turn to geographical aspects. There are three main considerations here. First, the extreme variations which existed even within small areas; second, pronounced regional differences in literacy; third, the generally superior literacy of towns and cities.

Aggregate figures for literacy are bound to disguise the rich variety which existed. We know, for example, that 54 per cent of men from the English county of Essex who subscribed an Association Oath in 1696 made initials or a mark. However, variations between parishes in the proportion of males who could not sign this anti-Catholic oath of loyalty were considerable. Within a radius of 10 kilometres in the north of the county there existed one parish where 41 per cent of adult males were illiterate and another with 71 per cent. Over England as a whole in the early 1640s the range was from just 9 per cent in one London parish to 94 per cent in certain parishes in Lincolnshire and Westmorland (Cressy 1980:73, 100–1). The geographical distribution of literacy in seventeenth-century England was very uneven, again a feature common all over Europe. In northern Italy, one Alpine valley such as Alagna might boast high literacy during the seventeenth century, while of another nearby it was said that only the clergy were literate (Viazzo 1983:163).

Substantial local variations in literacy are clear, and were related to the wealth, occupational structure, educational facilities, commercial orientation and cultural values of particular communities. Early modern Europe was far from being a homogeneous environment where literacy was concerned. We can extend this small-scale analysis to the understanding of regional differences. At one level the variations seem to have been almost random and tell us little about important cultural differences between regions. The Dala deanery of Iceland enjoyed 51 per cent reading ability among its parishioners in 1744-5 compared with a mere 23 per cent in the Arnes area (Guttormsson 1981:158). Yet, beneath the apparently anarchic variation there are patterns to be found. In seventeenth-century Ireland the northern and eastern regions were much more literate than the south and west, illiteracy in county Wexford being nearly twice the level obtaining in county Londonderry, for example. Male illiteracy in Provence at the beginning of the French Revolution was 68 per cent but in the adjacent Dauphiné it was just 51 per cent (Vovelle 1975:94). No clear and finely delineated line existed between an area where literacy was common and one where it was still unusual but there were certainly regional variations. Over France as a whole, departments in the north and east had levels of literacy far in excess of the remainder of the country: the 50 per cent level attained in the favoured regions by the late seventeenth century was not matched until 1866. In the Low Countries, illiteracy levels for males and females were one and a half times greater in the southern parts than in the north around 1800. The level for Brussels in 1845 had been reached in the towns of Holland as early as 1600 (Van der Woude 1980:258, 261-2). The place where a person lived might reinforce or counteract other environmental influences, as in the case of these differences between towns in different areas. Day labourers in one high-literacy area of France might be as accomplished in signing their *acte de mariage* as farmers in another with low scores. Artisans in different areas of France had widely differing levels of signing ability (Furet & Ozouf 1982:152).

In explaining the differences between regions of a particular country, rather than between one country and another, we must pay close attention not only to factors such as wealth, social structure and the availability of schooling but also to the languages used in different areas. Despite the development of nation states during the early modern period, Europe remained highly fragmented politically, administratively, culturally and linguistically. Most countries had a dominant, 'official' language such as English, French or Castilian in which education was conventionally provided. Alongside these existed both dialects and distinct languages such as Gaelic in Ireland, Scotland and Wales; Provençal, Breton, Poitevin and others in France; Basque, Catalan and some Moorish dialects in Spain. The implications of this linguistic diversity for literacy are discussed below. Put simply, education was commonly provided only in the main language of church, law and government, meaning that children who grew up among, say, Irish monoglots had to learn another language (English) before they could begin to understand the rudiments of reading and writing. Linguistic unity was an instrument of religious and political assimilation in countries such as Britain (including Ireland) and France, but this stress on uniformity had serious repercussions on literacy.

Scotland provides a clear example of this. Until the fifteenth century most Scots spoke Gaelic, a language quite distinct from English. During the sixteenth century a Scottish version of English spread quickly over most of the lowland areas of southern and eastern Scotland, and by 1700 Gaelic was confined to the Highlands and the western islands. To a large extent this change took place spontaneously as a result of greater economic and cultural intercourse between Scotland and her rich and powerful neighbour. However, it was also hastened by a deliberate policy of assimilation which was pursued with increasing vigour after the Protestant Reformation of 1560 and the union between the English and Scottish crowns in 1603. The Gaelic speaking areas in the seventeenth and eighteenth centuries were seen as Catholic and lawless, their clans a threat to the peace of the Protestant Lowlanders. Thus the educational campaign mounted by the state in the seventeenth century and aided by charitable bodies in the eighteenth sought to provide schooling only in English. This policy condemned the Gaelic-speaking areas of Scotland to deep illiteracy until well into the nineteenth century. Between 1660 and 1770 the average illiteracy of farmers in the Lowlands was just over one-third; in the Highlands and Islands the figure was over two-thirds (Houston 1985:70-83; Durkacz 1983).

In Highland Scotland, the overlap between subordinate language and illiteracy was nearly complete. Gaelic monoglots were condemned to low reading and writing abilities. This was not the case all across Europe and indeed in some areas it was the transitional, bilingual zones which were the least favoured. The Low Countries affords the best example of the detrimental effect of dual languages on literacy. In the northern provinces, Dutch was the principal language while in the south (what is now Belgium) Flemish and French predominated. In general, Dutch towns were far more literate than those in the southern Netherlands. However, the linguistically-mixed areas of both zones had the lowest literacy. Dutch-speaking communities in the French areas had literacy levels much lower than French-speaking ones. Around 1779 towns in the southern or Walloon area show 34 per cent male illiteracy and 50 per cent female compared with 43 and 55 per cent respectively for the Flemish speakers (Van der Woude 1980:258–60; Ruwet & Wellemans 1978:24–5). The issue was not simply one of language since areas like the southern Netherlands, the Basque country and Brittany had a strong oral culture which actively resisted written forms, especially if they were in an 'official' language (Furet & Ozouf 1982:297–8).

When making such regional comparisons, it is vital to specify the environment, for those who lived in towns of more than 2,000–3,000 inhabitants enjoyed higher levels of reading and writing ability than did country dwellers. For much of the sixteenth century the only literate people were the landlords and those who lived in towns. In the countryside around Nantes in western France, rural illiteracy hovered around 99 per cent through the whole century. The only men who could sign their names were nobles, officials and merchants, most of whom lived in the towns of the region. Two centuries later, in the 1740s, a national sample covering the whole of France shows that rural males were 65 per cent illiterate compared with 40 per cent of urban men; female figures were 87 and 60 per cent. Areas of France with nucleated villages were more literate than those of dispersed farmhouses or small hamlets: as a general, if not infallible, rule the denser the settlement of a region the higher the literacy. Michel Vovelle describes the countryside of eighteenth-century Provence as *'le ghetto culturel rural'* (Meyer 1974:346; Houdaille 1977:68; Vovelle 1975:113).

Towns almost invariably enjoyed superior literacy though size was important in determining the extent of the gulf between urban and rural signing. In central London during the 1750s, 92 per cent of bridegrooms could sign their names in full and 74 per cent of brides. Levels for the much smaller provincial town of Northampton were appreciably lower at 70 and 44 per cent but still superior to rural Bedfordshire's 52 and 28 per cent literate (Malcolmson 1981:95). Meanwhile in France, illiteracy in the smaller towns remained close to rural levels. Communities of less than 1,000 people in seventeenth- and eighteenth-century Provence had the same profile as deeply rural parishes. The next threshold came at about 2,000 people while urban concentrations of more than 10,000 could boast the highest scores. Spanish illiteracy was higher in towns and villages with less than 500 households where more than four-fifths of the population lived. Tax documents of 1635 show that about a third of male household heads in ports such as Santander and San Vicente de la Barquera were literate; slightly more than a quarter in the larger towns of the interior such as Medina de Pomar or Mojados. Villages near the main towns of Burgos and Segovia could reach 10–15 per cent but for the mainly rural parts of Galicia the figure never exceeded 10 per cent literacy (Vovelle 1975:99–104; Kagan 1974:23–5; Bennassar 1982:270).

The high literacy of European towns in the early modern period can be attributed to two principal causes: the type of people who lived and worked there, and the 'hothouse' effect of urban living thanks to the concentration of cultural features associated with reading and writing. Most urban centres performed a variety of functions but characteristically they provided services in the form of lawyers, doctors and educators, retail and wholesale trades and crafts of various kinds ranging from specialists like goldsmiths and coach-makers to humbler and more basic industrials such as textile workers and blacksmiths. These crafts, trades and services were not wholly absent from the countryside, but were less common than in the towns and not as specialised. We have already seen that artisans, tradesmen and professional men were more literate than the average peasant and should not be surprised to find that concentrations of such people produced a uniquely literate environment. However, enhanced urban literacy cannot be attributed entirely to the composition of town populations. For in these concentrations of people, men and women were constantly in contact with the instruments and the products of literacy.

Schools, and especially the post-elementary ones, were generally located in towns. Both density of places and variety of establishments were superior in urban areas. In Scandinavia, towns and cities contained almost the only schools until the nineteenth century. Iceland had its only two grammar schools, located at Hólar and Skálholt, transferred to Reykjavik (the largest town on the island with about 500 inhabitants) and amalgamated into one institution in 1801. This is an extreme example, but over much of Europe the quality and the quantity of urban educational provision was better than that available to rural people. A census of grammar schools in Spain during the 1760s revealed that villages of less than 100 residents which contained about a half of Castile's population contributed only 10 per cent of the schoolboys whereas 44 per cent came from towns of more than 1,000 *vecinos* (Kagan 1974:47–8).

For those with the ability to read and write, towns and cities afforded unique opportunities to participate in literate culture. It was in communities such as Antwerp, Amsterdam, Venice, St Petersburg, Augsburg and Nürnberg that there lived and worked the printers and booksellers who made and sold the products of literacy. City dwellers might find a publisher or a bookseller on their own street. Given that few early modern towns took more than half an hour to traverse on foot, books, pamphlets and broadsheets were never more than a short walk away for literate men and women with a few coins to spare. Amsterdam could boast 270 printers and booksellers in the last quarter of the seventeenth century. Bookstores blossomed in St Petersburg at the end of the eighteenth century: one sole establishment in 1768 but twenty-nine by 1800. Indeed, most Russian broadsheets and pamphlets of the eighteenth century used city life as their background since that was where the printers and the reading public were to be found. In England, the period after 1760 saw a proliferation of pocket-sized town guidebooks and of full-sized town histories at a time when rural guides were almost unknown (Ovsyannikov 1968:17; Clark 1983:106, 118).

Printers liked to work in towns. Christopher Plantin arrived in Antwerp in 1549 and stayed there thirty-four years to produce 1,500 different works and to employ, at the height of his fortunes in 1574, sixteen presses and fifty-five printers and journeymen. Plantin himself summed up Antwerp's attractions.

> No other town in the world could offer me more facilities for carrying on the trade I intended to begin. Antwerp can be easily reached; various nations meet in its market-place; there too can be found the raw materials indispensable for the practice of one's trade; craftsmen for all trades can be easily found and instructed in a short time.
> (Parker 1979:26)

Plantin's remarks point us towards the general function of towns and cities as intellectual entrepôts. The Dutch Republic was particularly significant here both because of its concentration of cities – no town was more than 25 kilometres from another – and because of its domination of European trade in the sixteenth and seventeenth centuries. Amsterdam was a commercial centre which linked several regional and national networks of commerce and finance. It became a focus for the exchange of information which was both a by-product and a commodity of trade, the seventeenth century seeing an expansion of the postal service, of specialist information-brokers (among whom Leo van Aitzema was the most famous), and of commercial newsletters such as the *Hollantsche Mercurius*. Among its functions, this sheet announced the return of the all-important East India Company fleet on which the fortunes of many merchants and financiers rested. The company (*Vereenigde Oostindische Compagnie* or VOC for short) had numerous stations in the far east which sent reports to their Javan headquarters in Batavia (now Jakarta) for collation and dispatch to Amsterdam. Small wonder that Amsterdam was a mine of information and a hothouse of literacy (Smith 1984; Gibbs 1971).

The importance of the urban environment in forcing literacy is apparent when we compare not simply aggregate levels but those prevailing among the same social groups in town and countryside. Such a comparison reveals that towns did not simply bring more literate people together, but also enhanced the reading and writing skills of those who might otherwise have remained illiterate. Urban priests who subscribed legal documents in seventeenth-century Russia were more literate than rural ones, and book holdings among clergy in towns like Nizhnii Novgorod (1621–2) were superior to those of their rural counterparts. At London in 1598, ninety-nine grocers were required to authenticate a receipt for repayment of a loan made by their company: ninety-eight did so with their full names, a figure without parallel anywhere else in England. A similar document survives dated 1606 in which the only illiterate person among 126 subscribers was a widow called Elizabeth Coles (Rappaport 1983:116). Urban living intensified the need for literate skills among all social groups.

Towns and cities concentrated literate people, presented them with schools, writing and books in relative abundance and demanded of them greater familiarity with reading, writing and counting. This is not to say that towns were a uniform social or cultural environment, nor that literacy was equally high in all their parishes. Printers and booksellers were concentrated in certain parishes or even in specific streets. Shops of German *Briefmaler*, who printed single-leaf woodcuts for an artisan and peasant audience during the seventeenth century, were generally located in the suburbs of cities like Augsburg and Nürnberg since it was easier to reach their customers. More up-market, the booksellers of Dublin were mainly to be found in Castle Street and Skinners' Row. Sixteenth-century Venetian book-men favoured the central districts of San Marco, Sant' Angelo, the Rialto bridge, Santi Apostoli, San Zanipolo and Santa Maria Formosa for their shops, while some hawked books from stands near the Rialto bridge or round the Piazza San Marco (Grendler 1977:5).

The effect of differences in residence according to occupation, wealth and social status is plain in the spatial geography of literacy in the towns. Early modern towns differed from those of the twentieth century in so far as the rich lived in the central parishes while the poorer classes, and especially industrial workers, tended to congregate in the suburbs. At Rouen during the reign of Louis XIV, merchants and professionals clustered in the western parishes near the Seine where ships unloaded and their goods were transferred into barges for the journey up the river to Paris. The eastern suburbs were the home of weavers and spinners, a poorer and less literate part of the town. Central Luxemburg had only 32 per cent illiteracy in the later eighteenth century, compared with the 62 per cent of the poor suburban parish of St-Jean Grund. Suburban parishes were usually more literate than the surrounding countryside which tended in fact to benefit from proximity to a high literacy environment. Rich town parishes of the southern Netherlands at this time could boast female illiteracy as low as 25 per cent; less favoured ones had figures close to 70 per cent (Ruwet & Wellemans 1978:30–1; Art 1980:270). In some areas of Europe, suburban and inner-city dwellers even spoke different languages. In Ruthenian areas of Poland, towns tended to be islands of Polish-speakers in a sea of Ruthenian-speakers (the local vernacular), but in bigger urban communities such as Lvov the outer parishes were inhabited by Ruthenian-speakers in the later sixteenth century while Polish was the prevailing tongue in central streets (Martel 1938:196–7).

Concentrations of literate people and the 'hothouse' effect made most towns centres of literacy. At the same time, urban job opportunities encouraged the more dynamic rural dwellers to take their skills and aspirations into the towns. Natural increase played a small role in maintaining and increasing urban populations: the most significant influence was immigration from the countryside. Between 1650 and 1750, London drew in and retained at least 8,000 people every year, while half of the populations of the French towns of Caen and Lyon were not born there during the second half of the eighteenth century. For some towns these migrants provided a boost to literacy levels. In the case of the growing textile town of Leeds in Yorkshire, immigrants were appreciably more literate than native-born people during the 1760s, and between 1760 and 1792 four out of every five men and women who moved into Rouen in France could sign their names (Yasumoto 1973:82–5; Grevet 1985:622–3).

These figures suggest that dynamic and possibly upwardly-mobile men came from other towns and from the countryside to make their lives in an urban environment. On a hypothetical 'cultural balance-sheet' these would represent a gain for the receiving town. This pattern was not, however, universal. Those who moved into mid-seventeenth-century Madrid from elsewhere in Spain were slightly less literate than the native born and only foreigners were clearly more accomplished than the indigenous inhabitants (Larquié 1981:152). Among natives of eighteenth-century Koblenz, there were 86 literate females for every 100 males, but the ratio for immigrants was 53 : 100, suggesting that immigration was selective of less literate women: domestic servants and prostitutes for the garrison. The same pattern of immigration characterised contemporary Bordeaux (Vogler 1983:445; Furet & Ozouf 1982:209–10).

The net effect of this type of movement on the town was probably slight, but migration could also bring cultural problems. The rapid rise in numbers experienced by the towns of Dordrecht, Rotterdam, Delft, Leiden and Haarlem in the Low Countries forced up illiteracy between 1600 and 1650. Ghent saw a 32 per cent decrease in the number of children receiving formal education between 1650 and 1789 despite an increase in the total population. For towns so affected, there was a cultural loss (Lottin & Soly 1983:294). Extremely fast population growth, especially that brought about by the immigration of unskilled workers into the manufacturing towns of the north of England, central Scotland, Belgium and north-eastern France from the end of the eighteenth century, tended to reduce aggregate literacy levels (Van der Woude 1980:261; Furet & Ozouf 1982:203–13; Sanderson 1983). Factory production did not require educated labour and could actually depress aggregate literacy levels in a town. Such an influx of people also strained educational facilities and therefore condemned a whole generation to illiteracy.

OLD AND YOUNG

Most migrants entered towns in the prime of life, commonly between the ages of fifteen and thirty-five. For most people this was the time of their lives when writing abilities were at their peak. Memory of what had been taught in school was still fresh, and opportunities to practice literate skills were expanding with their need to make their own way in life, both materially and socially. Indeed, some men and women were actually becoming more literate under these influences, adding to the manual skills which they had obtained while at school or in some cases learning for the first time what their truncated education had failed to teach them. The effect of non-scholastic education after the age at which formal schooling was likely to end is neatly demonstrated by the case of indentured servants who migrated to the British colonies of North America in the late seventeenth and early eighteenth centuries and who made up one half of total white migration there. David Galenson has analysed the indentures of 812 servants registered at the Middlesex Quarter Sessions court during 1683–4 and 3,187 registered in London between 1718 and 1759. The youngest servant was fourteen and therefore likely to have finished school. Mean age at indenture was about twenty for women and twenty-two for men. Servants came from diverse social backgrounds and from both towns and rural communities. Yet, even allowing for the impact of these factors, it is clear that the older they were, the more literate they became. Older servants could sign more frequently than younger ones, suggesting very strongly that they had picked up their abilities through practice rather than through schooling. This influence was not uniformly felt. Servants who had 'skilled' occupations were already more literate than their less skilled peers even at relatively young ages, and the rate at which their signing improved was slower. Most 'skilled' servants who were literate had become so before learning their trade or craft, but for the lower ranks among servants informal learning while in work was more important, producing increased literacy with age. Reasons for educating early in life are summarised in Campbell's *London Tradesman* of 1747.

> There are some Parts of Education that are useful and necessary ... The sooner these Helps are given, the greater and more lasting Effect they will have; and though the Child might acquire them in the Course of his Apprenticeship, yet it is more advisable to let him learn the Rudiments of them before he enters: By this Means, he is facilitated in learning his Trade, and acquires it with greater Ease.
>
> (Galenson 1981:824)

The effect of advancing years on literacy was not always a benign one. As people grew older they became more susceptible to blindness and debility which early modern medicine could do little to alleviate. Subscriptions to wills and comments made by scribes upon them illustrate the resulting damage. In a mid-seventeenth-century will which he had written, one notary recorded that Catalina Ortiz y Millan from Madrid suffered from an infirmity (arthritis?) in her right hand which prevented her from signing. Isabel de Albornoz had gone blind and could not take the pen which the scribe proffered for her use. Juan Sanchez, a priest from Grenada in Spain, was prevented from signing by the gravity of his illness (Larquié 1981:136). Some people had simply forgotten how to use a pen. Others on their death-beds may have felt the effort of signing their name not worth making. What is certain is that those above the age of sixty were much less literate than those in the prime of life.

These examples reflect a decay of signing ability caused by age-related disabilities. In other respects too, the older generations could be isolated from literacy. This is particularly apparent in those countries which conducted vigorous literacy campaigns. Directed at children, who were impressionable, rather than at their parents and grandparents, who were seen as obdurate and ignorant (at least by some observers), these campaigns had the short-term result of creating a literate youth while leaving the older people largely uneducated. The best examples of this come from the Scandinavian nations with their eighteenth-century reading campaigns. In the Swedish parish of Tuna in Västernorland, 370 persons were examined in reading and religious knowledge by the parish priest between 1688 and 1691. Of those aged over sixty, 47 per cent could not read; also 37 per cent of those in their forties but only 14 per cent of men and women aged twenty-one to twenty-five and just 2 per cent of the eleven to fifteen cohort (Åkerman *et al.* 1979:181). For a group of Icelandic parishes during the 1750s, we know that 45 per cent of the over-fifties could read the catechism well and 5 per cent could provide a decent explanation of it, compared with figures of 89 and 84 per cent for the fifteen to nineteen age band (Guttormsson 1981:151). What was happening was that the youth were receiving instruction in reading and religious knowledge from the parish priests, then passing it on slowly to their elders. Eventually, as the older members of communities died and as the literate younger generations came to take their place, the whole society became literate. Meanwhile, a 'generation gap' must have emerged. This phenomenon only appears in countries with rapid and successful literacy campaigns. By contrast, the literacy of grooms and fathers of brides, the latter roughly thirty years older, rose at the same pace over the eighteenth century in northern Italy (Duglio 1971:501).

CATHOLIC AND PROTESTANT

The importance of religion in creating both a demand for literacy and a drive from ecclesiastical authorities to instruct the people has already been discussed. To a large extent, Protestant and Catholic churches alike sought to win ordinary men and women from the traditional communal, medieval religious observances, deemed 'magical' and 'pagan' by the leaders of the Reformation and Counter-Reformation, and turn them into committed, individual religious believers imbued with God's Word. As we have already seen, Protestant parts of Europe usually enjoyed superior educational facilities to Catholic, with Calvinism particularly powerful as a force which encouraged the proliferation of schools. The implication of these differences for literacy has exercised considerable debate among historians. They generally agree that Protestantism and literacy were associated, and that the Reformed religion fostered literacy both through the provision of schools and the desire of individuals for direct access to the Bible. 'God's people were to be a literate people, taking in God's Word from the printed page.' (Stone 1969:79).

At the simplest level, this proposition is quite correct. In England, Protestant sects such as the Quakers were all able to sign their names on marriage registers after 1754 whereas two-fifths of men and two-thirds of women in the rest of the population could not (Stone 1969:80). Protestants also tended to be more literate than Catholics within areas where they co-existed, and countries where the Reformed faith was the official religion were usually more advanced in literacy than Catholic neighbours. The mainly Protestant Dauphiné community of Saint-Jean-d'Herans could boast 65 per cent literacy among its artisans around 1690 and 44 per cent among farmers; by contrast, Catholic Saint Ismier's craftsmen were 55 per cent literate, its peasants a mere 10 per cent (Chartier *et al.* 1976:105–6). The distinction between the faiths may have been greater in the sixteenth and seventeenth centuries than it was at later periods. A study of the cosmopolitan city of Amsterdam in 1780 shows the crude distinctions between denominations. Most literate among bridegrooms were the Calvinists (13 per cent illiterate) followed closely by Lutherans (14 per cent). Roman Catholics were half as illiterate again at 21 per cent with the small number of resident Jews nestling between the main categories at 16 per cent. The hierarchy for women is similar: 31 per cent illiterate among Calvinist brides, 35 per cent for Lutheran, 47 per cent Roman Catholic but a very high 69 per cent for Jewish girls. In the Maasland area of southern Holland a generation before this, the Catholic–Protestant gap was less for males (18 per cent compared with 13 per cent illiteracy) but greater for women (61 per cent for Catholics rather than 39 per cent). Protestants as a group were more literate than Catholics (Van der Woude 1980:262). Little, incidentally, is known of Moorish literacy in this period (Fournel-Guerin 1979).

The case for connecting Protestantism and literacy seems compelling. However, the nature of the relationship between religious affiliation and the ability to write is by no means straightforward. To understand why, it is essential to realise that Protestants and

Catholics were not distributed equally among all sections of society. This is particularly obvious among Calvinist minorities in Catholic countries such as Poland and France. Lutheranism made little headway in sixteenth-century Poland but Calvinists were much more successful in establishing a foothold, principally because of their policy of targeting important nobles and gentlemen who could espouse and protect the faith on their (substantially independent) estates. What this meant in practice was that Calvinism in late sixteenth- and seventeenth-century Poland was essentially an elite movement largely devoid of grass roots. A similar though less extreme social imbalance is clear among members of Calvinist congregations in late sixteenth-century France. Protestantism was a minority faith, concentrated in towns such as Toulouse and La Rochelle, drawing its adherents disproportionately from the middling ranks of society. The peasantry remained 95 per cent Catholic and, as Natalie Davis puts it, 'A printer, a goldsmith, or a barber-surgeon was more likely to disobey priests and doctors of theology than was a boatmaster, a butcher, or a baker' (Davis 1975:80; Davies 1979a). Protestants in these states were not drawn exclusively from the middling and upper classes, but they were recruited disproportionately from the most literate sections of society.

When we break down early modern populations into social and religious categories, the wide difference in aggregate literacy between Protestants and Catholics is substantially reduced. Among rural male leaseholders in north-west Ireland during the eighteenth century, Catholics were far inferior in literacy to Protestants. However, the papists held smaller and poorer plots of land than Protestants and this accounts for at least part of the difference. The economic and social standing of the Catholic population was lower than that of the Protestants who dominated landholding in Ulster. In this Irish example, religious differences remain the most significant differentiating factor in literacy profiles, more important even than wealth. The same is not true of rural areas of the Dutch province of Utrecht at the beginning of the nineteenth century. A gap of some 10 per cent existed between the literacy of Catholic and Protestant men as a whole. Among social groups composed of all denominations, the gulf was far wider. Between day labourers on the one hand and artisans and farmers on the other there lay fully forty percentage points. No significant difference existed between Catholic and Protestants in the latter group, but Catholic labourers enjoyed only three-quarters of the literacy of their Protestant equals (Van der Woude 1980:263). An association between Protestantism and enhanced signing ability certainly exists but it is not a simple one. Aggregate literacy levels in Protestant England were, for example, approximately equal to those in Catholic north-eastern France. Four-fifths of men marrying in the predominantly Catholic Mittelrhein area of Germany towards the end of the eighteenth century could sign, along with two-thirds of women, achievements clearly superior to contemporary England and marginally better than Lowland Scotland. And the ferociously Protestant Cévennes region of south-east France was highly illiterate (Graff 1987:188; Chartier *et al.* 1976:106). Other social and environmental factors could exert an influence as powerful as religion.

CHANGE

Structures of literacy among the people of early modern Europe reveal obvious patterns in spite of their rich variety. Literacy was clearly stratified depending on who one was and where one lived. When we turn to the dynamics of change, generalisations are simple at one level. Most important, the centuries between the Renaissance and the Industrial Revolution saw a fundamental shift in the relationship between people and print. The world of the fifteenth century was one of strictly circumscribed literacy in which elements of the gentry, nobility, clergy and bourgeoisie had the capacity to read and write, but the vast majority of the population was illiterate. Literacy marked out a small number of 'clerks' and those who needed reading, writing and counting for their jobs from the mass of their neighbours. Illiteracy was the lot of 95 per cent of the male population and all but a handful of females. Some areas of Europe had flourishing literary traditions, notably northern Italy, but the continent displayed substantial homogeneity in levels of literacy.

The world in 1800 was very different. Over most of north-western Europe, more than half of adult males could sign their names and still more could read a simple text. Whole social groups had command of high levels of functional skills – reading, writing, counting and languages – and there was no class wholly devoid of literate elements. Female literacy advanced less rapidly and did not reach the level of males as a group. Nevertheless, countries like England, Scotland, the Scandinavian cluster, Germany and north-eastern France could, in their own ways, boast *mass literacy* which set them apart from much of the Mediterranean world and vast areas of central and eastern

Europe. Mass literacy had arrived but it brought with it accentuated social and geographical stratification.

These central developments need to be seen in the context of the ways in which change was won. Most significantly, the growth of literacy was extremely slow. Literacy campaigns in under-developed countries in the 1960s, 1970s and 1980s have produced in a decade or less improvements in reading skills which took a century or more in early modern Europe. Furthermore, the change was gradual, irregular, hesitant and far from complete, even in 1800. Literacy certainly rose between 1500 and 1800 but it did so at different times and at widely varying rates in different areas and among separate social groups (Arnove & Graff 1987).

Literacy rose quickest in countries which espoused the modest goal of inculcating a capacity for reading and memorising basic religious texts. National literacy campaigns in the Scandinavian states took two to three generations to secure near-universal reading ability among their people. In the Swedish parish of Möklinta, just 21 per cent of the total adult population could read in 1614 but by the 1690s examination registers show a level of 89 per cent. The final drive to universal literacy could produce spectacular falls in ignorance over very brief time periods in parts of Scandinavia. Information survives about approximately 500 people who were tested for reading and religious knowledge at the time of their Confirmation in the Icelandic diocese of Skálholt. In 1754, 13 per cent of them were considered illiterate. Just four years later the percentage had fallen to less than a half and in 1760 a figure of nil is recorded (Kamen 1984:211; Guttormsson 1981:162). These two cases exemplify the fastest known rates of improvement. The level of skills required in these Lutheran tests was not high and we should not necessarily treat them as a reference standard. More typical of the almost glacial progress of literacy is Germany. Around 1750, 10 per cent of the population aged six or above could read with ease, 15 per cent by 1770 and 25 per cent by 1800 (Fabian 1976:166). These figures are not directly comparable with those from Scandinavia since they relate to a much higher quality of critical reading ability.

Developments in literacy came slowly and they were far from regular. The timing of improvements varied between countries and social groups and bursts of falling literacy were often punctuated by long periods of stagnation or even decay. Even adjacent towns in a small country such as the Netherlands could display quite different profiles of change. Brides at the towns of Leeuwarden and Groningen saw a steady reduction of about 30 per cent in their illiteracy between the first quarter of the seventeenth century and the last quarter of the eighteenth. For young women living in most other Dutch towns, the first half of the seventeenth century was a time of rising illiteracy and at Nijmegen the years 1650–1700 were also a time of mounting illiteracy. Progress was far from uniform and could be reversed for decades on end. At the same time, rates of change varied considerably over the centuries. Inability to sign among Amsterdam bridegrooms fell from 43 per cent in 1630 to 15 per cent in 1780. Between 1630 and 1680, illiteracy was cut by 30 per cent; a further reduction of 20 per cent (30 per cent down to 24 per cent) marked a slowing down of improvement between 1680 and 1730 but this picked up again in the half century to 1780 when a reduction of 38 per cent was recorded. The trend is similar for women (18, 12 and 27 per cent respectively), but the pace is slower (Van der Woude 1980:262).

A similarly erratic pattern can be detected in most European countries. The east Prussian peasantry were still steeped in illiteracy in the age of the Enlightenment despite their rapid progress: just 10 per cent could sign in 1750, 25 per cent in 1765 and 40 per cent in 1800 (Engelsing 1973:62). In Spain there is some evidence of falling illiteracy in the first half of the sixteenth century but progress was slow from the reign of Philip II until the second half of the eighteenth century. As late as 1860, Spain was still 75 per cent illiterate. In the case of southern England, the fastest rate of improvement for most social groups was during the reigns of Elizabeth and James I (1558–1625) whereas in the northern counties the years 1660–1720 were the most favourable times. Apart from occasional decades when rapid advances were made, the pace of change throughout the remainder of our period was slow. In some parts of Europe it was non-existent: Michel Vovelle describes the eighteenth century in Provence as a period of cultural stagnation when the graph of literacy was not surging into the nineteenth century but was instead '*une courbe brisée*' (Vovelle 1975:140). The eighteenth century was also a time of stagnation in the Massif Central, Brittany and Acquitaine, indeed at very low levels of literacy: Haut-Vienne in the Limousin remained among the ten least literate *départements* in France from the mid-seventeenth to the mid-nineteenth century. Italy, a highly literate culture (in the north at least) in the late middle ages, probably saw a contraction of education and literacy in the sixteenth and seventeenth centuries (Graff 1987:189). The literacy of Spanish women who gave evidence before the Inquisitions of Toledo and Cordoba fluctuated between nil and 7 per cent between 1515 and 1750, only improving to 18 per cent under the impact of the national literacy campaign of the later eighteenth century. Their husbands, fathers and brothers saw a substantial and sustained rise from 57 to 93 per cent over the three centuries from 1515 to 1817. Over large tracts of western Ireland, illiteracy remained above 90 per cent for women throughout the eighteenth century, a time when it had been cut by nearly a half in Scotland (Kagan 1974:23, 30; Rodriguez & Bennassar 1978:32; Furet & Ozouf 1982:30-1, 41-2; Vovelle 1975:140; Houston 1985).

Illiteracy declined for both genders and all social classes between 1500 and 1800, but it did not do so at equal rates for all groups. Indeed, the most characteristic pattern is not for simultaneous and uniform reductions in illiteracy among men and women, artisans and labourers alike. What usually happened was that literacy improved among the upper reaches of the social hierarchy and among men first, followed some time later by women and the lower orders. 'Ceilings' or 'plateaus' were reached by different groups at different times but it might take decades to move off them again. Take the example of one village in the Champagne region of north-eastern France. Male literacy at Vitry les Reims had climbed to 83 per cent by 1700. Only then could females drag themselves from no literacy at all to a figure of 60 per cent on the eve of the French Revolution. Over north-eastern France, the eighteenth century was 'the age of the take-off of female literacy *par excellence*' (Furet & Ozouf 1982:37-8); the rate of improvement at this time was much faster for women than men. Different social classes experienced distinct patterns of change even within the same area. In the larger towns of Provence the wives of artisans won substantial improvements in signing ability between 1660 and 1750, but the servant girls whom they employed saw none whatsoever during this period (Vovelle 1975:114). Illiteracy was halved among tradesmen who lived in Northumberland and Durham during the sixteenth century but there was a fall of only a few percentage points for the farmers of the region (Cressy 1980:159-63). Turin merchants cut their illiteracy by two-thirds between 1710 and 1790 but artisans could only manage a reduction of an eighth (Duglio 1971:509). There are exceptions to this pattern: contemporaneous improvements for all groups did occur in some areas, but the most common pattern was a staggered reduction in illiteracy led by males from the middling and upper groups in society, followed later on by women and the workers.

The dynamics of change, like the basic structures of literacy, reveal the intimate dependence of reading and writing on their social and material environment. Developments were sometimes accelerated, sometimes slowed down by the medium in which they took place. An understanding of context and of the ways in which people learned is central to a proper comprehension of the uses to which literacy could be put. The impact of literacy and of the book depended on the quality of learning.

CHAPTER EIGHT
The world of the book

Literacy itself is unimportant unless put to some use. Without practice, an individual's ability to read and write will atrophy and decay. Without a social, economic and cultural context, the mere fact of reading or signing is irrelevant to the historian. We have already covered some of the situations in which reading and writing might be beneficial to individuals but have devoted relatively little space to book reading. Printed literature is central to the lives of those living in modern developed countries. The printing revolution of the mid-fifteenth century and the explosion of publishing which followed it brought the printed page into the forefront of both popular and elite culture, creating a huge potential for both new reading and new patterns of thought. Rare and precious in the fifteenth century, books had by 1700 (if not earlier) become common all over western Europe. At the same time, political, commercial and religious change confronted more and more people with writing. If we are to assess the significance of literacy we must examine how many books were produced, what subjects they dealt with, how much they cost, how they were distributed, who owned books, who read them, what topics were most popular and, finally, what impact the printed word had upon the mental world of early modern men and women.

BOOK PRODUCTION

Until the fifteenth century, books had usually to be copied out longhand, meaning that they were few and expensive. Printing had existed in Europe for generations before the birth of Johann

Gutenberg in the form of fixed wooden blocks. Gutenberg's outstanding contribution to the development of printing was the invention of movable metal type coupled with developments in ink which would adhere to this and modifications to the screw press which made for greater flexibility in operation and improved legibility of the finished product. Printing by movable type began in Mainz in 1439 but spread quickly to other major commercial centres: Cologne in 1464, Basel 1466, Rome 1467, Venice 1469 and to Paris, Nürnberg and Utrecht in 1470. It later spread to intellectual centres such as prominent university towns. Indeed, the period from *c*.1450 to *c*.1550 marked the most dynamic phase: 'the creative century' according to Steinberg (1974:12). By 1480, more than 110 towns had presses; by 1500, 236 centres could boast one. Presses proliferated though the high cost of paper (two-thirds of the cost of production) and uncertain markets meant that failure rates among printing enterprises was high; some survived by moving from town to town, seeking out ecclesiastical or lay patronage for their skills. Important innovations during the creative century included the development of italic and other type-faces, Greek and Hebrew printing, production of musical scores and the introduction of pocket editions. Hebrew printing flourished in early sixteenth-century Italy following the expulsion of the Jews from Spain and Portugal in the 1490s. Primitive copyright libraries were created – Francis I ordered the Parisian printer Robert Estienne to give him one copy of every Greek book he produced – and the growth of competition is neatly attested by the apology of a Parma bookman who accounted for the numerous errors in a book by pointing out that it had been rushed out 'more quickly than asparagus could be cooked' (Steinberg 1974:119).

The expansive phase had come to an end by the third quarter of the sixteenth century. Peripatetic presses settled in the main administrative and marketing towns with privileges increasingly fixed in law: the monopoly of English printing granted to the London Stationers' Company in 1557 is a signal example. It became cheaper to produce books in the eighteenth century but there were few technical changes introduced between the sixteenth and nineteenth centuries. The main development of the period *c*.1550–*c*.1800 was the growth of specialisation in the printing, publishing and distribution of books. The volume of publication, on the other hand, expanded to enormous levels.

Printing made relatively slow progress during its early years, but book production increased dramatically after the 1480s. In Spain, roughly 300 editions were produced between the introduction of movable type (*c.*1472-3) and 1489, but double that number appeared during the 1490s and 1,307 in the years 1501-20 (Norton 1966:117, 125). Some 5,100 titles were published in England alone between 1486 and 1605. Perhaps twenty million books were printed in Europe before 1500, and 150-200,000 editions between 1500 and 1600. Except for proven best sellers such as Luther's works, which might demand an edition size of 4,000 copies, the average print run was probably about 1,000. In other words, 150-200 million copies may have been turned out during the sixteenth century (Febvre & Martin 1976). The number of editions produced and volumes printed increased dramatically during the sixteenth and seventeenth centuries to reach awesome levels by the time of the French Revolution. In the century between 1711 and 1811, approximately one million New Testaments were sold in Germany alone, plus two million complete Bibles, ten times as many as had been bought there between 1534 and 1626. During the eighteenth century, three million titles were produced in Europe as a whole; allowing for multiple editions this meant that roughly 1,500 million copies were printed and this total excludes popular ephemera. Towards the end of the eighteenth century somewhere between two and five million books a year were being printed in Germany alone (Gawthrop & Stauss 1984:50; Ward 1974:62). Western Europe was the leader in printing. Muscovy by comparison was a late starter and the level of production was low. Less than thirty titles had been produced there by 1612 and just 500 by 1700. At the time of Peter the Great's coronation, yearly output was about six or seven titles, but five new presses were set up in St Petersburg between 1711 and 1727 by which date the average had risen to forty-five. The growth in output continued to accelerate, reaching 500 a year by 1790 when the Empire could boast thirty publishing houses (Marker 1982:270, 277; Simmons 1977:47-9). Only three Norwegian towns supported presses in the eighteenth century (Lindberg 1981:228).

Part of the increase can be accounted for by a proliferation of printing shops or presses. Forty-two titles were produced at Geneva between 1533 and 1540, but the influx of 130 Protestant refugee printers into the city in the 1550s raised that number to 527 editions 1550-64. The lifting of the Stationers' monopoly on English printing in 1695 was followed by the establishment of presses in thirteen provincial towns before 1725. Rationalisation also took place. Paris in 1644 had 75 printing shops with 180 presses compared with 51 shops and 195 presses in 1701 (Darnton 1984:9; Febvre & Martin 1976:192, 196, 315). More than 1,000 printers and booksellers made a living in France in 1781. More men took up jobs in the printing industry: there were seventeen *Briefmaler* (literally letter painters) living in Nürnberg in 1571 compared with twenty-seven in 1599, and those describing themselves as *Formschneider* (cutters of wood blocks) increased from five to nine. The average number of volumes produced by a printer in a given year also grew. Sixteenth-century printing had been a small-scale affair. The biggest firms in Venice at that time (Giolito, Giunti and Manuzio) turned out between ten and twenty titles a year (originals and reprints) but the bulk of active enterprises printed between four and six editions a year. The names of 500 publishers feature on the title pages of Venetian printings during this century, though there were only three or four dozen who were producing at least a title a year for any length of time (Grendler 1977:4–5; Alexander & Strauss 1977:17–18).

Publishing was a widespread enterprise in some countries. Thirty-one permanently located presses are known to have existed in Spain before 1510 and an unknown number which moved from town to town. Forty-nine Italian towns had a press at some point between 1501 and 1520. Germany and the Austrian lands too had numerous presses. As early as 1480, fifty German towns had a press. All the Imperial free cities had at least one press in the early seventeenth century, Prague was a multi-lingual publishing centre and provincial towns as modest as Dobrovice and Königgrätz could boast presses (Norton 1958:xiii; Schulte 1968:69; Evans 1979:102). Other nations had a more centralised publishing industry. France's printers were grouped particularly in Paris – seventy-five printers operating 180 presses in 1644 – those of Russia were to be found in a handful of major towns such as Moscow, Kiev and St Petersburg, even in the early eighteenth century, and Iceland's only press before 1772 was alternated between the diocesan seats of Skálholt and Hólar. Certain towns were famous for specific types of publishing – Burgos in Spain and Troyes in France for chapbooks – or as distribution centres – Frankfurt-am-Main and Leipzig. Trends differed between countries. Production rose steadily in France between the mid-seventeenth century and the mid-eighteenth but was much less rapid in its growth than Germany after 1750 where the population are said to have been seized by a frenzy for reading (*Lesewut*) (Darnton 1986:8).

The spread of printing by movable type and the organisation of publishing has been extensively studied and outlined in detail in books such as Febvre and Martin (1976 trans.). Its significance too has been discussed since the fifteenth century. Changes in the medium of literacy, from syllabic to alphabetic writing in the ancient

Mediterranean world, from written to printed texts in the fifteenth and sixteenth centuries, from type and paper to electronic technologies in the twentieth century, have all involved fundamental transformations in patterns of thought and communication. The importance of printing was not lost on contemporaries. Martin Luther spoke of print as 'God's highest act of grace' and the Elizabethan Francis Bacon believed that along with gunpowder and the compass, printing had 'changed the appearance and state of the whole world'. Governments were not slow to realise the potential of printing: James IV saw Scotland's first press (at Edinburgh, 1507–8) as a way of promoting his government through the printing of legal texts, Acts of Parliament, chronicles and service books. The epilogue to Diego de Valera's 1482 *Coronica de España* deplored the scarcity of manuscript texts and praised printing; two decades later the Spanish crown was eagerly fostering printing (Norton 1966:117). In seventeenth- and eighteenth-century Russia, the state was the main force behind the propagation of print. Among the other contemporaries who appreciated the significance of making books cheaper and more available was Tomasso Garzoni who, in the 1599 edition of his *Piazza Universale*, claimed that printing had made esoteric knowledge available to all and had brought to light volumes of classical and humanistic literature which might otherwise have been condemned to obscurity. More conservative in his outlook was the Dominican Filippo della Strada who cautioned that print could spread unacceptable political and religious ideas to the vulgar (Lucchi 1978:593, 595).

Modern scholars too have discussed the significance of the invention and dissemination of printing across Europe. Most distinguished of these is Elizabeth Eisenstein, writer of a monumental two-volume work, *The Printing Press as an Agent of Change* (1979), the major conclusions of which are summarised in a substantial article and a brief volume (Eisenstein 1968; 1983). Eisenstein's argument centres on the fact that print can produce more books at cheaper prices than manuscript copying, that it fixes concepts and facilitates the cumulative development of ideas, and that the new modes of thought which it requires alter both attitudes and human relationships. First of all, printing dramatically reduced the number of man hours needed to produce a volume and therefore made books more accessible both in terms of numbers and cost. 'More abundantly stocked bookshelves increased opportunities to consult and compare different texts and this also made more probable the formation of new intellectual combinations and permutations.' (Eisenstein 1968:7).

Men could experiment with new ideas and form new ways of thinking. Furthermore, existing ideas were now available in a *fixed* and certain form, making cumulative intellectual advances easier and systematic progress more rapid. At the same time, learning by doing became less important than learning by reading, and the mental world of those steeped in oral culture was changed by familiarity with regular numbering, systems of dates, indices and the other trappings of printed volumes. Reading could be private and introspective, separating individuals and reducing the importance of communal participation. Thus printing touched the very core of everyday experience. It also eased economic developments: standard printed works helped with efficient planning and rational calculation of profit; printing created new advertising possibilities. In the sphere of politics, print made possible the standardisation of language sought by increasingly powerful states and fixed both rights and obligations of rulers and subjects in an unprecedented way. Fixed, definite and international rather than drifting, vague and local, printing ultimately restructured cognition and all human relationships.

Eisenstein's ideas are fascinating, her arguments about printing's potential are persuasive. She was influenced by the great Walter J. Ong who has recently extended and refined his ideas, claiming that orality and literacy require different sets of mind, that 'writing restructures thought' (Ong 1986). Writing and print promote objectivity, encourage exploratory thinking, separate the known from the knower, interpretation from data, past from present, learning from wisdom. However, the importance of the advent of printing is not as straightforward as it might appear, and its impact depended both on existing forms of communication (written and spoken) and on established intellectual tastes. Print was undoubtedly important in changing the ways in which people thought and, indirectly, in shaping economic, social and political developments in the early modern period. Yet its impact was neither immediate, nor direct, nor certain. The changes it won were slow and contingent, dependent on other features of society as much as it altered them. Printing itself may have been in part a response to an existing desire to promote mass communication for economic and political purposes. Like education and literacy as a whole, printing's importance depended on the existing social, economic and political context.

Eisenstein's arguments depend on the nature of presentation of books, their numbers, content and the ways in which they were understood. In appearance and content, considerable overlap existed between the forms of manuscript books and those of printed volumes. True of France, England and Germany, this was also the case in Russia where the creation of a specific 'print' form did not occur until the seventeenth century. The form and content of printed books continued to follow that of their manuscript predecessors even during 'the creative century'. Hand copying was still important during the early seventeenth century: it was geographically more widespread, better integrated into distribution networks and, not surprisingly, most Russian libraries of this period continued to be composed predominantly of manuscript books and most printed volumes would have been imported since there are no known books printed in Muscovy until 1564; in the west, printed books were in the majority by 1550. Moscow, and later St Petersburg, were the only centres in which large numbers of uniform printed editions were available to the reading public and then only in the eighteenth century (Marker 1982). Even in the west, manuscript books on esoteric subjects which did not attract publishers would continue to be important to scholars and students. For a limited market, it might make more commercial sense to continue copying since it was not difficult to run off a few hundred brief volumes by hand in a large copying shop of the kind found in late fifteenth-century Flanders (Labarre 1971:395).

Without print, it is hard to imagine the intellectual ferment of the later seventeenth-century Scientific Revolution, the debates on social and intellectual topics during the Enlightenment or the surge of revolutionary sentiment across Europe after 1789. Between *c*.1450 and *c*.1650 the expansion of printing made many more volumes available in the international language of learning, Latin, and thus made the ideas contained in them more accessible to the European elites who had command of it. From the middle of the seventeenth century, the rapid increase in vernacular output made ideas more widely available but broke up the unity of intellectual life created by Latin, a unity which was to some extent preserved by the adoption of French as a diplomatic and scholarly language in the eighteenth century. While ultimately new ideas did develop through the medium of print, many sixteenth-century volumes were reprints of books which had long been available in manuscript and others perpetuated facts and ideas which were either old-fashioned or simply wrong. Censorship and the dominance of politics and the church by traditionally-minded figures meant that established, acceptable ideas were propagated in print rather than innovative ones.

In the early years, the advent of print did little to change the titles available. More than three-quarters of books printed before 1500 were in Latin and 45 per cent were religious in content, indicating that demand came principally from scholars and clergy: titles such as the Bible, Thomas a Kempis' *Imitation of Christ* and Augustine's *City of God* were the most popular. Voragine's *Golden legend* went through eighty-eight Latin editions, eighteen French, five English, two German, two Czech, thirteen Flemish and six Italian in the late fifteenth and early sixteenth centuries alone. Classics too sold well, including 126 editions of Aesop's *Fables* before 1500 and sixty-one of Juvenal's *Satires* (Febvre & Martin 1976:245–55). Publishers were in business to make money, and it is hardly surprising that books gave their audience what they wanted to read, which often meant simply perpetuating an existing body of knowledge. Twice as many volumes were published about the Turks during the sixteenth century as about the Americas, and there was virtually no literature on Africa. Illustrations were of considerable, if diminishing, significance. The 1498 edition of *Tristrant* had eighty woodcut depictions but the editions of the 1550s had fifty-five or less and that of 1570 had none at all. Illustrations were sometimes employed for their appropriateness rather than strict accuracy. The 1493 Koberger edition of Hartmann Schedel's *Liber Chronicarum* had 1809 illustrations but only 645 woodcuts were used: any one walled city was, for example, used to depict Rome, Paris, Jerusalem or whatever (Steinberg 1974:158). In fairness, this Nürnberg edition was not trying to be a work of modern scholarship. In form and content it was a medieval chronicle and its use of illustrations followed the same guidelines as the selection of examples and settings in the oral narrative tradition: employ whatever was at hand or whatever seemed appropriate by way of example or setting. However, if books like this represent the world map of early modern people, then they had a distorted and old-fashioned perception. Publishers preferred to print old favourites such as the fantastic Mandeville's *Travels* or Boemius' *Geography*, the latter reprinted seven times in French alone between 1539 and 1558 without any mention of north America. Early printing did not accelerate the spread of new knowledge or ideas, but popularised old beliefs, strengthened existing prejudices and gave authority to fallacies and specious arguments (Febvre & Martin 1976:278–9, 282). As late as the third quarter of the eighteenth century, the catalogues of 500 private libraries in France show only one copy of Rousseau's *Social Contract* and Enlightenment ideas reached the educated elites by indirect means: book five of the more popular *Emile* rehearsed Rousseau's arguments (Darnton 1971a:215). What seem fundamental texts to modern scholars may have been comparatively unimportant in the spread of new ideas to contemporaries.

Printing developed in phases and its influence was neither immediate nor continuous. Its huge potential took perhaps a century to be realised and, as we shall see, it was arguably not fully developed until the eighteenth century. Printing created a vast reservoir of potential intellectual stimuli whose development depended on the social, intellectual and political circumstances. Its influence, like that of education, was slow, contingent and selective.

CENSORSHIP

The potentially revolutionary impact of the book was, for example, limited by controls on what could be published and sold. In all the countries of Europe, censorship existed in one form or another throughout the early modern period. Nowhere was the freedom of publishers to print whatever they thought the market would bear recognised either in principle or in practice. The Dutch press, the least restricted of any and a provider of banned literature to every European country, was not allowed free comment on domestic politics, while the independent Swiss cantons entered into an agreement in 1776 that they would suppress criticism of authorities in other jurisdictions as well as their own (Smith 1979:79, 93). Countries like France were relatively free of censorship until the vicious 'truth war' between Huguenots and Catholics in the 1560s even if scriptural writings had to be passed by the university of Paris's theology faculty as early as 1521. Francis I protected Rabelais against the Parlement de Paris and the Sorbonne, though attacks on the court in the affair of the Placards during the 1530s provoked a censorious backlash. Nor did Spanish authorities become strict until the threat of Protestantism appeared most serious during the 1550s, and Venetian censorship was not at its peak until the 1560s. Authorities tried to curb inflammatory religious propaganda after the Thirty Years War and were sometimes prepared to entertain criticisms of publications for which their subjects had been responsible. Czar Alexis, father of Peter the Great, protested that he had been described as a mere Grand Duke in a Dutch paper while the town council of Nürnberg complained that a report of plague in that part of Germany carried by the *Haarlemsche Courant* in 1713 was ruining trade (Baschwitz 1938:102).

163

Strict or lax, censorship was universal and could be effected by three means: direct control by the church, secular intervention by royal or local officials, and printing monopolies. In countries like Iceland where all the presses were run by the church until the eighteenth century, the printers and the supervisory personnel worked cheek-by-jowl and were in some cases the same people. Administratively, the third option was the easiest and was used with success in England, where the London Stationers Company held the monopoly of printing from 1557 until 1695, in Ireland where the royal Print-Master General had a monopoly from 1609, and in France throughout our period. The state's political interests were served by giving a monopoly of printing to a guild whose economic concerns would ensure that they forced out illicit publishers and policed what was being printed. Book production in France was heavily centralised, making it easier to supervise by the authorities in Paris, and the 3,000 ordinances and decrees regulating the Parisian publishing industry in the eighteenth century alone testify to the importance which royal government attached to it. Paris had a monopoly of new titles which meant that provincial printers in Rouen, Lyon, Caen and other centres had to rely on reprints of existing ones, albeit sometimes with alterations. Stockholm bookbinders' guild obtained a monopoly of the sale of bound books which was not finally lost until 1787 (Lindberg 1981:229-30). Monopolies also served a fiscal purpose, since the recipient usually had to pay the crown for the privilege, and a political one, since they encouraged printers to settle in politically important but commercially inhospitable areas. The highly lucrative monopoly of printing playing cards was much sought after. Philip II granted a share in the proceeds of monopoly of Nebrija's Latin grammar, *Arte grammatica*, to the *hopitales general*, Madrid's major poor hospital, in 1602 as a way of funding poor relief (Bennassar 1982:272; Thomas 1979). A variation on censorship for fiscal reasons was restriction of whole types of output by economic means. In the later eighteenth century, the English government tried to stem the flood of radical propaganda by placing a stamp tax on pamphlets which would price them beyond the reach of ordinary people (Walvin 1984:96-7).

Most towns exercised some control over what was printed by their burgesses, representing the local and mainly secular version of censorship. Authorities tended to concentrate less on the politically polemical or theologically unorthodox than on libellous works which might damage the closely-knit fabric of urban life (Chrisman 1982:28-9). Those in politically sensitive areas – the Imperial free cities of Germany such as Cologne and Nürnberg – had established codes of practice to govern printing, though the fragmented nature of the early modern German states made censorship, and indeed primitive copyright regulations, difficult to enforce. In the Spanish towns of Valladolid and Ciudad Real, control of the press after 1502 was vested in the presidents of the royal tribunals or *Audiencias*, while in the other principal towns such as Burgos this job was performed by the bishop (Norton 1966:119). During the 1700s the chancellor of France, Pontchartrain, employed inspectors to seize anti-Jesuit, pro-Jansenist, anti-war and pro-Protestant literature: they mounted 142 successful raids between 1700 and 1706. Provincial publishing in France was subject to even closer scrutiny after 1760 through the appointment of 120 censors (Birn 1981:159–61). A state-controlled board was set up in Portugal in 1768 to administer censorship, though its concerns remained mainly religious (Marques 1972:415).

If denounced for printing defamatory or inflammatory material, a publisher might face the death penalty. Sixteenth-century Venice had its own officials who enforced the censorship of the church, and a civil court, *Esecutori contro la Bestemmia*, which could order the burning of proscribed titles (Grendler 1975). Venice, ostentatiously different in many respects, nevertheless typified the towns of Spain and Italy which had local, secular censorship combined with local and national church Inquisitions. A list of banned volumes (*Index*) was printed periodically, though the papal index was only accepted in full by Venice in 1569; approved books on the other hand were identifiable by an official *Imprimatur*. The various Inquisitions produced their own Indices, varying in length and the sorts of titles proscribed: the Spanish Indices (the most important issued in 1551, 1554, 1559, 1583, 1584, 1612, 1632 and 1640) were, for example, more liberal than those of Rome (Kamen 1965:98).

The censorship of the Inquisitions has achieved notoriety, thanks to Protestant polemic and the hindsight of more 'enlightened' ages. Cardinal Ximénes of Spain is said to have burned more than a million Moorish books during the reconquest of Granada at the end of the fifteenth century. Yet, for all their power and variety, the mechanisms of censorship were of limited significance in altering intellectual development. The effectiveness of censorship was limited by two principal facts. First, the ready international market in books and pamphlets meant that a title banned in one country could be obtained fairly easily from another. In England, banned pornography was obtainable from France while Frenchmen who wanted news or comment critical of their regime had only to look to the Netherlands. Despite inquisitorial censorship, the Moriscos of Aragon kept and read censored books in the sixteenth century. Scribes copied out Korans and clandestine schools passed on the traditions of Islamic culture (Fournel-Guerin 1979). The tribunal of Logroño informed the Spanish *Suprema* during the 1790s that 'the multitude of seditious papers coming from France makes it impossible to initiate prosecutions against all the people who introduce, keep, and distribute them'. Two decades earlier, a priest proclaimed of banned Enlightenment literature that it was 'sought after at any price ... read with ardour and delight, and devoured ... with the hunger of a disordered appetite excited by novelty and prohibition itself' (Kamen 1965:268-9). In sixteenth-century Netherlands it was said that men consulted the Index when looking for an exciting book to read.

Second, fluctuations in the zeal with which illicit books were sought out and the limited manpower and effectiveness of any bureaucracy in early modern Europe made total or consistent control impossible; this was particularly noticeable in sixteenth-century Venice. Some censorship was highly effective: the publishing of Jewish books stopped completely in Venice after the purge of 1553, and Jesuit censorship of Protestant works in central Europe worked well during the seventeenth and early eighteenth centuries. In general, censorship was imperfect and its impact on scientific and cultural advances was slight. The sixteenth-century Roman Inquisition had little effect on classical scholarship, history, law, literary criticism, logic, mathematics, medicine, philology or rhetoric, while in the whole early modern period no scientific books were ever placed on the Spanish Index (Grendler 1977:288; Kamen 1965:301; Márquez 1980). Of the seat of the papal Inquisition in 1739, a French traveller opined that 'Freedom of thought on religious matters and sometimes even freedom of speech is at least as great in Rome ... as in any town I know' (Doyle 1978:157).

As many as 200 million books and chapbooks were published in Europe during the sixteenth century alone. Demand for print must have existed to fuel such a vast production and for the determined it was always possible to get the books. The other side of 'censorship' was to foster certain kinds of output in order positively to shape opinion rather than simply suppressing the unacceptable. Indeed, many of the developments in printed literature, notably in newspapers and broadsheets, came about through the political will of governments. Propaganda was probably more important in shaping public opinion than proscription of certain literature. Periods of political, military and religious crisis provoked an outpouring of print. Martin Luther's famous pamphlet, *To the Christian nobility of the German nation*, sold out its first edition in exactly seven days and within two years had been through thirteen editions. The catalogue of pamphlets and broadsheets in the royal library at 's-Gravenhage in the Netherlands shows that from levels of a few dozen a year the number of such works rose into the hundreds at times of fear and suspicion such as 1578–9, 1607–9, 1618–19 and 1647–8. Indeed, the Thirty Years War was one of the most productive periods of propaganda publication. Fifty-four pamphlets and broadsheets describing just one battle – the Swedish victory at Nördlingen – are known to survive and European archives are full of evidence of the flood of claim and counter-claim which was part of this vicious conflict. More than 4,000 political lampoons, *Mazarinades* (so-called after the royal minister), circulated in Paris between 1649 and 1652, more than 15,000 religious, social and political commentaries in England between 1640 and 1661 (Febvre & Martin 1976:291; van Deursen 1978:90–3; Langer 1978:238; Kamen 1984:216). As we shall see shortly, developments in the content and format of periodical literature were partly attributable to political initiative. Censorship was universal and while it was always possible to get forbidden books, legal restrictions had the effect of filtering out specific books or categories of literature from certain types of source, an important consideration when discussing reading tastes in early modern Europe.

BOOK DISTRIBUTION

The volume of publication grew enormously throughout the early modern period. Warehouses bulged with bales of heterogeneous reading material from Bibles to bawdy pamphlets. The next question is clearly how they made their journey from attics and barns into the hands of the readers. Some sort of distribution network, however informal, was needed so that men and women could enjoy the products of the revolution in printing. Fortunate individuals had their own ready-made outlets. As early as the 1470s, a Dominican called Petrus Nigri had his evangelical book addressed to the Jews published by Conrad Fyner at Esslingen; some sales he handled himself, others were made through his home monastery in Würzburg. During the same decade a group of Perugian booksellers banded together to publish books and have them sold through their stalls in Rome, Naples, Siena, Pisa, Bologna, Ferrara and Padua (Sprandel-Krafft 1983; Febvre & Martin 1976:225). More commonly, wholesale and retail outlets were organised separately. Their variety almost defies classification though we can make some generalisations about phases of development. The discrete categories of typefounder, printer, editor, publisher and bookseller which came to exist by 1800 were blurred and overlapping in the early decades of printing. Sometimes the functions were performed separately, at others they were conducted by one and the same person or on the same premises: one noted authority (P. Grendler) uses the term 'bookmen' to encompass the many facets of the trade. Broadly speaking, we can distinguish shops, chapmen and subscription as the principal outlets to the reader, and fairs and personal links between publisher and retailer as the key to the wholesale trade (Steinberg 1974:215–32). The German book trade offers an example of developments during our period. The century between 1450 and 1550 was characterised by cash sales, an identity between printer and publisher, and distribution by travelling pedlars. Protestant authors, for example, distributed their own and friends' books in the 1520s and 1530s. The distinctive features of the years 1550–1750 were that sales on an exchange basis became common and book fairs became the accepted mode of transaction for traders. Literary patrons of booksellers were un-important after the mid-seventeenth century. After 1750, publishing and selling came increasingly to be separated, sale or return developed and bookshops proliferated (Ward 1974:92).

The market for books was for much of our period a restricted one, dependent on the purchasing power of the reader and the availability of transportation. In small and geographically favoured countries such as England or the Netherlands, this was not a problem. Isaac Thompson claimed in 1766 that his *Newcastle Journal* reached readers in 188 towns and villages in the north of England (Wiles 1976:90). Books were nevertheless heavy, bulky, fragile and expensive to transport. In 1778 the director of postal services at Rotterdam complained to Etienne Luzac, editor of the extremely popular French edition of the *Leiden Gazette*, that his packages destined for France were far too heavy. He suggested either reducing the weight of the bundles or paying for a second horse to carry them or having the paper printed in France (Gibbs 1971:334). As a result, orders for books dispatched by publishers tended to be small. In the later seventeenth century, Guillaume de Luynes sent twenty-four copies of Primi's *Histoire de la Guerre de Hollande* to booksellers at Lyon, five to one at Nantes, eight to one at Reims, six to Bordeaux and four to Douai. Lyon was a highly significant town for the book trade and was the location of the first major book fair in Europe. Fairs in strategic locations such as Lyon or later Frankfurt-am-Main attracted many buyers and sellers anxious to exploit their range of choice, efficient transport facilities and financial services. Lyon was the market for Italian, German, Swiss and Flemish publishers; major Italian publishers like Giuntas, Gabiani and Portonari all had branches there. Via the Loire valley and Toulouse, books were transported to different areas of Spain, Medina del Campo, Burgos and Valencia being the principal distribution points (Febvre & Martin 1976:220–30).

Bookshops were uncommon in the sixteenth and seventeenth centuries, confined to state capitals and to the larger provincial cities. During the eighteenth century their numbers increased substantially but they retained their mainly urban location, and tended to be situated in particular streets or quarters. In eighteenth-century London, the 'mercuries' or sellers employed by the main metropolitan newspapers were often the wives or widows of printers who kept small shops in areas such as Charing Cross (Harris 1978:91). In Russia as late as 1750 the two bookshops belonging to the Academy of Sciences, one in St Petersburg and one in Moscow, accounted for the vast majority of domestic sales (Luppov 1981; Marker 1982:280–1). While Russia was acquiring bookshops, some western cities began to contain specialist sellers. The first French bookshop was opened in Berlin in the early 1700s, the first English one in Hamburg in 1788. The communications network in eastern Europe was even slower and less developed than in the west. Those who wanted books relied more on direct order from the west and on borrowing and lending circles. The importance of different forms of distribution and access to printed literature varied across Europe according to transport facilities, the extent of urbanisation and the proportion of active readers in the population.

Once a book had been published, its potential audience had to be won over. In some cases the market was fairly certain: almanacs, Bibles, topical news-sheets and certain recreational literature sold easily. They were the bread and butter of ordinary printers. Some publishers only produced works to order, assured by their contract that they would not be left storing quintals of unsold print. An alternative which was pioneered in the early seventeenth century but reached its heyday during the eighteenth was publication by subscription. The supreme merit of this arrangement was that author and printer did not have to sink large amounts of capital into production, stocking and distribution: the audience was 'captive, tame, pre-committed' (Rogers 1972:1539). A sixth of all new German books published between 1770 and 1810 were subscription volumes (Darnton 1986:11). Unsuccessful attempts were also made to prevent the all too common pirating of editions by subscription publishing. For most specialist works, this was the preferred means of funding because of the necessarily small and dispersed audience. A Spanish translation of the Dutch political periodical *Mercure Historique et Politique* appeared in 1738 with 1,000 subscribers on the Iberian peninsula and a further sixty copies a month shipped to the Spanish colonies in the New World. German translations of English literature afford another example. Johann Joachim Bode's translation of *Tristram Shandy*, published at Hamburg in 1774, was subscribed to by roughly 600 north German professional men and 43 women (Gibbs 1971:348; Fabian 1976:166–7). Enterprising publishers were able to extend the system to include what were known in England as 'number books'. Smollett's *History of England* and Milton's *Paradise Lost*, for example, were sold a few pages at a time bound in cheap blue paper. Serial publications made these long and expensive books accessible to a wide market. Some were distributed weekly by the same men who delivered newspapers (Wiles 1976:98–9).

Particularly fascinating are the means used to disseminate illegal literature. We have seen that all countries of Europe operated some kind of censorship in the early modern period, ranging from the official Index in Spain and Italy to the more lax but still evident regulations of the Netherlands or some of the Swiss cantons. Restrictions on the sort of material which could be printed and sold did not, of course, prevent clandestine publication and distribution. Indeed, the more extensive the censorship, the more ingenious and daring became the clandestine book trade. Take the case of Italy at the height of the Counter-Reformation. Protestant bookmen such as the Venetian Pietro Longo had contacts with printers in key towns like Basel in Switzerland. In the 1570s and 1580s he carried contraband titles with him along with legitimate merchandise into Venice where its passage through customs inspections was 'eased' by sellers like Zilettia and Valgrisi who also helped to distribute the illegal books to Protestants in Venice and its region. The clandestine trade could prove lucrative, especially for occult works, but it could also bring heavy fines and imprisonment or worse. Longo was drowned by order of the Inquisition for his heresies and smuggling in 1588 (Grendler 1977:188, 193).

Smuggling flourished all over Europe, even in the century of the Enlightenment. Catholic countries which could be reached with ease from Protestant havens such as the Netherlands or Switzerland were particularly vulnerable to infiltration by illegal titles. Italy is one obvious example, the other being France. Some publishers existed almost wholly to fill the demand for banned books in French, known generically in the trade as *livres philosophiques*. The archives of the *Société Typographique de Neuchâtel* for the later eighteenth century provide fascinating insights into the clandestine book trade between Switzerland and France. Take the example of Faivre de Pontarlier, described in the association's records as a hard worker who lived on his wits. Faivre shipped crates of books by horse-drawn wagon from his storehouse in Neuchâtel to a secret location in the village of Les Verrières on the Swiss side of the border. He then employed teams of porters and mule drivers for the back-breaking task of lugging bales of books across mountain trails into France where he had a hidden warehouse near Pontarlier. This was a dangerous job, since the porterage had usually to be done at night over perilous mountain paths. Worse, the porters might risk a stretch in the galleys if they were caught with banned books. They were paid in cash and drink, the latter, one assumes, particularly welcome under the circumstances. French customs officials at the Frambourg post were either bribed or duped with fraudulent *acquits à caution* (discharge notes). Once in France, the books were crated once again and sent in wagons to Besançon or to other distribution points where dealers bought them for sale in Troyes, Lyon or Paris. This was an expensive and slow process fraught with difficulties. Books might be seized, abandoned by the porters or damaged: most publishers shipped books as unfolded, printed sheets which would not receive a protective binding until they were sold to a reader. Smugglers like Faivre had to undertake to reimburse their clients in full for any books lost in transit. For those prepared to pay the understandably high prices, this network gave opportunities to enjoy illicit political, religious or pornographic works (Darnton 1971a; 1976).

With the possible exception of book smugglers, the most colourful characters in the book trade were the chapmen. Itinerant pedlars brought a whole range of goods to many rural areas where transport and communication networks were poor or where the nearest sizeable town was too distant to be easily reached. Before the eighteenth century, provincial bookshops were rare in most parts of Europe; in Norway, Sweden, Iceland, Finland and Russia they were almost unknown until the nineteenth century. Those who wanted printed material had either to order it specially or to rely on mobile retailers. Indeed, the same holds true for many consumer goods. In Sweden such chapmen were called *gårdfarihandlarar*, literally tradesmen who travel to farmsteads, or by local names: in Västergötland the slang was *knallar* (Dahl 1959). These men (and sometimes women) traded mostly in craft products such as cooking utensils and clothes not available locally. However, many also carried a few books and pamphlets as part of their wares. In sixteenth-century Italy, humble itinerants who specialised in the lives of saints were called *leggendaio*, in Russia *ofeni*, in Germany *Jahrmarktströdler*, while in France the word *colporteur* describes the peripatetic trader. Illegal in some countries such as Sweden, chapmen were officially licensed in France, though they were stigmatised in a decree of 1660 as 'people who sell almanacs, ABCs, gazettes, little tales of *Mélusine* and the *Quatre Fils Aymon* to abate boredom, vulgar songs, dirty and nasty idle farces, and disgusting drinking songs' (Martin 1978:86). Only forty-six recognised *colporteurs* existed in 1611, though there must have been hundreds more who operated outside the licensing system. The number was restricted to 120 in 1725 but by 1740 four times that number had licences and in 1848 the figure had jumped to approximately 3,500 (Capp 1979:271; Bollème 1965:64-5). Sellers of broadsheets, newspapers, pamphlets and books were almost an itinerant vocational group. A German broadsheet of 1630 shows one of them, clutching fistfuls of sheets in both hands; more are crammed into a large sack on his back; his pockets and waist pouch bulge with pamphlets and there are even papers stuffed into his hatband and garters (Smith 1979:18; Langer 1980:238).

More settled sellers also existed in towns, these often the dregs of urban society. Provincial pedlars could be relatively prosperous, but in the bigger towns impoverished, transient hawkers did most of the selling of cheaper (and sometimes illegal) papers, sheets and pamphlets. In Venice, humble traders bought and sold second-hand books from open-air benches on the Rialto bridge or peddled religious pamphlets at the doors of churches. The hawkers advertised their wares by reading pamphlets and newspapers aloud from barrels, benches and street corners: a contemporary estimated that there were some 300 street hawkers crying their wares in London in 1641 (Grendler 1977:6; Capp 1985:200). Even blindness did not prevent some Spanish street sellers from presenting a resume of their merchandise to potential customers. One bi-weekly published between 1786 and 1791 was called the *Correo de Madrid o de los ciegos* after its blind distributors. A clear, hearty voice was possibly more important than eyes to streetcorner sellers (Schulte 1968:108).

Those who worked in print shops were themselves unusual both for their high literacy and for the way they worked closely together in factory-like conditions. Printers and their journeymen and apprentices were among the most organised and articulate of industrial workers. Solidarity was maintained by strong guild ties, though printers and publishers were not above pillaging the resources of their fellows: in 1703, Jacques Collombat was convicted of pirating titles owned by eight different colleagues. Journeymen were vocal in their condemnation of exploitation by their masters. In the second half of the seventeenth century the number of master printers was halved in Paris, meaning that each master had more journeymen and that these employees were increasingly proletarianised since their chances to become masters in their own right had been substantially reduced. Workers in the book trade were unusually vocal in asserting their rights and privileges. A century later (1776), Paris bookbinders struck for their working day to be reduced to fourteen hours (Partner 1976:91; Birn 1981:163). Yet even in the sixteenth century, apprentices and journeymen were precocious in asserting their rights. Those in Elizabethan London were allowed one copy of each book which they could then sell, but they also (and illegally) used spoiled or surplus sheets to bind up extra copies, a sort of early 'black economy' (Johnson 1946). Printers were, furthermore, unusually mobile. Geneva attracted 130 refugee printers and booksellers in the 1550s while two-thirds of the 364 known to have been active in the northern Netherlands between 1575 and 1630 had come from southern Flanders and northern France (Parker 1979:250). Printing and purveying of books meant that the bookmen were themselves leaders in social and intellectual change.

In modern developed countries, book purchase is extensively supplemented by borrowing from public libraries or from friends. Book lending certainly existed on an extensive but unquantifiable scale in early modern Europe. Together with reading aloud, this meant that the potential reading public was far larger than most documentary sources suggest – how substantial we shall assess shortly. Public libraries were rare: medieval libraries were private and closed, created for monasteries, ecclesiastical officials or academics. University collections and private libraries were on occasion opened up on an individual basis to scholars. One such was the library of the Academia Gustaviana, set up by the Swedish king in 1632, and later to become Tartu university. In the later seventeenth century, the books were accessible for three hours a day on Wednesday and Saturday.

Students were granted a twice-weekly visit to the library 'for looking through its good books and reading them, and making abstracts of them'. Students were not supposed to borrow books, a hangover from the days when the staff read books and passed their contents on to students in class, but the lending register for the years 1692–1707 shows otherwise. Indeed, staff and students were not the only borrowers: doctors, clergy, army officers, city councillors and other townspeople were among them. Bremen 'public' library in 1660 was open only on Wednesdays of alternate weeks (Ward 1974:103). One depiction of the university library at Leiden in 1610 shows rows of books chained to shelves and students standing up to read from shoulder-level counters, protected against the cold by heavy cloaks and against cramp by a foot rail (Darnton 1986:13).

Private libraries of the seventeenth century came to form the core of later public ones. For instance, the library of Pescia in Tuscany was based on the collection of Romualdo Cecchi, who died in 1648, bequeathing his volumes to the cathedral chapter for general use (Brown 1982:196). Systematic efforts were made from the middle of the seventeenth century to create national libraries. The granting of legally-binding copyright to certain English libraries in 1663 helped to provide a core of books though we should recognise that legal protection of authors and publishers through copyright legislation was not introduced in England until 1710 (Ward 1974:93–8). Libraries like the French Bibliothèque Nationale became a monument to the increasingly powerful and centralised absolutist monarchies of the later seventeenth and eighteenth centuries. Libraries were still not 'open' even in the eighteenth century and the first real lending library in Britain, that attached to the shop of the Edinburgh bookseller Andrew Ramsay in 1725–6, was an offshoot of a commercial enterprise (Steinberg 1974:255–9). The ducal library of Wolfenbüttel, whose borrowing register dates back to 1666, did lend more readily than most and during the 1760s the number of books borrowed every year doubled; borrowers from social levels below the professions begin to appear at this time. Berlin had a public library from 1704 but these institutions were far from common in Germany until the last quarter of the eighteenth century. St Petersburg imperial library, founded in 1795, became open to the public after 1814 (Darnton 1986:11; Ward 1974:107).

The seventeenth century was the great age of private libraries. In the eighteenth century it became more common to club together to buy books which would be kept for consultation and borrowing by members of reading societies. In eighteenth-century Ulster (Northern

Ireland), three sorts of group purchase existed: subscription libraries; county reading societies patronised by artisans and schoolteachers who pooled books; and societies which did not keep a library but disposed of the books once read. All had the common aim of spreading the cost of buying and avoiding duplication as far as possible. Some were highly successful, including the Downpatrick literary society, founded in 1793 and able to boast 827 volumes by 1804, and the Doagh book club in county Antrim, set up by a local schoolteacher in 1770 but burned down by anti-Radical elements in 1798. At least a dozen reading societies existed in Ulster by 1800 (Adams 1980). A variation on this theme was the circulating library. These flourished in England from the 1740s onwards, members paying on average three to five shillings a quarter and the money being used to buy books which were lent out. There were 122 circulating libraries in London in 1800 plus 268 in the rest of England (Porter 1982:253; Hamlyn 1946–7). In all cases, members had to pay to use the library, though it might be 'seeded' by a philanthropic figure. The library for the lead miners of Wanlockhead in southern Scotland was founded by the owner after a serious labour dispute in 1756, but attracted little interest and few members from the workforce until the 1780s.

Membership of reading societies was generally select and prestigious. One adult in 500 belonged to a reading society in Germany at the turn of the nineteenth century. There were two such bodies in the German town of Wunstorf whose total complement was around sixty in the mid-eighteenth century, some 4 per cent of the total population. Schaffhausen reading society's membership amounted to 1 per cent of the town's population in 1770 or 10 per cent of the burgesses; those of Mainz in 1788 had 300–450 members among some 22,000 inhabitants (Fabian 1976:166; Ward 1974:105–6; Engelsing 1973:63). Much less exalted were coffee houses where newspapers and periodicals might be available: Vienna had at least sixty by 1760. Humbler still were informal groups of Swabian peasant women who got together to read the Bible and pray together as a way of resolving generational conflicts and reconciling themselves to a life of toil (Gawthrop & Strauss 1984:54).

Private libraries were more common than public. As we might expect, any collection of books which had any financial value, and especially any which were worth compiling into a catalogue, would belong to members of the upper classes. Catalogues survive for 377 private libraries in late fifteenth- and sixteenth-century France. Of these, 28 per cent belonged to churchmen, 33 per cent to lawyers, 18 per cent craftsmen and tradesmen, 8 per cent soldiers and the rest to other nobles and professional men (Febvre & Martin 1976:263). Some 'libraries' numbered only a few books: just 9 per cent of all inventories from the town of Amiens during the seventeenth century mention fifty or more titles and half of the artisans whose inventories show they owned books had a single title; 90 per cent of all the single volumes were religious and of these four-fifths were Books of Hours (Labarre 1971:262). Other libraries were extensive. When don Fernando of Aragon, duke of Calabria, died in 1550 he left 795 titles, a quite exceptional number by the standards of contemporary Spain. The library of Jörgen Seefeldt at Ringsted, captured by Charles X of Sweden during his invasion, contained 26,000 volumes and was probably one of the largest anywhere in Europe. More typical was the collection of Johann Langepeter, pastor of Kapellendorf in northern Thuringia (Germany), who reported seventy-seven titles when asked about his literary possessions by his superiors in 1570. Or Jehan Myramont, a student at the University of Toulouse who around the same time made a hasty departure from the town leaving five dirty shirts, two torn doublets, a sheaf of lecture notes, twenty-seven books and an unpaid bill for three years' lodging (Bennassar 1982:276; Hermannsson 1929:52; Strauss 1980:161–2; Davies 1983). Extensive studies have been conducted into libraries belonging to some of the more prominent figures of early modern Europe, in order to discover the sorts of intellectual influences which shaped their attitudes and actions.

Book distribution suffered from the problems of slow and (overland) expensive communication common across Europe. This explains why most booksellers had their businesses in towns. Wholesale could be by private means, at fairs or through the increasingly common shops of the eighteenth century which reflect growing specialisation in the book trade. Sales to ordinary people were made by those who physically brought the literature to them, though the better-off usually ordered specialist volumes from a merchant since stocks were limited in range. Until the eighteenth century, private libraries numbered their books in dozens rather than hundreds. If people did not buy or borrow books informally, there were few public libraries open to them before the eighteenth century, at which time groups of interested individuals came increasingly to form themselves into subscription or reading societies. The difficulties of access to books reflect and perhaps explain an important feature of reading in the sixteenth and seventeenth centuries which we shall discuss shortly.

NEWSPAPERS

We have seen how censorship was supplemented by positive attempts to shape opinion by propaganda. Indeed, new forms were tried during our period in order to 'inform' the political nation about events, objectives and (supposed) achievements. The best example is the development of the newspaper from its origins as a commercial information sheet to the status of a provider of more or less hard news of the kind which twentieth-century readers associate with the medium. Newspapers were born of merchants' need to be informed about political and economic conditions in the areas with which they traded. Intelligence was received from business representatives and semi-professional *rapportisti* or *avvisatori*, and collated by town authorities or by private companies like the Fuggers. The resulting news-sheets were available in both manuscript and print from the end of the fifteenth century. As late as the seventeenth century, merchants and gentry in Norway sought out handwritten newspapers and manuscript versions were still available in eighteenth-century France and Germany. Circulating as *Avvisi* in Venice or *Zeitungen* in Augsburg from the 1550s, they provided a model for later newspapers. The development of newspapers is another example of the interplay between institutions and social groups in the development of literacy and its products (Baschwitz 1938:100–1; von Klarwill 1924; 1926; Høyer 1982:16).

Modern newspapers developed through four stages. First came sheets describing a single event: 'relations' such as the early sixteenth-century Spanish *Relación de lo que pasó al Emperador en Bornes [Worms] con Luthero en 1521*. *Relaciones* in Spain were usually one-off single sheets folded once or twice. One or two a year survive for the reign of Charles V, nearly four for the early years of Philip II, more than five for his later years, twelve for the first half of the reign of Philip III and twenty-six for the second part. Not all were 'hard' news: some in verse told of sightings of monsters while one of 1617 from Granada was a report of a nun who, after twelve years in a convent at Úbeda, suddenly became a man after vigorous exertions (Ettinghausen 1984:1–3, 12). For the years 1599–1614, 159 different news-sheets survive and many more must have been published and all the copies lost. The second phase was characterised by the publication of a series of relations as a *coranto*, a form in which the Dutch specialised. During the 1620s, Jacob Jacobsz. produced a French *Courant d'Italie et d'Almaign* pirated in Spain by Andres Mendoza as *Correos de Francia, Flandes y Alemania*. These sheets were regular (if infrequent) and kept to fixed titles. Next came the 'diurnal' which purveyed regular news about a particular event or body for a brief period: Robert Coles and Samuel Pecke's 1640s *Perfect Diurnall of the Passages in Parliament,* for example. Fourth came 'mercuries' such as the *Mercurius Gallo-Belgicus* published in Latin at the end of the sixteenth century (Smith 1979:9–11; Schulte 1968).

These phases were not discrete and sequential since forms overlapped over time. Every European country has at least some claim to have published the first 'modern' newspaper, including, for example, King Mathias of Hungary's *Dracola Waida* (Devil Prince) in 1485 and the 1609 Augsburg relation. In fact, there was no Augsburg relation of that year but there were two weekly papers with that title, one published in Strasbourg and the other in Wolfenbüttel (Ries 1987). Debate on this issue is clouded by problems of definition: is permanence of title, nature of content or regularity and frequency of appearance the most significant criterion? There is more agreement over the importance of the early seventeenth century in the development of regular newspapers. France had the weekly *Gazette* from 1631, Florence from 1636, Rome from 1640 and Madrid from 1661. Newspapers proliferated in the decentralised German states during the seventeenth century and these territories were much more productive than France or England which did not see similar expansion until the eighteenth century. Germany had over 200 newspapers before 1700, the Netherlands as many as thirty but France and England effectively only one (Ries 1982). The first regular daily was produced at Leipzig in 1660 (*Einkommende Zeitung*), though it was not until 1749 that Denmark had its first 'permanent' newspaper, *Berlingske Tidende*, and the first regular, if short-lived, Finnish language paper was not started until 1776. Spain's first daily, *Diario Noticioso*, was started by the prolific Francisco Nipho y Cagigal in 1758 (Thomsen 1982:3; Kamen 1984:218; Høyer 1982:16; Schulte 1968:91). Indeed, the later eighteenth century marks the second major phase of development. Countries already well-endowed with newspapers saw a further proliferation while in the northern and eastern states sheets and pamphlets began to be available on a regular basis. Provincial England had thirty-five papers in 1760 but fifty by 1782 with total circulation doubling to nearly 400,000 copies a year. Paris got its first daily paper in 1777, but the first Latvian newspaper (*Latweeschv Awihse*) came as late as 1822 (Vīksniņš 1973:157).

The significance of the early seventeenth century for the development of regular newspapers lay in improved communications, growing demand for political and economic news and a heightened awareness among political authorities of the part which the proper manipulation of information could play in ensuring success abroad and peace at home. Propaganda came of age during the Thirty Years War. Part of the development of newspapers came spontaneously, part was orchestrated. Popular demand for commercial and then political news increased the numbers, regularity and variety of news-sheets and pamphlets. In England, the Netherlands and the Austrian Habsburg territories, development was largely organic, but in France, Denmark and Russia it was closely determined by the aims of absolute governments. These latter states were determined to convince outsiders of the strength of their regime and those within its boundaries of the legitimacy and efficacy of their policies. Sixteenth-century propaganda had been rhetorical and overstated, but that of the seventeenth and eighteenth centuries was increasingly sophisticated and imaginative, using reasoned persuasion to win over a better-educated and more aware public. Serially published news periodicals mark a signal adjustment to new patterns of taste and political culture (Solomon 1972; Klaits 1976). France's *Gazette*, the principal newspaper of the seventeenth century, was wholly given over to official propaganda. Peter the Great was determined that his policy of westernising the manners, dress and attitudes of his Russian subjects and the military development of his empire should be aided by the creation of a state-controlled press. The Russian *Posolskii Prikaz* (department of embassies) took seven Dutch newspapers alone in the early eighteenth century and employed a battery of translators to scan Europe's news-sheets (Gibbs 1971:338). Normally liberal governments turned to the press in times of crisis as a way of shaping public opinion. Prussian authorities prevented the import of uncensored foreign papers but allowed native publishers considerable freedom. This changed completely during the Seven Years War when Frederick the Great would brook no criticism of his policy (Smith 1979:65; Burke 1978:262–70).

Not all of the opinion-shaping content of newspapers was conscious, articulated propaganda. Spanish *relaciones* of the reigns of Philip II, III and IV illustrate the selective presentation of news. They tended to proliferate in years of prominent national successes such as the defeat of the Turks at Lepanto in 1571 or at times of celebration such as royal visits. Unpleasant news tended to be filtered out (except for acts of God), publishers working on the assumption that bad news is no news. They 'put out a consistently reassuring interpretation of reality that is strikingly at variance with the messages of contemporary satirists, moralists and reformers'. The content may have been inspired by the government, but it is also possible that people preferred not to recognise that Castile was in serious economic difficulties and that the Spanish empire was encountering growing military problems in the early seventeenth century. Presenting a picture of stability rather than change, *relaciones* were 'less reports, selecting and distorting a set of events in the real world, than accounts put together after the manner of literature according to a sense of what is necessary and appropriate' (Ettinghausen 1984:14–16). They reflected the existing power structures, boosted morale, fostered loyalty to the crown, united diverse parts of Spain by emphasising joint nationality, related victories and miracles which showed that God and Spain were synonymous. Arguably, people propagandised themselves.

Newspapers could also serve separatist causes.The 1778 *Dublin Evening Post* represented nationalist sentiment against English domination, and the first Hungarian language newspaper (*Magyar Hirmondó*) of 1780 was followed by a wave of patriotic, anti-Habsburg imitators (Smith 1979:92). Indeed, the press was used as an agent of change as well as a means of preserving existing social and political structures. The radical English Levellers used cheap print to propagate their ideas in the 1640s and the later eighteenth century saw an expanding use of printed propaganda for radical causes in England and Europe. Scandinavia had newspapers independent of government from the middle of the eighteenth century. In 1743 the chevalier de Mouhy told his employer, the lieutenant-general of police, that 'the true cause of the discontent' against Louis XV's government and of the 'agitation of the people' lay in the widespread reading of hostile broadsheets and gazettes (sometimes called *lardons*) smuggled in by France's enemies (Kaiser 1983:623). No country was 'watertight' and this example illustrates the ambivalent role of printing and literacy in that once the printed material was available and a reading public existed, it was impossible to exert total control over the uses to which it could be put. The problem posed by topical printing for the authorities was summed up by Charles II of England's official censor Sir Roger l'Estrange when he opined that reading newspapers 'makes the multitude too familiar with the actions and counsels of their superiors, too pragmatical and censorious, and gives them not only a wish but a kind of colourable right and licence to the meddling with the government' (Burke 1978:270).

BROADSHEETS AND CHAPBOOKS

The growth of newspaper output shows how commercial needs in the early stages of development were built upon by political will in the seventeenth century and then, as we shall see, by true mass demand in the eighteenth century. Newspapers became cheaper and more common in the seventeenth century but until the century of the Enlightenment they can hardly be termed a mass medium. It is also unlikely that the majority of substantial volumes could have commanded a truly mass market. With the exception of religious texts, most books were either too expensive or too abstruse for the ordinary man or woman. The only real mass medium in the sixteenth century was the illustrated broadsheet and in the seventeenth and eighteenth centuries the pamphlet or chapbook. Given the low levels of education available to the majority of the population, a medium of communication which used visual symbols rather than print or which kept the number of words to a palatable minimum was likely to reach much larger audiences than substantive literature. Popular literature was often illustrated in the early years of printing: a third of all volumes printed in Europe before 1500 were so embellished (Steinberg 1974:158). What scholars understood from writing and print was communicated to ordinary people by pictures. It is, for example, unlikely that more than 10 per cent of the population of Luther's Germany could read his work for themselves and most of these would have been middle-class urban males. Vernacular religious literature in late fifteenth-century Italy was semi-theatrical in presentation, showing the contemporary emphasis on visually-oriented spirituality (Schutte 1980:16–17). At a time when literacy was restricted to a small minority of men, most people gained their knowledge of the ideas of the Reformation by looking and listening rather than reading.

What they viewed were illustrated woodcuts. A picture was cut into the end grain of a block of wood, coloured (if at all) by hand and printed on to single sheets of paper using a press. Russian broadsheets and pamphlets were called *lubki* after the limewood blocks from which 3–4,000 copies could be printed before deterioration. Broadside sheet almanacs were the precursors of modern wall calendars, posters the harbingers of the political graffiti of the twentieth century. Some woodcuts were crude and simple but expert practitioners could produce definition close to that which could be obtained by engraving metal. Some were pictures alone but many combined word and image, and in all cases the symbolism was rich and powerful. Human, animal, monster, medical, morbid and mechanical images were used to impart religious and political propaganda as well as social comment and pure entertainment. Peter the Great may have issued a picture of a barber cutting off the beard of an Old Believer as part of his westernisation campaign following his 1705 decree banning beards, though it may also have been a satire put out by his opponents. Old Believer propaganda, on the other hand, showed Peter as a cat, a crocodile, a witch-baby and even Satan. At the start of the Thirty Years War, the failures of Frederick of Bohemia were shown in broadsheets which portrayed him building a house on sand or digging his own grave.

These broadsheets were not simply illustrations to accompany a text, but contained the central message in their images. 'Like homemade gin', writes Scribner (1981a:5), the woodcut 'was cheap, crude and effective'. The range of subjects they covered was substantial and changed relatively little over time. A major study of German single-leaf woodcuts has shown that, between 1550 and 1700, religious matters accounted for a third of all surviving broadsides, a fifth were 'folklore and superstition', a seventh involved social comment while the remainder dealt with politics or offered calendars, advertisements, maps and portraits (which were the only growth area between 1550–99 and 1600–1700) (Hanebutt-Benz 1983; Langer 1978:238–9, 248; Alexander & Strauss 1977). The heyday of the broadsheet was in the sixteenth and the first half of the seventeenth century in western Europe. It was still a very popular medium in eighteenth-century Russia where western themes were adapted for propaganda by the Orthodox church or for entertainment purposes. The largest category of early seventeenth-century *lubki* were religious. Callot's depictions of Punch and Judy were introduced to Muscovy in the second quarter of the eighteenth century and Russianised as the beak-nosed *Farnos*. Drink, taverns and drunks were popular themes in Russian broadsheets of the period: one, set out like a hagiographical icon, depicts nine scenes of what can befall the enebriate. *Lubki* of the early seventeenth century were primarily directed at upper-class audiences but by the eighteenth they found their way on to the walls of humbler townspeople and became common among the peasantry only in the nineteenth century, by which time they had long been out of fashion with the elites (Ovsyannikov 1968; Brooks 1985:63).

In Germany, *Flugblätter* were broadsheets. With more pages and more print, chapbooks and pamphlets (*Flugschriften*) were the most significant mass media of the second half of our period. Known as *Skillingtryck* (farthing prints) in Sweden, *Literatura de Cordel* in Spain (also *pliegos sueltos* or 'loose pages'), and as *Fatras* or the *bibliothèque bleue* in France (because of the cheap blue paper in which the pamphlets were bound) this cheap, brief and ephemeral literature circulated extensively. It is hard to overestimate its popularity. Chapbooks were priced low enough to be afforded by ordinary peasants and labourers or even by servant girls. Output was correspondingly huge. In Spain, mass production of chapbooks began in the 1510s while as early as 1548 Guillaume Godard, a Paris bookseller, died leaving a stock including 1,000 ABCs, more than 10,000 verse chapbooks, 275,000 service books and 148,000 Books of Hours (Martin 1978:73). Teachers all over Europe complained that their charges loved nothing better than to waste their time reading idle and frivolous tales, romances and fables rather than studying Godly and improving texts. The range of topics covered was enormous, and almost any title which was available in a bound volume would have an approximate equivalent in chapbook form: from reprints of medieval romances such as *Amadis of Gaul* to condensed versions of contemporary bestsellers. Defoe's 1719 *Life and Most Surprizing Adventures of Robinson Crusoe* (a substantial volume of more than 400 duodecimo pages) was available some years later as *Voyages and Travels: Being the Life and Adventures of Robinson Crusoe of York, Mariner*, a pamphlet which ran to just eight pages and did not take the reader much beyond the hero's shipwreck! Shortened editions or serial publications were targeted at a market close to that of the full version but Crusoe was closer to the mainstream chapbook in being fragmented, 'hasty, formulaic, with no sense of tempo or climax, and no relation beyond plot outline to the original text' (Rogers 1985:168, 171, 196). This volume was, incidentally, extensively translated and pirated in eighteenth-century Germany. Not all popular literature was a vulgarised and condensed version of 'serious' books, but popularisation of sophisticated material involved breaking it up into short, simple, autonomous units; shortening sentences and paragraphs, increasing the number of chapters, dropping complex sub-themes and the development of characterisation; clichés were substituted for elegant prose, a few short, simple words for extensive vocabulary (Darnton 1986:23). Brevity and simplicity were not necessarily related, therefore, and some pamphlets were addressed to highly sophisticated and restricted audiences. *Lettre aux révérends pères Jésuites au sujet d'une thèse soutenue au collège de Louis-le-Grand à Paris* was for educated

Parisians interested in the Jesuit controversy of the 1700s (Birn 1981:167).

Genuinely popular pamphlets dealt with religion, death, success, ruin, violence, power, vice, love, travel, crime, miracles, marriage, injustice, fashion, politics, war, history and medicine. Most popular in France were chapbooks dealing with traditional piety, morality and practical guides such as the *Calendrier des Bergers*, a sort of abridged encyclopedia in which a shepherd offers cures for moral and physiological ailments, traditional medical lore, recipes, prayers and fiery accounts of hell, refurbishing and rehashing old and familiar truths. Marvellous topics were very popular and people seem to have delighted in the grotesque: monsters but also gastronomic extravagances which must have represented an exact reverse of their meagre everyday fare. Histories were often jingoistic and, because they were published to cash in on recent events such as the defeat of the Protestants at the battle of the White Mountain in 1620, gave as much space to these events as to, say, the birth of Christ or the Norman conquest. Farce and crude humour, known generically as *Tabarinades*, included Grosley's finely-tuned, if obscene, *Description of Six Kinds of Fart*. Some were in prose, some in verse – certain Spanish chapbooks related current affairs in verse. Most shared brief chapters, frequent repetition, summaries and a slow rhythmical progress suited to those who were used to oral forms such as ballads and church litanies. Some were illustrated, some text only (Martin 1978).

One important variety of chapbook was the almanac. Originating in fifteenth-century Italy, almanacs also took root in Spain in the sixteenth and the genre flourished in Germany and the Netherlands until the late seventeenth century, in France until the nineteenth. Almanacs contained two strains, the first involving accessibly presented intellectual astrology and the second representing a set of generalised beliefs in heavenly influence. Like the *Calendrier des Bergers*, these were handbooks-cum-diaries, essentially tables or calendars of terrestrial, astronomical and astrological events with predictions for the future; they might also contain medical or farming hints, weather forecasts, lists of fairs, tides and interest rates. Prognostications, dismissed by Rabelais as drunken fantasies, were a popular subset of almanacs, their readers clearly untroubled by the repeated failure of the foretold millennium to arrive. English almanacs were usually borrowed from continental examples until the early seventeenth century but then began to develop on their own, in contrast with French publications of this type which ceased to develop at about the same time. Interest in astrology was on the wane

in Europe from the mid-seventeenth century but flourished in
England. English almanacs were much more practical than French,
their agricultural information, for example, including during the
seventeenth century new techniques from Holland being tried out by
leaders in the field (Capp 1979; Sührig 1981). The popularity of these
almanacs was huge. The *Badische Landeskalender* was produced in
runs of about 20,000 a year towards the end of the eighteenth century
while in England the phenomenally popular *Vox Stellarum* or 'Old
Moore' was being printed by the London Stationers' Company in vast
quantities: 107,000 for 1768, 220,000 for 1789 and 353,000 for 1800
(Engelsing 1973:58).

Literature for the masses was mostly brief and basic with a stress on
visual aspects and on potential for being read aloud. More
demanding literature was read by ordinary people but their limited
education frequently did not equip them for it. At the same time, most
volumes beyond simple pamphlets were beyond the means of many of
Europe's men and women.

THE COST OF BOOKS

The virtue of libraries, informal borrowing and reading societies is
that they reduced the cost of access to printed literature. In the century
after the invention of movable type, printed books were very
expensive though probably much cheaper than their manuscript
predecessors. In 1500 the earl of Kildare in Ireland paid the large sum
of twenty cows for a manuscript medical text (Ó'Cuív 1976:518). Just
how expensive is clear if we assess the proportion of income which a
worker would have had to set aside to buy various categories of books
and pamphlets, or how much food he and his family would have to
forgo in order to substitute the mental satisfaction of reading for the
more down-to-earth pleasure of a full stomach. Most people in early
modern Europe lived close to the poverty line, their disposable
income was small and purchases of any substantial volume would
have been beyond their reach. In the early years of the Reformation in
Germany, few could dream of owning a Bible. A New Testament
published in 1522 cost the equivalent of a week's wages for an
ordinary artisan, and the first complete German Bible (1534) the
equivalent of more than a month's earnings for a common labourer
(Gawthrop & Strauss 1984:116). The top end of the price range was
occupied by specialist texts on law, surgery, science and the classics,

all far beyond the reach of the bulk of the population. Lesser publications were more affordable: a basic arithmetic would cost a Frenchman the same as half a loaf of bread in the 1530s, a sermon on poor relief roughly a whole loaf, but buying an account of the siege of Rhodes would mean postponing the purchase of a new pair of children's shoes. Even in the seventeenth and eighteenth centuries, when books had become cheaper in real terms, a sixteen to thirty-two page recreational pamphlet from the *bibliothèque bleue* would cost the same as a pound of bread or about 10 per cent of a manual labourer's weekly income. Even the lowliest publications were not a negligible expenditure for ordinary people (Davis 1975:212).

An expensive luxury in the sixteenth century, books became more affordable as time went on. By 1711, the cost of a German Bible had fallen substantially in real terms to just one and a half days' wages for a labourer thanks to technological improvements in printing (Gawthrop & Strauss 1984:49). Yet, the barriers of cost to widespread book-ownership remained. Religious works, drama and recreational material (usually in unbound form) were relatively affordable, but illegal titles smuggled into France or Italy continued to command high prices and some of the new reading available was priced for a middle-class market. Building on developments in Golden Age Spain, early eighteenth-century England witnessed the rise of the novel as a literary form, possibly the most significant development in literature during the early modern period. Writers such as Defoe and Fielding offered substantial novels such as *Robinson Crusoe* and *Tom Jones*. A first edition of *Robinson Crusoe* cost about five shillings, half the weekly wage of a day labourer, a quarter that of a skilled craftsman (Watt 1972:45-6).

There were, of course, ways round the high cost of certain books. One strategy was to buy the volume with others: *ex libri* annotations in French and Italian books of the sixteenth century sometimes include the phrase *et amicorum* alongside the owner's name, implying that the volume was shared with others (Davis 1983:83). Another option was to purchase it, read it, then sell it again if it had not already fallen to pieces: a ready traffic in second-hand books existed and people seem usually to have kept only works of reference, books of sentimental or religious value such as family Bibles, or particularly valuable volumes such as an illustrated Book of Hours. Publishers and booksellers helped by reducing the selling price and by finding ways of spreading the cost over time. James Lackington set up a major second-hand bookstore at Finsbury Circus in London in 1774 and pioneered the practice of remaindering publishers' surplus stock (Porter 1982:95). Widespread pirating of popular works in eighteenth-century Germany made them cheaper and more accessible. Novels could be made more accessible by serial publication or by splitting one tome into several smaller volumes: Fielding's *Tom Jones* was produced in a six-volume edition though its total cost was still more than a week's wages for a labourer.

BOOK OWNERSHIP

Given the cost of books, and especially of bound volumes valuable enough to be mentioned in inventories and strong enough to survive use and misuse, the restricted social distribution of ownership is understandable. In early sixteenth-century Paris, 105 of the 173 inventories of movable possessions at death which mention books refer to the estates of men who worked in the law or bureaucracy, seventeen were those of medical men, eleven clergy, two teachers, thirty-eight merchants and booksellers (Schutz 1955:6). Of 4,442 inventories of inhabitants of nearby Amiens (1503–76), 887 mention books. Of these, 143 relate to clergy, 259 to merchants, 144 to lawyers and nobles and 32 to doctors (Labarre 1971). Book ownership was mainly the preserve of the professional classes in urban France at this period. It was also more common among men than women: just 140 of the 887 Amiens inventories belonged to wives and widows, and in the Spanish town of Valencia during the seventeenth century 34 per cent of male inventories mention books compared with 16 per cent of female (Bennassar 1982:275).

As prices fell in real terms, book ownership became more evenly spread throughout society, though it remained heavily biased towards the middling and upper ranks. Artisan ownership of books was almost unknown in Paris at the start of the sixteenth century, except among printers, but by 1560 the proportion of craftsmen whose inventories contained books had risen to levels which were not exceeded until the second half of the seventeenth century. Among Valencian artisans, the average number of books per inventory between 1490 and 1518 was three but this had risen to five during the next half century. Around 1700, 28 per cent of merchants' inventories at Frankfurt-am-Main contained no mention of books, but this figure had fallen to 16 per cent by 1750 (Engelsing 1973:46). Wealth and social standing remained an important determinant of ownership. At

Amsterdam in 1700 it is possible to compare taxable wealth with patterns of book ownership. Those in the top category, with average net wealth of about 72,000 guilders, had an average of 138 books each, while at the lowest taxable levels (*c*.3,000 guilders, well above the poverty line) the average was six, but this disguises the fact that the majority of inventories with books show nothing more than a Bible and a hymn book (Faber 1980:152–3). The continuing expense of the Bible in some parts of Europe meant that the most common book in the ordinary household was the psalms: a quarter of homes in an Icelandic sample between 1748 and 1763 had a Bible but two-thirds a psalm book (Guttormsson 1981:138). Indeed, while book ownership in countries like France, Spain and England had ceased to be the preserve of elites and professional groups by *c*.1600 and had spread well down the social hierarchy by the end of the seventeenth century, in Finland it was not until the second quarter of the eighteenth century that urban inventories other than those of clergy, teachers and merchants record books and not until the closing decades that artisans finally came into possession of volumes worth recording (Lindberg 1981:237–8).

The sorts of books which people owned can be crudely compartmentalised into those used for entertainment, those necessary to their spiritual welfare and those to their wordly prosperity. One Parisian woman who lived in the sixteenth century died leaving a Book of Hours, a Lancelot (epic) and a book on how to make jam. Half the books recorded in Amiens inventories of the seventeenth century were of practical use (Schutz 1955:11; Labarre 1971:398). Full and wide-ranging libraries were very rare at any social level before the eighteenth century, and collections were dominated by religious works and/or reference books. True of the Calvinist Netherlands and Catholic France, it was also the case in Lutheran Germany and Orthodox Russia. Fifty-five book owners left inventories of their possessions in the Franconian town of Kitzingen-am-Main during the seventeenth century: twenty had five books or less, twenty-four had between six and twenty titles, nine had twenty-one to fifty, one had sixty-two and one could boast seventy-four (Weyrauch 1985:469). While these dominant patterns persisted throughout our period, reading tastes were in fact extremely varied among those who moved away from the staple fare. Those who sought out contraband titles in sixteenth-century Venice showed a fascination with the occult, interest in which was fostered by curiosity, greed, desire for power, wealth and success. Humanist titles were also very popular among those hungry for knowledge about intellectual developments taking place in northern Europe but banned in the southern Catholic nations by the Inquisition (Grendler 1977:196–7).

Given the problem of omissions from inventories and catalogues and the scarcity of library catalogues, historians have tried other methods to discover the literary tastes of the reading public. One approach is to investigate the trade in clandestine books. The presence of censorship in all European countries meant that certain titles could not appear in public or legal documents. However, records relating to booksellers who specialised in the clandestine trade make it possible to add a further facet to the picture of reading tastes. One such specialist was Mauvelain who operated an undercover 'trade in the taboo' from Troyes east of Paris. From the archives of the Swiss printers who supplied him, we know the sort of titles which Mauvelain ordered for his customers and can build up a sort of 'best-seller' list of prohibited titles for this area of eighteenth-century France. Top of the list by far was *Les Fastes de Louis XV*, a political libel with eighty-four copies requested; in descending order of popularity after this were the *Muses du Foyer de l'Opéra* (pornography), *La Chronique Scandaleuse* (scandal), *La Papesse Jeanne* (religious satire), *L'Espion Dévalisé* (political libel), *Dialogue des Morts* (topical politics) and the *Portefeuille de Mme. Gourdan*, all with thirty-one or more volumes ordered. The fifteen most popular titles were all concerned with politics, pornography and scandal, and the number one best-seller was, not surprisingly, a mixture of all three (Darnton 1976:49).

No one source affords an absolutely true-to-life picture of reading tastes and, indeed, different sources sometimes reveal contradictory patterns. Nevertheless, there is enough overlap between the different perspectives offered by inventories, publication records and book-sellers' stocks to allow a convincing montage to be created. Religious literature was of central importance in the early years of printing. Between 1465 and 1501 about a fifth of Italian incunabula were in the vernacular and thus available to ordinary people. Religious titles account for 35 per cent of this vernacular output at Bologna, 46 per cent at Venice and 70 per cent in Florence. Moral treatises, works about the life and passion of Christ and the Virgin, and works depicting models of religious piety were particularly popular, notably Tommaso Gozzadini's *Fior di Virtù* which went through forty-two editions 1465–94 (Schutte 1980:8–16). During the sixteenth century, the most significant trend was an increase in the proportion of religious material in publishers' stocks. Religious titles accounted for about a fifth of the Imprimaturs for new books issued by the

Venetian Inquisition between 1551 and 1575 compared with one-third between 1578 and 1607. The house of Giolito counted religious titles as 7 per cent of their output in the 1540s but ten times that level by the 1570s (Grendler 1977:132–4). The proportion of religious titles fluctuated depending on the political and religious climate: 29 per cent of 169 titles published at Paris in 1598 compared with 38 per cent of 456 in 1645 (Kamen 1984:213).

The most significant shift in reading tastes after the middle of the seventeenth century was an increase in the proportion of historical, scientific and fictional titles at the expense of religious works. At Speyer in the Rhineland the number of religious books mentioned in inventories decreased by 32 per cent between the 1750s and 1780s (Vogler 1983:448). Leipzig book fair catalogues of newly-printed works show that 19 per cent of titles were religious literature for the layman in 1740, 11 per cent in 1770 and 6 per cent in 1800, while novels, drama and poetry increased from 6 to 16 per cent and then reached 21 per cent in 1800 (Ward 1974:33). Given the continuation of a strong demand for religious material, especially cheap Books of Hours, psalters, catechisms and lives of saints, it is probable that the new secular demand was a supplement to existing tastes as much as a substitute for them. Conceivably, the rural masses and urban lower classes retained a taste for traditional material while the middling and upper groups sought out the newly fashionable novels and periodicals. If the new taste for the secular and profane took root principally among the middling and upper classes, the polarisation of taste between social groups may have been enhanced during the eighteenth century.

This change should not be exaggerated. Half of the 1,034 titles recorded in seventeenth-century inventories from the German town of Braunschweig were religious, and fully two-thirds of the 691 at Kitzingen-am-Main (Weyrauch 1985:469). Nearly one-third of all those dying in Amiens during the seventeenth century and whose inventories mention books had only a Book of Hours (Labarre 1971:397). The first purely secular Moscow-printed book did not appear until 1647 and in England religion accounted for an average of 200 titles a year throughout the eighteenth century: *Pilgrim's Progress* had been through 160 editions by 1792. On the eve of the French Revolution, 63 per cent of the volumes published in provincial France (excluding Paris) were religious in flavour, mostly practical, devotional works such as liturgies and Books of Hours rather than high-flown theology (Watt 1972:55; Brancolini & Bouyssy 1970:11).

A new taste for the profane is clear in the growing demand for pornography. Markets for libertine pictures and literature had always existed, but the seventeenth century saw an expansion of production and the development of a ready international trade in erotic tales. The French *Ecole des Filles* (1655) was quickly translated into English as *The School of Venus*: Samuel Pepys bought a copy in 1668 and, after reading it 'for information sake', records that he burned it. The popularity of the genre made it an attractive target for moralist fraud: a spoof *Ecole des Filles* was produced, the first twenty-four pages of which promised a spicy dialogue between mother and daughter, thereby sucking in the reader for the remaining 120 pages which told how to expunge unclean thoughts and deeds by prayer, masses and confession. Taste was moving away from the more artistic, allusive tales of professional whores made famous in the classic early sixteenth-century dialogues or *ragionamenti* of Aretino towards more explicit and domestically-situated material such as Defoe's *Moll Flanders*. In eighteenth-century France, enterprising publishers produced pornographic political propaganda, *Libelles*, about Louis XV and XVI's court and especially about Madame Du Barry whose career from a brothel bed to influential mistress of Louis XV made her the perfect target (Foxon 1964).

Book ownership was very restricted in the late fifteenth century but gradually and intermittently spread down through society during our period to feature among the possessions of growing numbers of humble people by the end of the eighteenth century. Religious literature remained important even in 1800 but secular titles became increasingly significant and with them came other changes in reading tastes.

BOOK READERSHIP

Sold by shops, chapmen, hawkers or directly by publishers, we have followed the path of books, pamphlets and broadsheets from the printing house into the hands of the reader. The concept of a reading public among writers was an eighteenth-century development and until then serious writers tended to produce for patrons, and only polemicists and hacks wrote for a mass market. Books were, however, finding their way into the homes and hands of growing numbers of ordinary people and the literacy figures we have outlined reveal a large potential readership even in the seventeenth century. Plausible

191

connections can be posited between the production and distribution of books and the extent of the early modern reading public, associations which we must investigate very closely in order to discover the extent of book reading, its social distribution, the sorts of titles which readers preferred and the possible impact of literacy on the thoughts and deeds of ordinary men and women in sixteenth-, seventeenth- and eighteenth-century Europe.

Direct evidence of readership is rare and never simple to interpret. Ownership of a volume did not necessarily mean that it was read: some Books of Hours, hand-illustrated or decorated with silver, semi-precious stones and mother-of-pearl buttons, may have been bought and kept as much for decoration or investment as for devotional purposes. Books were fragile and those which survive or were recorded in inventories represent an uncertain proportion of those produced and used. Borrowing and lending was certainly widespread but we have only anecdotal evidence as a way of estimating how extensive. A collection of extracts from popular prophecies published in Germany in 1522 exhorts the reader to pass the pamphlet to others when finished and to discuss its contents with them (Scribner 1981a:6). One sixteenth-century Italian miller, whose mental world we shall examine shortly, borrowed from priests, women and kinfolk while belonging to a reading circle which included a painter and a farmer. The miller, Menocchio, obtained Voragine's *Legendario de Santi* from his uncle, Domenico Gerbas, but we know that since it had 'become wet, it tore' (Ginzburg 1980:30-1). Six of the eleven books which Menocchio possessed were borrowed and it is possible that people might have read what they could get their hands on rather than volumes in which they were particularly interested.

We know that by buying or borrowing, people had access to a large volume of printed material. The next step is to determine the size, composition and tastes of the reading public. Estimates of the proportion of the population who could read are of only marginal use here, since this ability did not mean that a person can necessarily be described as a reader. Teaching methods concentrated on particular texts and on rote learning rather than on instilling critical understanding; reading and writing represented a strain for many 'literate' people. Necessarily, the reading public must have been smaller than the numbers of those able to read. The sixteenth-century Spanish writer Cervantes posited the existence of a reading public among peasants and labourers in his *Don Quixote*, but made no attempt to assess its size. Contemporaries made guesses and claims about the extent of the audience for newspaper and periodical literature, though the financial interest of some in boasting a large circulation should make us wary of their assertions. The Englishman Addison said in a 1711 issue of the *Spectator* that the paper had twenty readers for every copy sold. Issues would be borrowed, read in coffee houses, barbers' shops and anywhere time had to be killed; the second-hand market was probably enormous. This would mean that one English person in every eleven read the periodical, almost certainly a wild exaggeration. The 1798 *Anti-Jacobin* started to cash in on fears generated by the French Revolution, had 2,500 subscribers but claimed between 17,500 and 50,000 readers, depending on the optimism of the editor (Watt 1972:39). Thomas Abbt also reckoned on 1 : 20 as the ratio of copies to readers of newspapers and periodicals in Germany in 1765, though another contemporary went as high as 1 : 40 or even 50. The *Hamburgische Correspondent*, the most widely read political newspaper in Germany and Austria during the 1780s, was published in editions of 21,000 and was therefore potentially read by between 400,000 and one million people (Engelsing 1973:56–60).

Direct estimates of this kind are rare and of questionable reliability. Book subscription lists offer an alternative insight, this time into the stratification of readership. There is no guarantee that subscribers actually read the book in which their names appeared: some perhaps subscribed in order to advertise their social and literary standing. However, subscription lists do show that the reading public was a highly stratified entity. Pat Rogers has analysed lists in two early eighteenth-century publications, one a translation of the *Aeneid*, the other Oldmixon's *History of England during the Reigns of the Royal House of Stuart*. The subscribers shared certain common features: they were overwhelmingly male and drawn from a close-knit circle of wealthy and highly-educated persons. But the precise social breakdown differed and the subscribers to Vergil were generally younger than those who took the history book. Far from homogeneous, the reading public was 'a sharply stratified array of separate audiences' (Rogers 1972:1540). In eighteenth-century Germany there was a market for reading material in English and French, but nobody would pretend that this was anything more than the upper crust of the literate public. Similarly, the account books of Jean Nicolas, a mid-seventeenth-century Grenoble bookseller, show that his sales were mainly to lawyers, officials and members of the local *Parlement*; purchases by other elements of society were infrequent (Martin 1978:70).

There were three regular reading publics: a limited number of 'unlettered' general readers; academics and reviewers; the educated upper classes. To these might be added the bulk of the barely literate population who were attracted to devotional and recreational chapbooks and pamphlets. In eighteenth-century Germany, and indeed over much of Europe, the reading public was specific to certain social groups and environments and it grew in layers rather than evenly across the whole of society. The urban upper-middle classes were the most precocious, the reading habit spreading down through successive layers of urban society in stages until, at the end of the eighteenth century, only the rural masses and town-dwelling labourers had still to be assimilated. The latter groups were not necessarily illiterate, but their educational standards, pockets and tastes meant that they sought out very traditional literature such as Bibles, psalm books, almanacs and chapbooks rather than the new and varied material which, as we shall see, the middling and upper ranks had begun to crave (Fabian 1976:168; Engelsing 1973:64–5).

The particular audience intended by the author and publisher can be inferred from statements in the preface of a text. Books and pamphlets might be targeted at a specific section of the population. Some contain dedications which set up the framework for understanding the text and establishing the context in which the author wished it to be seen. In 1570 the printer Antoinette Peronet dedicated a translation of Marcus Aurelius to the provincial governor of Lyon in return for patronage and protection. The book was an expression of goodwill, a request for aid and an offer of advice on the art of good government (Davis 1983:75, 78). Others were deliberately coy about their contents. The 1794 chapbook, *Le Messager Boîteux de Bâle*, asked educated men and those who have read widely not to judge the almanac too harshly, since it was really intended for the lowest classes who were not in the habit of reading a great deal. French medical pamphlets of the eighteenth century were sometimes directed to sick countryfolk far from professional healers (Bollème 1969:11–12, 65). Addresses to 'the ordinary reader' cannot always be taken at face value, since they were a standard apology for basic presentation. One English medical pamphlet of the sixteenth century was directed to the commonality, but in its suggestion that tennis was a useful form of exercise it probably had scant relevance to the lives of the masses. Indeed, most surviving collections of popular chapbooks were made by gentry such as the Englishman Samuel Pepys and by aristocrats. Francis I, king of France, had a copy of the 'model' almanac, *Grand Calendrier et Compost des Bergers* (Slack 1979:257–8; Davis 1975:191). There was no hermetic seal between elite and popular culture in the sixteenth century and it is possible that all classes read chapbooks, but the 'romantic revival' of the late eighteenth century stressed peasant values and made the reading of *Volksliteratur* chic. Similarly, *The Ladies Diary*, founded in 1704 and selling 30,000 copies a year in the 1750s, was extensively read by men (Capp 1979:246). The intended or assumed audience was not always the actual one.

The *bibliothèque bleue* had one important feature in common with more substantial and demanding volumes: it was not meant to be read swiftly and silently but to be perused closely and probably rendered aloud. The most significant development in reading during the early modern period was the shift from this intensive reading to extensive. The timing of this change varied across Europe, beginning in the late seventeenth century but concentrated in most western countries during the eighteenth century. From what we have seen of book ownership, borrowing and reading, it is clear that for most literate people, reading until the eighteenth century was an *intensive* affair. A few volumes were closely examined, and perhaps studied more than once. Devotional literature in particular was read repetitively. English Quaker meeting-house libraries of the late seventeenth and eighteenth centuries lent out books on average once a year to any given individual. The same is true of a mid-eighteenth-century Scottish library, that at Innerpeffray in Perthshire. Between 1747 and 1757, 241 books were borrowed by 130 individuals, two-thirds of whom only borrowed once during the eleven years. Even the most avid borrower took out just one volume a year over this period. Particularly interesting is the case of John Roben, a weaver. In April 1754 he took away a religious text called *Gospel Revelations*, returned it, then borrowed it again in January 1755. At Christmas of the same year he picked *The Fulfilling of the Scriptures*, but seven months later returned to his favourite *Gospel Revelations* (Houston 1985:174–9). There is an interesting parallel with a reading society in the contemporary German town of Trier. The society had eighty-three members but only two-thirds of these ever borrowed books in the years 1783–93 and eight readers account for around half of the total number borrowed. The others presumably sought out the company which the reading society had to offer as much if not more than its books (Engelsing 1973:63). The Scottish example illustrates the important general point that apart from courts, noble households and scholars, men and sometimes women were in the habit of reading in detail a narrow range of books, carefully poring over them for every nuance. People came into contact with a limited number of texts though these may have circulated widely. Thanks to their comparative scarcity before the seventeenth century, bound volumes may have been treated with awe. Literates and illiterates alike were influenced by the settings in which they saw books, especially in churchs and law courts, settings which lent authority to books through their rituals.

Two main developments in reading tastes came during the eighteenth century: the search for novelty and a more extensive approach to reading. Both were made possible by improved communications, better marketing and new printing and paper-making techniques which made production cheaper. The craving for the topical and the new rather than ancient wisdom is shown in the development of periodical literature. Desire for quick and easy access to information stimulated titles such as Francesco Nazzari's 1668 *Giornale de' Letterati* and encouraged further development of pocket editions of works for travelling *conoscenti* and *dilettanti*. Readers looked for more and more varied material. Scholarly periodicals were on the wane as well-educated readers in countries like Italy came to demand literature on current affairs such as the *Gazzetta Veneta* or *Caffè*. Venice had sixty-six journals and forty-four almanacs at one point or another between 1661 and 1797, Russia more than a hundred 1755–1800 though most of these enjoyed small circulations and brief lives (Georgelin 1978). Periodical literature developed particularly rapidly in Germany. Typical were the moralist weeklies growing in popularity from the 1720s, periodicals such as *Der Patriot* and *Die vernünftigen Tadlerinnen*, the latter said to be available in eighteen towns, the former in forty. Twenty-eight new moralist weeklies were set up 1741–5 in Germany, twenty-seven 1746–50, forty-four 1751–5. German journals of the late eighteenth century wrote of a craze or mania for reading and *Das gelehrte Teutschland* listed 4,300 living authors in 1776 ready to meet that demand (Ward 1974:23, 60; Darnton 1986:9). In England, topical pamphlets such as bishop Sherlocke's *Letter from the lord bishop of London to the clergy and people of London on the occasion of the late earthquakes* (1750) sold well as did the periodical *Gentleman's Magazine* (Watt 1972:39).

During the eighteenth century the growth of newspaper and periodical literature encouraged recurrent, *extensive* perusal of printed matter by providing new material and thus fostering a climate in which novelty was demanded. As far as full-scale books were concerned, skimming for ideas became increasingly common. The second major development of the eighteenth century was the rise of the novel, a (fictional) prose narrative of everyday events. Cheaper than full folio editions, novels moved away from the traditional, eternal and invariant themes so common in chapbooks to become more firmly rooted in everyday life. Written in the vernacular, the novels of Defoe, Swift, Dryden, Pope, Addison and Fielding offered direct commentary on everyday life (Craig 1975:136, 154, 158; Watt 1972; Knight 1985:936; Fabian 1976:169–72). Historians of literary development see the novel as a dependent, uncertain and psychologically elementary form until the nineteenth century but acknowledge the significance of the period after the 1680s in its development, and also the importance of the 1770s with the publication of three very influential novels: *Pamela, La Nouvelle Héloise* and *Die Leiden des Jungen Werthers* (Darnton 1986:9). Before the eighteenth century, authors mixed factual writing with fictional work. Hans Grimmelshausen (who died in 1676) was a producer of calendars as well as the author of the famous *Simplicissimus,* and in the tales of Eberhard Happels traditional moral and didactic strains remained prominent. Pioneered in England, the form did not catch on in Germany until the mid-eighteenth century and cannot be seen as genuinely 'popular' until the early nineteenth: readers would have had to have a wide knowledge of other literary products to derive the maximum enjoyment from early novels (Ward 1974). Reading extensively in novels purely for pleasure came only at the end of the eighteenth century in Germany, as it did in Finland; until then books had to have a practical or edifying content (Lindberg 1981:237–8).

There was not one 'reading public' in early modern Europe but several, each with different tastes and capacities. Readership moved down the social scale over time and people were reading a much wider range of material in 1800 than they had even a century before. What influence did this have on the ways in which they thought and acted?

UNDERSTANDING

Printed matter of all kinds was widely read throughout early modern Europe. Men from the middling and upper groups in society, people who lived in or close to a town and those who inhabited the more economically and politically developed states of western Europe almost certainly participated in a widespread and highly diverse literate culture. We have located books and pamphlets and broadsheets in the hands of ordinary men and women, and we can be certain that some at least actually read this material. Analyses of literacy conventionally stop at this point. Breakdowns of book production or sale or ownership tell us about the relative popularity of different genres but not about how influential certain titles were compared with others. Concentrating on ideas and their transmission in print, historians tend to shy away from any detailed investigation of the way in which facts and concepts were received by the reader. They conventionally assume that early modern people read and understood the printed page in the same way as twentieth-century scholars. This is a very dangerous assumption. After all, there are three major actions involved in reading. First, the need to identify and recognise printed words. Second, achieving a proper understanding of the meaning intended by the author. Third, using the meanings and understandings derived for some further purpose. These processes are: a response to graphic signals in terms of the words they represent, plus a response to text in terms of the meanings the author intended to set down, plus a response to the author's meanings in terms of all the relevant previous experience and present judgements of the reader. Put simply, the ability to read does not automatically bring with it a clear understanding of the text and certainly does not imply the capacity for independent or original thought. The whole issue of understanding is crucial to our knowledge of the ways in which ideas about religion, philosophy, science and politics influenced the early modern world. The way in which readers fashioned meanings from texts is, however, an extremely complex topic.

In order to determine the ways in which ordinary men and women understood the products of literacy, we need two pieces of information. First, some idea of the quality of reading skills and, second, insight into the intellectual and cultural background of the reader. As we noted in the introduction, 'literacy' represents a spectrum of skills between the bare ability to read and the capacity for composition in more than one language. Only rarely can the historian find sources which allow the delineation of that spectrum. The Toledo Inquisition asked those who stood accused before them about their upbringing, their travels and their beliefs. It also enquired whether a man could recite certain prayers and rehearse the essentials of Christian doctrine. Some Spanish bishops required communicants to display basic religious knowledge of this kind before enjoying the rite, and at the 1601 synod headed by cardinal Rojas this also became a requirement for marriage. Before 1550, 37 per cent of men were 'good' at reciting the four prayers (Ave, Pater, Salve, Credo) but 25 per cent failed completely. For 1600–50 the figures were 82 and 5 per cent respectively. Between 1565 and 1574, 40 per cent were good at reciting the Ten Commandments and 45 per cent 'bad' (wholly ignorant) compared with 70 and 8 per cent respectively 1600–50. By the reign of Philip IV the majority of males who came before the Toledo

Inquisition possessed this *'bagage théolgique minimum'* (Dedieu 1979).

Similar evidence is available on a fuller and more systematic basis in northern Europe since for most Scandinavian countries registers survive of parochial literacy campaigns: *sjæleregistre*. During the seventeenth century, the Lutheran church of Denmark (which also controlled Norway and Iceland) and of Sweden (of which Finland was a dependency) demanded that priests provide instruction in religion and reading for their flocks. Since one had to demonstrate proficiency in these fields in order to enjoy the church's services, notably marriage and communion, the clergy were ordered to test children and adults alike on a yearly basis, and to keep registers of the levels attained. We know, for instance, that of seventy-six adult male householders in part of Iceland (1748–63), 62 per cent could read well (*Læsedygtige*), 33 per cent were quite ignorant (*Kan ikke læse*) while the remainder had some limited ability (*Ringe læsere*) (Guttormsson 1981:149). These tests were to a considerable extent subjective, depending solely on what the clergyman thought of the candidate based on his or her presentation of a brief passage. It is also plain that at least part of the skill was in memorising the catechism or the Ten Commandments or the Creed. Furthermore, set passages for reading aloud were from known religious texts; unseen reading was not required. Finally, descriptions of people 'reading with understanding' should be treated with caution, since their interpretation of passages could be memorised in the same way as much of the rest of the test. These religious registers tell us about the lowest levels of literacy but cannot be interpreted as evidence of critical understanding.

These Scandinavian registers are the closest we are likely to get to a systematic assessment of reading ability. In our search for evidence of understanding we must leave aside quantitative analysis and turn to more qualitative, illustrative and anecdotal material since only this can provide the sorts of insights we desire. Some authorities have argued that popular literature was written to be understood in one particular way. Bollème argues that the French *bibliothèque bleue* shows a collective mentality which changed little between the fifteenth and nineteenth centuries and which desired the entertaining and the useful from its reading. Chapbooks, for Bollème, were written by and for the people and served no other purpose. Ordinary people were certainly subjected to multiple insecurities and threats to their life and happiness from natural and human agencies. Perhaps they used chapbooks as an innocent way to forget their problems. Themes such as the inversion of the normal social and political order could, if read 'aggressively', help to free peasant minds from oppression and injustice. More sinister interpretations are possible, however. Robert Mandrou put forward the view that chapbooks were composed by the alienated lower orders as a substitute for class consciousness: popular literature was essentially escapist and prevented ordinary people from understanding the harsh realities of their exploited lives. However, he also tended to imply that author, printer, seller, pedlar and censor conspired to enforce submission to authority and hierarchy through popular literature, thus legitimating the existing social and political order. Robert Muchembled developed these views, claiming that the *bibliothèque bleue* was written by members of the elite as a way of pacifying the masses: 'like drugs', chapbooks 'tranquilized a popular world that was alienated, crushed by taxes and tempted by revolt' (Muchembled 1985:292; Bollème 1965:70–89; Mandrou 1975). The chapbooks certainly contain a very basic, 'conservative' world picture but their origins and content are far from simple.

The debate centres on the authorship, intent and content of the chapbooks and on how they were understood. Was literature for the people also of them? Most pamphlets were written by the educated middle classes, including the clergy who wrote most of the religious tracts destined for a mass readership in late seventeenth-century England. However, most popular literature was hybrid in form and content. Detailed study of one particular chapbook reveals that different themes could co-exist in a single text. Francois Lebrun has analysed *L'Enfant Sage à Trois Ans Interrogé par Adrien Empereur de Rome*, first known in 1516 and popular in numerous editions until well into the nineteenth century (Lebrun 1984). The format is questions and answers resembling that of the catechism systematised by Calvin in 1541: assorted worthies question the child. The content is a mixture of fantasy, sound religion and social comment. The questioners are composite medieval figures including a duke, archbishop and knight, and while the text is theologically sound on infant baptism and salvation according to the tenets of the Catholic church, it allows the reader to drift into fantastic situations in the text. There is no questioning of the social order and the values expressed are deeply traditional: when questioned about the hopes of farmers for salvation, the child answers that 'most will be saved because they live by honest toil and God's people eat the fruits of their labour', unlike the deceitful tradesmen. *L'Enfant Sage* had a religious purpose, but it is neither an imposition by the elites nor a spontaneous expression of popular culture. Like much literature before the emergence of the novel as a clear literary form in the early eighteenth century, it was designed to be useful as well as entertaining and was almost certainly written by an educated man. Some elements of the chapbook were based on traditional folk culture, some on a vulgarisation of elite literature and some on a specific religious viewpoint which the church wanted to put across. There is thus evidence to support both points of view, though it is clear from the frequency of riot that the *bibliothèque bleue* did not completely anaesthetise popular political sensibilities in seventeenth- and eighteenth-century France. Discussions of the role of popular literature in social stability and change run into difficulties over the issue of understanding and of identifying which components of a text are the most meaningful to the reader.

Discovering the intention of the author is child's play compared with assessing the impact which his work made on the mind of the reader. One example from the records of the Venetian Inquisition highlights the problem. In 1574 the tribunal examined an elderly lawyer and druggist, Marcantonio Valgolio, who had a shelf of banned books, most of them written by humanists. Admonished by the judge that his eighteen prohibited titles would foster evil in his mind, Marcantonio replied cleverly that this would only be the case if the reader's intention was mischievous (Grendler 1977:197). In a very real sense, understanding depended on the existing mental world and readers seem to have looked for works which would reinforce their own point of view, or to have read books for ideas which confirmed those they already had. Before he became a Quaker, the Yorkshireman Josiah Langdale deliberately refused to read books owned by an early employer of his, lest he be 'drawn to the Belief of the Quakers'. The physical layout of the text may also have been important to the way it was understood. Some Englishmen were apparently influenced by the astrological almanacs they read. Richard Shanne, a Jacobean yeoman, entered astrological rules into his family memorandum book. Henry Best recorded that he delayed gelding his lambs until the full moon had passed. Shanne seems to have copied from almanacs, but Best's beliefs in lunar influence were strongly rooted in popular wisdom. Perhaps he only chose certain ideas from his reading. Indeed, the evidence which we possess strongly suggests that reading was a very selective process and that readers only took on board certain aspects of the intellectual content of a text. Once read, the ideas were transformed by the existing mental climate of the reader (Thirsk 1983).

The fullest and most fascinating picture of this active process of selection and transformation which we have in print is Ginzburg's study of the mental world of a miller, christened Domenico Scandella but known to his friends as Menocchio. Born in 1532, Menocchio lived at Montreale, a small hill town in the Friuli district of Italy until he was denounced to the Inquisition as a heretic in 1583. Recognised by his neighbours as a reader and a vigorous debater, he was questioned intensively by the tribunal on and off over a period of years. His testimonies reveal the world picture of an ordinary person during the sixteenth century. Menocchio cannot be seen as 'typical' of all early modern people: he was very much an individual possessed of a cosmology which seems bizarre to the twentieth-century reader but which in the broadest terms illustrates the process of understanding which must have occurred in the minds of the common people. He may indeed typify the imperfect command of the self-taught reader and thinker which helped to create misunderstandings of printed literature.

Menocchio owned or borrowed at least eleven books ranging from a vernacular Bible through the Decameron and Mandeville's travels to the Koran. He read others borrowed from friends and neighbours but steadfastly asserted that 'my ideas came out of my head' rather than from either books or discussions with other people (Ginzburg 1980:27, 28-31). To some extent this is true, since a close comparison of the passages of the books which he mentioned with the conclusions which he derived from them reveals significant gaps and discrepancies. For example, Menocchio had read in the *Historia del Giudico* (a fifteenth-century religious poem) that it was good to give charity to a beggar (in the story, the beggar was in fact Christ). He went on to make the connection that if Christ is a neighbour and a beggar, it would be better to love one's neighbour than to love Christ since He could exist in all one's neighbours and was certainly more accessible in that form than in others (Ginzburg 1980:36-41). Interpretation involved more a change in the emphasis of the text rather than outright distortion, and the sense was altered by over-stressing certain marginal ideas. Menocchio did not passively accept ideas from a book nor the opinions of others. The way he read was 'one-sided and arbitrary', heavily influenced by the literal, materialist emphasis in popular thought in the sorts of interpretations he made. Some ideas he ignored completely in the printed texts he consulted, others he altered significantly. Some books, such as Mandeville's travels, helped hugely to expand his mental universe to encompass pigmies and cannibals. Others, such as *Il Fioretto della Bibbia*, provided him with the linguistic and conceptual tools to express his view of the world, albeit a view comprised not of discrete ideas but of a mass of composite elements. Menocchio pondered phrases for years, ruminating them until they had been assimilated, transposed or even completely remoulded. A critical or analytical approach to reading was unusual but active interpretation was normal, so that the concept of a fixed 'source' with unequivocal meaning is difficult to maintain (Ginzburg 1980:44–7, 60–1). Menocchio is a particularly naive version of a common process of selective reading. Deeper immersion in print, discussion of ideas with others might eventually help to resolve some of the possible errors in interpretation but, for the self-taught, ambiguities must have remained strong. Jean Ransom, a merchant from La Rochelle, provides an example of a more educated reader. The letters he wrote between 1774 and 1785 show that he read Rousseau and tried to shape his personal, family and business life according to Rousseau's writings. Ransom certainly absorbed Rousseau's message and the letters he wrote to the great man show him striving to live exactly as Rousseau intended (Darnton 1986:6).

Similarities in patterns of behaviour are evident between modern men and women and their early modern counterparts, but it would be a mistake to suggest that patterns of thought were the same. What slender evidence we have shows a mental world very different to our own, one shaped by reading and writing but also formed by cultural influences such as intense religious belief and magical assumptions now all but absent from modern developed countries. The mental world of the early modern person should not be written off as irrational, his or her understanding as inferior. It was, however, different to our own. It is important that we recognise how broad is the range of abilities implied in 'reading' and also the selective process involved in understanding of texts. Other features too determined the spread of ideas in print and we shall now turn to these.

CHAPTER NINE
Language and culture

COMMUNICATION

Understanding is a complex issue, and the ways in which ideas were transmitted were very varied. Visual, aural and literate media were intermingled and the mental world of the reader was crucial to the reception of ideas. The practices which served to bridge the gap between literates and illiterates could only bring some of the products of writing and print to the unlettered. Inability to read and write could cut off men and women from developments in literate culture and consign them to intellectual backwaters. Yet this was not the only barrier to a culture shared by all. Differences of language and dialect militated against any such uniformity. In the sixteenth century the vast majority of printed literature was available either in Latin or, in Russia, Church Slavonic, both of which were understood only by a small elite. Of the 6,000 books in Oxford's Bodleian library around 1600, just thirty-six were in English (Thomas 1986:101). The triumph of the vernacular as a literary medium certainly made literature more accessible. Eight of the eighty-eight books published at Paris in 1501 were in French, thirty-eight of 269 in 1528, seventy of 332 in 1549 and 245 of 445 in 1575 (Febvre & Martin 1976:321). This development came later in Germany. In 1650, the ratio of Latin to German books sold at the Leipzig and Frankfurt book fairs was 71 : 29 but by 1700 that ratio had been reversed to 38 : 62 (the 1680s was the key transitional decade), 28 : 72 in 1740 and just 4 : 96 by 1800 (Steinberg 1974:118; Knight 1985).

However, as one barrier was overcome, another was erected. During the seventeenth century, books came increasingly to be printed in just one of the vernacular languages which obtained within the borders of

204

a state, leaving the speakers of dialects or of different tongues with a restricted or even non-existent body of literature upon which to draw. Italy in the fifteenth and sixteenth centuries illustrates a problem common to much of Europe: 'There was,' as Harvey Graff writes, 'an Italy of many dialects but no true literature, and an Italy of courtiers, oligarchies, and the learned, with one language and one great literature.' (Graff 1987:89; Burke & Porter 1987). For the literate, print helped to unify cultural experience, but for the millions who did not possess the language of literature there might be little change in their intellectual horizons. The map of Europe was pock-marked by 'black holes' of illiteracy, but it was also blotched with linguistically distinctive areas which were important barriers to cultural integration. As the geographer Sebastian Munster noted in his *Cosmography* of 1552: 'Formerly regions were bounded by mountains and rivers ... but today languages and lordships mark the limits of one region from the next, and the limits of a region are the limits of its language.' (Parker 1979:35).

Linguistic unity within the boundaries of a state was relatively unusual in sixteenth- and seventeenth-century Europe. In some parts of the Austrian Habsburg lands, German vied with Czech, Serbian and Croatian; in the Swedish empire, Swedish with Finnish and German (among others); in Scotland and Ireland, English (or Scots English) with Gaelic; in Spain, Castilian with Basque, Catalan and Moorish. The official language was made the medium of communication in the church (when Latin was not in use), law courts and bureaucracy and it was in that language that the vast bulk of vernacular literature was printed until the end of the eighteenth century. A more pressing problem was the huge variety of dialects which existed across Europe. Despite developments in trade and communications, European society remained highly localised, one feature of this being the diversity of vocabulary, intonation and phraseology used by the inhabitants of a particular area. Even England, where the only separate language, Cornish, had been driven out by the time of James I, was divided into dialect zones. Travellers remarked on the problems which ordinary people had in understanding the natives of a different county and one said of Tyneside that: 'They speak very broad: so that, as one walks the streets, one can scarce understand the common people, but are apt to fancy oneself in a foreign country.' One prose and verse chapbook, printed by J. Kendrew of York in 1809, offered *Specimens of the Yorkshire dialect. To which is added, A Glossary of such of the Yorkshire words as are likely not to be understood by those unacquainted with the dialect.*

205

Socially aspiring bourgeois provincials of eighteenth-century Scotland and England responded well to newspaper advertisements which promised to eradicate traces of dialect and train them in 'standard' English. It became increasingly fashionable for grammar books and pronunciation guides in later seventeenth-century Germany to offer examples of 'proper' pronunciation and expression, thus creating a distinction between 'fancy' and 'common' speech. Even the great Martin Luther fought to throw off the traces of his own lower Saxon dialect (Malcolmson 1981:94; Schenda 1985:449; Febvre & Martin 1976:322). Dialect differences were less of a problem in the vast Russian territories than in countries like Italy, though the communication difficulties occasioned by fluidity in language (the fluctuating relationship between Church Slavonic and the more vernacular East Slavonic) and alphabet were not finally removed until the end of the eighteenth century (Auty 1977a:32–6; Franklin 1985:2).

While the sprawling states of central and eastern Europe contained great variety, even small countries might encompass several different languages and dialects. The Netherlands, that great political, religious and intellectual melting pot, offers an excellent example. In the core provinces during the sixteenth century there were two languages, French and Dutch, and the dialects based on them such as Walloon, Picard and Flemish. In the eastern lands, Low German was spoken and written while to the north, in isolated Friesland, Fries was spoken. Even Dutch was divided between that spoken in the east (Oosters) and West Dutch which was later to become dominant (Parker 1979:35–6).

Linguistic and dialect differences had social as well as spatial dimensions. Broadly speaking, the urban middle classes and the gentry and nobility in the countryside were less prone to use dialect and were more likely to speak and read the dominant official language in multi-lingual zones. Male members of the Welsh gentry spoke, read and wrote Welsh, English and Latin thanks to their education in grammar schools, universities and Inns of Court. They were able to participate in pan-European Renaissance culture and to acquire a breadth of outlook far wider than their social inferiors. In France, the nobility of the north-western provinces had abandoned the local dialect, Breton, in favour of French (*langue d'oeil*) as early as the twelfth century though, in Ireland and Highland Scotland, Gaelic was only superseded by English among the gentry during the later seventeenth and eighteenth centuries. The Norwegian nobility spoke Danish rather than their own tongue, those of Finland preferred Swedish and the Lithuanian upper classes opted for German. Eighteenth-century developments in publishing in Iceland, such as the monthly *Islandske Maaneds Tidender* (set up by Magnús Ketilsson in 1773; it folded in 1776), were nearly all in Danish because the market was made up by officialdom and the educated elite who understood that language best (Cullen 1980:18; Kessler 1976; Hermannsson 1918:6–7).

Officials of church and state too might conduct their affairs in a language which was not that of their clients. What this meant was that in some circumstances those with knowledge of more than just the local language or dialect would have acted as translators for the monoglots, in the same way as literates could mediate the products of literacy for illiterates. At the end of the fifteenth century, the city fathers of Montreal, to the west of Condom in south-western France, could not understand correspondence in French and had to have it translated into Gascon while the local bishop, Antoine de Pompadour, employed a clerk to translate petitions and letters in Gascon into French for him (Loubès 1983:317). On the other hand, local officials working in the Habsburg monarchy during the eighteenth century had to be bilingual in German and the native tongue of their area. Schoolteachers and religious instructors in contemporary Norway would usually have been native Danish speakers who could also manage Norwegian. Sweden had an elite cadre of Russian-speaking interpreters who worked in diplomatic negotiations, interrogated prisoners of war, translated the Lutheran catechism into Church Slavonic and collected political, military and economic information from Russian travellers and businessmen. Religious missions to Greenland or Lappland during the eighteenth century were of necessity staffed by men with a spoken knowledge of the language of the indigenous population and who were able to translate basic religious works for them (Burian 1970–1:86; Tarkiainen 1972).

Knowledge of more than one language gave these 'brokers' a position of power in local communities. The overlap between high social status and bilingual skills reinforced the dominance of the gentry and nobility over their monolingual peasants. Yet even ordinary people might enjoy some standing because of their ability to translate. Irish peasants who spoke English seem to have done so very poorly, taking a Gaelic sentence and translating it inaccurately into English, but a humorous literature existed which would have required an awareness of the differences of grammar and vocabulary between Gaelic and English and the potential for error. This suggests that a bilingual population existed. In the Mediterranean and the

Baltic, phrase books helped merchants in the rudiments of conducting business. Finally, there were some parts of Europe where the population was induced by their circumstances to become multilingual. In the hills of northern Italy, men required a knowledge of Italian for dealings with bureaucracy, and of German and French if they wished to emigrate temporarily from their village or trade with neighbouring areas (Bliss 1976:556–7; Viazzo 1983:168).

Separate dialects and languages came increasingly under attack by governments during the early modern period. The lack of a uniform tongue within a state was, correctly, equated with the persistence of provincial loyalties which weakened or actively opposed the consolidation of centralised power. From the early sixteenth century onwards, more and more states began to demand uniformity in the language of church and government, working on the assumption that if speech was different, then hearts and minds must necessarily also differ. Leading the field in the search for linguistic unification was the French crown with its 1539 ordinance of Villers-Cotterets establishing standard French (the *langue d'oeil* used in the north and east of the country) as the official language of the law courts. France had numerous dialects and languages – Poitevin, Picard, Gascon, Provençal and Breton, for example – and uniformity was not achieved overnight. In 1668, Louis XIV set up a *Collège des Quatre-Nations* on the model which his former minister, Mazarin, had outlined in his will, the aim being to educate gentry boys from the extreme north-east and south-west of France in French and to brainwash them into accepting central domination of the ostentatiously separatist homelands. The campaign was still active in the eighteenth century, when Rolland D'Erceville, spokesman for the Parlement de Paris, expressed the hope that educational expansion and an insistence on the use of standard French would hasten national integration (Febvre & Martin 1976:272; Trenard 1980:99; Leith 1977:17).

France was just one of the European states formed in the late medieval period from an amalgam of distinct provinces. The problems of diversity and the drive for integration through uniformity of language, laws and government were common to all of Europe. In the seventeenth century the Swedes tried actively to assimilate provinces of the Finnish frontier, but confined their cultural imperialism in Finland to an insistence that Swedish should be the language of education (Whittaker 1984:7). From 1607, James VI and I sought to eradicate the Gaelic tongue spoken by his Scottish Highland subjects because of its association with the unacceptable religious and political aspects of that region: Catholicism, clans and military organisation. And in the vast Habsburg territories of central Europe at the middle of the sixteenth century, Ferdinand I's reforms of government and the courts involved a substitution of German for Latin. However, Czech remained the administrative and legal language of Bohemia until the 1620s (when only some 10 per cent of the population there were German speakers) and it was not until the late eighteenth century that German became generalised as the language of government, official communication, military command and the courts in all but the Italian and Belgian provinces of the empire. After the first partition of Poland (1772), the Austrian authorities tried to insist on teaching in German in the schools of Galicia 'to contribute to the unification of provinces varying in national structure and religions, into a single, strong State organism'. And Joseph II spoke for generations of fellow rulers when he extolled in 1785 the 'advantages which the whole state will gain if the different provinces of one and the same government are more closely united with each other through the common language' (Krupa 1981:82; Burian 1970-1:84-5).

The decline of certain minority languages and dialects was not always the product of a deliberate drive for conformity on the part of secular authorities. In fact, straightforward proscription of a language seems to have had little effect on its survival or decay. Certain languages and dialects persisted throughout the early modern period, others experienced erosion and decline. What determined their differing fortunes were their political standing, the extent to which literature was available in the minority tongue and the relative significance of the dominant language in economic and social life. Take the case of the replacement of Ruthenian by Polish as the language of the middling and upper classes in zones such as Lithuania, Byelorussia and the Ukraine. Until 1696 legal documents had to contain an introductory and concluding clause in Ruthenian but after 1640 it was rare to have a whole document written in Ruthenian: usually just the beginning and end with the bulk of the document in Polish. This was not by any means compulsory. There was no institutional reason for nobles, clergy and bourgeoisie to drop Ruthenian in favour of Polish unless they had lost faith in their native tongue for other reasons. Leaders of the Russian Orthodox church realised the weakness of local vernaculars when they selected a language of service and literature to combat militant Counter-Reformation Catholicism and opted for Church Slavonic as their weapon (Martel 1938:54-66; Jakobson 1955:33).

Sometimes we can pinpoint the reasons for loss of confidence in a tongue. Sir John Davies commented that the spread of English criminal assizes across the whole of Ireland caused a movement away from Irish from the reign of Elizabeth: 'because they find a great inconvenience in moving their suits by an interpreter, they do for the most part send their children to schools, especially to learn the English language'. And in the reign of James I, the chronicler Connel ma Geoghagan wrote of his fellow authors: 'Because they cannot enjoy that respect and gain by their said profession as heretofore they and their ancestors received, they set naught by the said knowledge [of bardic culture], neglect their books, and choose rather to put their children to learn English than their own native language' (Ó'Cuív 1976:529).

The early modern period witnessed a contraction in both the geographical areas where separate dialects and languages were used and in the social spread of the users. However, the rate at which this change took place varied considerably. In Spain, the dominance of Castilian was quickly achieved in Valencia and Aragón during the fifteenth and sixteenth centuries, but it remained a foreign tongue in Catalonia, the Balearic Islands, the Basque lands and in much of Galicia (Bennassar 1982:259). The main period when Irish suffered at the hands of English was the seventeenth century while, in Highland Scotland, Gaelic retreated most rapidly during the eighteenth and nineteenth centuries.

Languages and dialects which avoided decay were, broadly speaking, those which had a practical use for religious, cultural, legal, administrative and economic purposes. Breton, for example, was not taught in schools, but there was a mainly religious literature which helped to perpetuate it. Two-fifths of the stock of 30,000 volumes held by the Quimper printer Marie Blot in 1777 were in Breton. Breton survived as a medium of religious instruction and in the theatre, oral culture and chapbooks (le Menn 1985:230, 239). In England, Cornish existed in the south-west during the sixteenth century, but was forced out of existence by the sheer power of English as the language of trade, law and government. Similarly, the decline of Gaelic cannot be wholly explained by oppression, poverty and the sell-out of the middle and upper classes to English in Scotland. Lack of printed literature was a crucial determinant of its poor fortunes. Slightly more fortunate was Irish, the widespread use of which as a written (if not printed) language distinguished it from Scots Gaelic and allowed it to revive as a focus of nationalist feeling in the late eighteenth and early nineteenth centuries (Cullen 1980). By contrast, Welsh, which was formalised as a language of religious worship by the publication of a Bible and Book of Common Prayer in the 1560s, enjoyed greater stability and permanence. English did make headway in Wales during the seventeenth and eighteenth centuries, notably in the towns and by the westward spread of the bilingual zone in the east of Wales, but Welsh retained a much stronger position than Gaelic in Ireland or Highland Scotland (Durkacz 1983). Perversely, the low educational standards of the Moors or Moriscos in sixteenth-century Spain helped to preserve their Arabic language and culture relatively untouched by the spread of Castilian.

The story of subordinate languages was not always one of stagnation or decay. During the second half of the eighteenth century the developing nationalist movements of eastern Europe began to foster the use of their local languages and dialects as a way of asserting their independence from central, imperial power. The Finnish Aurora society, founded in 1771 by Henrik Gabriel Porthan, sought to promote national consciousness by fostering language and oral traditions. The period after 1814 saw the rise of 'New Norwegian', a recreation of ordinary speech before the Danish takeover. In Hungary from the 1790s, nationalists tried to promote Magyar in public life rather than German or Latin, and in 1805 fourteen county assemblies decided to conduct all official correspondence in Magyar. The first 'best-seller' in Magyar was the 1788 *Etelka* extolling Hungarian virtues and denigrating German cultural influences (Whittaker 1984:8; Bárány 1966:29, 34; Tazbir 1982).

Linguistic and dialect variety were not the only obstacles to pan-national or pan-European culture. Print lettering was not uniform during the sixteenth century. The two main faces in use in western Europe were Gothic or 'black letter', which dominated the first century of printing, and Roman face, also called Latin or 'antiqua' face. Italic face was developed in Italy from the late fifteenth century but was never particularly significant except for highlighting text. Roman type only became dominant over most of western Europe by the end of the sixteenth century, stagnation in the development of Gothic typefaces from the early seventeenth century announcing its surrender to Roman type as the principal literary face. Germany, Scandinavia and parts of eastern Europe held on to Gothic type until the eighteenth century – the first known Danish book to be published in Roman type came in 1723 – when intellectuals came to realise that Gothic face was provincialising their culture for wider markets. Communications difficulties could be considerable. Acts of Parliament and proclamations from the English crown used Gothic type in the early sixteenth century, as did elementary teaching aids, making it difficult to gain familiarity with Roman type (Thomas 1986:99). The indigenous population of Greenland during the eighteenth century read and wrote in Roman letters whereas most Danish literature was in Gothic and both traders and officials of Norwegian and Danish extraction used Gothic (Gadd 1985).

In western Europe the only significant deviation from conventional Latin script was the use in German states of the Gothic. Even here, Latin words and some proper names were written in Latin script in otherwise wholly Gothic manuscripts. Forbidding as the heavy Gothic letters are to a modern reader, the easy interchange of the two scripts in manuscript and printed records suggests that their co-existence presented no barrier to communication. This is less clear east of the river Elbe. Russians and Finns used calendars made of wood (*birka*), multi-faceted sticks a foot or two long notched to mark days and marked with signs (often pictograms connected with agricultural tasks) and cyrillic letters to show saints' days and festivals. Printed calendars which became more current in the eighteenth century retained the form and letters (Smith 1983:283). An important change took place during the reign of Peter the Great, involving the introduction of a streamlined, civil alphabet called by printers 'secular face'. During the eighteenth century, ecclesiastical face (which was to secular what Gothic was to Roman in western Europe) came increasingly to be confined to religious works as the simplified alphabet was used to print new works: the first book using this typeface was a geometry text of 1708 (Simmons 1977:49; Auty 1977a:36).

In Poland the position was more complex and more fluid, especially during the sixteenth and seventeenth centuries. Court documents of the Grand Duchy of Lithuania show a gradual replacement of cyrillic by Latin over this period. Unlike Galicia to the south, ruled by Casimir the Grand, Ruthenian was not banned outright in Lithuania but was gradually pushed eastward by the spread of Polish. We can date the transition quite precisely in the documents. The nobles who signed contracts and agreements did so in cyrillic until the 1580s when they began to use Latin script. By 1620 the only ones who signed in cyrillic were the lesser nobles. Of twenty-three from the Kiev region who petitioned the king in 1629, only six did not use Latin letters. The transitional phase can be identified in a paper relating to the purchase of a building by a religious order, dated 7 June 1590 and registered at the tribunal of Vilna. The text is in Ruthenian; of the fifteen signatories, six use cyrillic letters followed by a legal clause in Ruthenian, while the other nine employed Latin characters with a Polish formula. Russia, Poland and eastern parts of the Holy Roman Empire were the only areas of Europe where language divisions were accentuated by the different scripts in use (Martel 1938:54–9).

The implications of linguistic and dialect divisions were profound. Martin Luther, for one, tried to encourage the standardisation of High and Low German dialects (the former spoken in the south of Germany, the latter in the north) so that his message would be easier to transmit in print. Yet, areas in which a dialect or minority language obtained were often poorly served by printed literature. Flemish, spoken by 90 per cent of the population of eighteenth-century Brussels, was a culturally marginal language: the fifteen major periodicals available there were all in French and of 218 stage plays put on in the middle years of the century, 95 per cent were in French and the rest were in Italian (Lottin & Soly 1983:293). Only a handful of books were printed in Breton or Basque during the sixteenth century, these usually religious in nature. Some agricultural tracts were printed in specific Italian or German dialects at this time, but most agricultural literature was in Latin or one of the mainstream tongues such as Tuscan or French (Beutler 1973). Two centuries later (1788–89), 76 per cent of French books were produced in the north-eastern half of the country, with Toulouse and its hinterland the only part of the Midi where substantial production and demand existed (Brancolini & Bouyssy 1970:19, 32). Even if they could obtain the full range of literature through the rudimentary distribution networks, inhabitants of these zones had not only to be literate but also to be versed in a language which was probably not the one which they spoke in everyday life. As with education, the transfer of ideas through the medium of print was seriously inhibited by linguistic and dialect divisions. The triumph over much of Europe of English or Tuscan or standard French or German or Polish tended, in many areas, to mean that town-dwellers spoke a different tongue to that of rural peasants while the rural gentry and nobility were distanced from their lower-class neighbours by speech as well as education, wealth and life style. Social as well as intellectual divisions could be widened by the expansion of printing and of literacy.

INNOVATION

Communication of ideas through the medium of print was an

innovation of the late fifteenth century, and historians have claimed that it marks a revolution in intellectual and practical life. Reading printed material is said to create new possibilities for thought and action. By breaking through the barriers erected by 'irrational custom' and traditional oral transmission, printed books create fresh opportunities for individual and societal improvement and help substantially to hasten economic change. Intellectual contact and cross-fertilisation of ideas were certainly facilitated by printing, but when it came to imparting practical knowledge the influence of print and writing were less straightforward. We know that commercial development enhanced the demand for literacy and was itself fostered by the expansion of educational facilities. The largest sector of the early modern economy was not, however, overseas trade. Agriculture was the biggest industry and substantial developments in manufacturing did not come until the eighteenth century. Production of food was crucial to the economic well-being of a country and was central to something as basic as whether its people lived or died. The famines which affected many parts of Europe until the eighteenth century were a direct result of population pressure coupled with basic farming methods and low output. With the exception of the Low Countries and areas of northern Italy, intensive, high-productivity farming was uncommon during the sixteenth century. During the seventeenth and eighteenth centuries there were major improvements in both organisation and techniques which increased output in certain regions of Europe so dramatically as to merit the title of an 'agricultural revolution'.

Literature on agricultural improvement existed from the medieval period, and has been studied for the sixteenth century by Beutler. These early tracts were written by gentry for gentry and were concerned with the growing of basic foodstuffs. Fairly typical was a Polish treatise by one Gostomski, offering information on how to run an estate, presented as a set of epistles advising how to raise rents, market produce and instruct peasants. Most were in prose, though some verse editions exist, including the early sixteenth-century *Coltivazione*. Some were in Latin and 622 editions were reprints of ancient authors such as Vergil and Pliny. Konrad Heresbach's *Vier Bücher über Landwirtschaft* was in fact first published in Latin in 1570, and was modelled on the Georgics. The practical usefulness of such volumes cannot have been great, and it is hard to escape the impression that many were little better than coffee-table books. Even vernacular editions were not particularly useful to the masses, written by highly educated Italian and German authors and presented in terms which were probably alien to the ordinary working farmer. Not all texts were like this. Some tried to be simple and practical, one even claiming to have been tested 'on the ground' by two Nîmes gardeners. Agricultural literature certainly existed in the sixteenth century, but it is difficult to believe that it was of any great significance in bringing about agricultural change (Beutler 1973; Thirsk 1983:295).

Only in the seventeenth century did pamphlets begin to appear on specialist topics such as gardening and tree growing, and only in the eighteenth was there any extensive body of literature on experimental methods. England and Holland led the field in agricultural improvements during these centuries, their dissemination aided by a large body of literature on new methods. Arthur Young, the famous eighteenth-century agricultural improver, divided print on agriculture into two categories: the genuinely useful written by working farmers and the rubbish composed by dilettantes for journals like the *Museum Rusticum* (Fussell 1932:419). The former could certainly prove useful, and there are surviving examples of agricultural pamphlets marginally annotated by farmers using information obtained from practical experience of trying the recommended methods or from discussions with farmers or from reading other literature (Thirsk 1983:305). Yet, we must be cautious about extrapolating from one or two examples to the whole process of disseminating new ideas on agriculture. Recent research on seventeenth-century England indicates that the channels by which new ideas and methods were conveyed were much more complex. Innovation travelled by two methods. Gentry and richer yeomen farmers, the rural elite, read about novelties in books or in correspondence with other 'opinion leaders' elsewhere in England. They introduced the innovations first and by this medium ideas travelled over long distances and were introduced into an area. Extensive adoption of new techniques such as turnip husbandry depended on these opinion leaders showing other yeomen and husbandmen the means and merits of their improved farming. Personal contact and the mobility of labourers trained in the new husbandry were more significant than reading and writing in the widespread dissemination of innovations. As William Ellis put it in his *Modern Husbandman* (1744): 'It is certain that no teaching of Arts and Sciences comes up to the practical way of doing it; and, therefore, Ocular Demonstration is the quickest and best Way of introducing new improvements in Husbandry.' (Overton 1985:216–17). Literacy was significant, but in a very particular way which was vitally complemented by traditional methods of learning by seeing and doing. Some eighteenth-century farmers scouted around for trained labourers and tenant farmers from other counties with experience of new methods in order to train their existing workforce, recognising the difficulties created by traditional conservatism and the importance of example in changing those attitudes. The influence of literacy and print depended on social contacts, cultural traditions and existing methods.

We can make the same point about inventions and new technology in industry. Until the end of the eighteenth century no part of Europe can be described as industrialised, though pockets of industry did exist. Most manufacturers were small in scale, decentralised, rurally located and used simple machinery which involved little fixed capital. However, important changes in technique were taking place during the seventeenth and more especially the eighteenth century. The ways in which they were introduced and systematised again illustrate the complexity of the relationship between printed means of communication and the human agent.

The Italian historian, Carlo Cipolla (1972), has brought a very pertinent example to our attention. In 1607, Vittorio Zonca published his *Nuovo Teatro di Machine et Edificii* which featured illustrations of a hydraulic silk mill, a *filatoio*, capable of increasing significantly the output of manufactured silk. This book was available to the eager English as early as 1620, but they were not able to build a copy until decades later when an industrial spy called John Lombe 'found means to see this engine so often that he made himself master of the whole invention and of all the different parts and motions'. Lombe ran a great risk, since the Piedmontese government had decreed that seeking or revealing such information was punishable by death. They recognised that without practical instruction, the mere reading of books would not enable competitors to build and run the mill. This simple example illustrates that practice and demonstration were every bit as important as the reading of printed material when it came to propagating innovations. The printed word was undeniably an important channel for the diffusion of new technology but we should not overestimate its effectiveness.

As was the case with agricultural change, mobility of skilled labour was of great significance in disseminating novel industrial techniques. Most of the prestigious royal manufactories in eighteenth-century Spain were worked by English, French and Dutch artisans. In the sixteenth and seventeenth centuries, Protestant refugees from religious persecution in France and Flanders took new clothmaking skills to Holland and England; to Scotland and Scandinavia they took metalworking and clockmaking developments. Eighteenth-century Swedish and Flemish craftsmen were attracted to Russia in order to introduce the technique of casting iron guns. Some of the Swedes had originally come from Flanders which was a technological leader in the sixteenth and seventeenth centuries. In the eighteenth century, England was the most advanced nation, and it was from her that many European nations obtained their new technology. As early as the 1690s, Swedes worried by Russian competition came over to learn from the English. Men like Odhelius and Swedenborg were followed by other legitimate information gatherers: Schröderstierna made 200 pages of notes on Birmingham manufactures in 1749. As the pace of technological change accelerated, secrecy became more important and downright spying more common. Austrians, Germans and Russians were all active, as were the French, one of whom posed as a naturalist in the 1760s to spy on mining and metallurgical enterprises. The importance of literacy in all this was considerable, but we must remember the warning of the Frenchman Trudaine de Montigny in 1752 that 'the arts never pass by writing from one country to another; age and practice alone train men in these activities' (Harris 1985:130; Mathias 1975). Inventions could be transferred in print, but skilled labour was also important and, in the case of indigenising new technology, people were crucial.

In a sense, the most effective 'improving' texts were those which recognised the importance of example and leadership, and which therefore tried to show the educated how to direct opinion and work among the masses. A good example is an article on education and economic change awarded a prize by the Tuscan *Accademia dei Georgofili* in 1775. The author, Francesco Pagnini, recommended that landowners and rich farmers should be given the best available education both in order to combat their own indifference and ignorance, and so that they could instruct the peasantry. Interestingly, he did not believe in offering a similar education to the rural masses. For them, a training in docility, obedience, hygiene and morals would create a mentally receptive and physically capable labour force which would quietly accept the direction of its social and intellectual superiors (Ricuperati & Roggero 1977:260). Established, socially prestigious figures in a community could act as 'brokers' or opinion leaders who would influence discussion and innovation. There was, of course, no guarantee that their views would be adopted, or that their ideas would spread beyond limited social groups, but the mix of demonstration and literate media seems to have been the most successful means of disseminating innovations.

All this assumes that the content of innovative literature was accurate and new. Neither quality was universally present and, indeed, much of the literature on subjects such as agriculture was either wrong or impractical. In the case of medical books and pamphlets, those which sold best seem frequently to have confirmed the prejudices of the reader rather than introducing him to discoveries and breakthroughs in medical knowledge. Among 153 medical titles published in England between 1486 and 1605, the largest category was that of remedies. Designed for use at home by laymen, these offered little in the way of explanation. This is hardly surprising since many of the most popular titles were written not by physicians but by lawyers, clergymen and officials. By offering *any* advice at all, the texts helped to reduce anxiety on the patient's part. However, the body of literature on medical subjects simply perpetuated an existing body of knowledge rather than spreading a new one. The leading authority on the subject concludes that sixteenth-century medical literature 'was not a major factor in the provision of medical knowledge and treatment, but of ancillary help to a relatively small elite of practitioners and laymen' (Slack 1979:273).

The significance of personal demonstration and practical experience to technological change and economic development highlights the place of aural, oral and visual forms in everyday life. Increased literacy was important, but again it was tempered by existing cultural forms and social practices. As an agent of economic change, literacy and literature depended on personal demonstration, social contacts or divisions and on deep, often oral traditions to which we shall now turn.

ORAL CULTURE

The world of books is one which the twentieth-century reader understands very well. What was written and printed between the Renaissance and the Industrial Revolution and has survived to the present day can be dissected, scrutinised, admired and criticised by scholars. Written words bear silent witness to the vast volume of correspondence which took place between businessmen, lawyers, bureaucrats and soldiers. Millions of printed books speak volumes for the intellectual curiosity of Europe's readers and thinkers. Because the material on which historians of this period work is written or printed, and because literacy is so crucial to modern economy and society, research tends to focus on the products of literacy. The words of ordinary men and women as they went about their everyday lives have been lost in the utterance. Yet for the vast majority of early modern people, what was spoken and heard, seen and experienced was far more important for social and economic life than what they read or what they wrote. This is clear from the preceding discussion of the dissemination of innovations. To measure just how important is, of course, impossible for the very reason that face-to-face interactions generally leave no trace in surviving written records. Transcriptions, even if verbatim, cannot provide us with the full force of the spoken word with its pauses, stresses and cadences. Most important lessons in life were probably learned by seeing and doing, but if we are to assess the part played by oral communication in shaping the social, cultural and intellectual lives of the common folk we must rely on incidental and sometimes anecdotal information. These types of source are by no means inferior to the hard, quantitative material which has provided most of the detail so far for they help us to fill in the significant contours of experience which are sometimes lost in mere figures. Indeed, they hint at a rich and densely textured world of meanings and understandings every bit as important as that of written culture.

There was no firm dividing line between oral and literate culture. The two were face-to-face all over early modern Europe, their interaction eased by a number of factors. First, there was the prevalent practice of reading aloud, both when alone and in company. Medieval society had prized the idea that knowledge and books were best shared, and in Muscovy the verbs 'to read' and 'to listen' could be used almost interchangeably of a written text. When children were taught to read, they were expected to articulate the words, and this habit seems to have stayed with them into adulthood. In 1570 Arthur Chapman, a thirty-year-old blacksmith from Wolsingham in the English county of Durham, was called before the diocesan Consistory Court for misbehaviour in church. He admitted that he had been attending morning service in his parish church one Sunday, and defended himself by allowing that he had been 'reading of an English book or primer, while ... the priest was saying of his service, not minding what the priest read, but tending his own book ... Marry, he read not aloud to the hindrance of the priest ... but the priest after the first lesson, willed him ... to read more softly.' He later added that he had owned the primer for more than a year and was presumably using odd opportunities to improve his grammar, spelling and vocabulary since he could already sign his name in full (Raine 1845:231–2).

Reading aloud to oneself could be a very personal event, and may explain why many working-class readers preferred to follow their hobby in the open countryside. It also had wider social implications, for reading aloud in a group could be a way of transmitting ideas and information contained in written or printed material to illiterates. Some popular literature was clearly designed to be read out to an audience and street pedlars sometimes advertised the contents of sheets and pamphlets by doing so. In early sixteenth-century Germany and Muscovy, the verb 'to read' could also mean 'to read aloud'. Some works advised those who could not read or who had only rudimentary literacy to seek out a more accomplished friend to read out the harder passages. Popular propaganda for the German Reformation was often a hybrid form with printed words and pictures mixed; the process of transmission was probably also hybrid. A Nürnberg clerk called Erasmus Wisperger was arrested in 1524 for reading a proscribed religious work aloud in the marketplace (Scribner 1981a:6). Few communities, however small and remote, can have lacked at least one person who could read, write and count, even if that person was the local priest or landowner. Comparison of a plan of the parish of Montin in Savoy and family ties shown in parish registers with literacy from notarial registers reveals that every illiterate family in the community had at least one literate kinsman living close by to whom they could turn (Siddle 1987). During the 1640s, the English gentleman Adam Eyre recorded in his diary occasions when, on behalf of one or other of his friends and neighbours, he drew up a petition, framed an apprentice indenture, made out a draft contract for the sale of some land and read out some writings which had been brought to him. Another Lancashire man, the apprentice Roger Lowe, was paid by his friends for writing love letters, wills and bonds either in cash or in ale. The famous sectary, Ludovick Muggleton, a contemporary of Eyre's, was aware that his followers might not be able to understand 'print-hand' and would have to have his message read aloud to them (Reay 1985:6). Eighteenth-century Parisian illiterates could go to one of several public reading places to hear news being read out for a small fee. Professional gossips, *nouvellistes*, told listeners of court or diplomatic affairs from their accustomed benches in the Tuileries or Jardin de Luxembourg (Smith 1979:47–8).

Reading in private required time, light and, in winter, warmth: how much more congenial to read aloud or to listen with friends in a tavern or barn. Anabaptists at Augsburg in the 1520s and Cologne in the 1530s sometimes preached in inns (Scribner 1984:242). Some forms of sociability created particularly favourable opportunities for experiencing vicarious literacy. The German *Spinnstuben* or spin-ning circles are a good example. Conducted in the winter evenings, these formalised gatherings of young men and women began with the sexes separated. The initial male assembly was called a *Gunckel* and typically involved the youths in set emulations of their elders. Thus the lads smoked their pipes, played cards, argued about politics and read the newspaper aloud. Only later did boys and girls meet. *Gunckel* and *Spinnstube* included a whole range of sociabilities, one of which was reading aloud and listening to texts. In southern France a similar institution existed in the form of the *viellée* or evening gathering. During the sixteenth century, the material which was read aloud at these meetings was rather old-fashioned, according to Noël du Fail, who wrote literary works such as the *Propos Rustiques* (1547) set in a peasant village, Aesop's *Fables* and *Le Roman de la Rose*. Those charged with reading out such texts might also have to change standard French into local dialects. Both the *viellée* and *Spinnstube* were probably special occasions and there must have been many more informal gatherings of family and friends where reading aloud occurred (Medick 1984:334–5; Davis 1975:196–8, 210, 213). Elementary teaching methods depended on rote learning, and even the rhetorical style of the Jesuits tested memorisation and delivery as much as understanding and the capacity for independent thought. Literacy could be an aid to oral communication rather than a substitute for it.

Oral and literate culture interacted in these sorts of environments. The exchange was a fruitful one and by no means one way. Oral culture often provided the basis for what was written down, while printed texts fed back into the oral tradition to be retold and perhaps subtly changed. Interactions of this kind are clear in much of the ballad literature which was collected by amateur ethnographers during the eighteenth and nineteenth centuries. Sometimes portrayed as the pure waters of oral tradition, songs and tales did not in fact spring unpolluted from the depths of popular memory. Instead, oral and literate forms contributed to each other in differing ways over time. In Ireland and Germany, for example, some tales began in a written form in the medieval period, were adopted by oral tradition in the fifteenth and sixteenth centuries, then passed into and out of manuscript until they were eventually printed during the nineteenth and twentieth centuries. Eighteenth-century Iceland had three versions of the story of Griselda from the Decameron, all very similar, which had been introduced from Holland. The initial transfer was probably oral but the tale was then written down. This particular story was never printed in chapbook form in Iceland as it was in most other countries, but was propagated in prose or in verse *rímur*. Perhaps the best example of interactions between cultural forms are jokes. Seventeenth-century collections of jests and witty stories were made by men who went round taverns, coffee shops and private houses. Written down and then printed, these jokes fed the conversation of readers in the same environments in which they had been found (Ó'Cuív 1976:537; Hermannsson 1914). Much of the effect of a joke depends on the way it is told, and there is unfortunately no way of reproducing this on paper. Nor, for that matter, can we be sure that a jest, or any other oral form, was accurately recorded and reproduced in writing or print. Were conversations faithfully reported in form as well as content? Were sermons printed exactly as spoken? Were those who wrote down ballads in touch with the roots of the tradition or did they mediate it according to their own experience?

Representatives of the oral tradition such as ballads would almost certainly have remained unknown to modern historians had they not been collected, written down and often printed by those who saw it as their duty to record what seemed to be either a curiosity or the last remnants of a threatened culture. The early eighteenth-century commentator Pálsson, for example, believed that all the old women of Iceland who could remember the ballads were dying out. Many of the tales the amateur ethnographers gathered were designed to be nothing more than entertaining. Interesting differences appear in the sorts of ballads preferred by men and women. In early nineteenth-century Norway, men preferred humorous tales, women magical ones; in eighteenth-century Scotland, men regaled audiences with martial stories and songs, women with more marvellous ones; Faroese men opted for heroic ballads, women for those on love, chivalry or the supernatural. There is some evidence that women were the repository of the ballads and, indeed, most were written down by men listening to women – the famous Icelandic compiler Árni Magnússon, for example. The Englishman John Aubrey recalled that as a child his nurse recited a ballad version of the history of England from the Norman Conquest to the reign of Charles I. Women told their tales in the home whereas the menfolk enjoyed the quasi-professional status of public singers and tellers (Grambo 1983:121; Ólason 1982).

Ballads and tales were not purely recreational, but could serve important social and political ends. Singing at work about topics close to their lives helped to reconcile women to hard labour, resolve generational conflicts, unburden themselves of worries about husband and family, assimilate news about the living and remember the dead. For the whole community, a song about the virtues of past nobles might serve to highlight the shortcoming in a present landlord and thus help to alleviate feelings of injustice. A tradition of Gaelic political poetry began in later sixteenth-century Ireland, nurtured among men who had been exiled to Catholic Europe. The Irish bardic tradition contains a number of long political poems composed between *c.*1630 and *c.*1660 dealing with the partiality of the English courts, confiscations, transportations and the brutalities of troops; these are rhetorical and atavistic, offering little in the way of constructive alternative. In any case, most tales were of a conservative nature because of the structure of patronage. In seventeenth-century Scotland, spiritual songs helped preserve (illegal) Catholicism among the Highlanders, and the significance of the Gaelic poets as political propagandists was recognised by Charles II who retained Iain Lom MacDonald as his bard to compose and disseminate loyalist, episcopalian ballads (Ó'Tuathaigh 1980:158; MacInnes 1950:32, 37). Ballads show the ways in which oral culture could mould itself to a variety of practical ends; they were not simply entertainment.

Oral culture is often portrayed as an unchanging morass of immemorial ideas. Interchanges between written and memorised forms must cast doubt on this notion and, while inertia was a prominent feature of oral culture, the material which was transferred by speaking and listening was adapted to context and was far from invariant. Ballads which moved from one country to another tended to undergo creative adaptation which gave them a distinctively local or national flavour: Faroese imports from Denmark or Irish borrowings from England and France, for example. Not all ballads and tales were tailored to the experience of the hearer since some relied for their effect on exotic settings. Legends of giants, which originated in Norway, were popular in the folklore of the Orkney islands to the north of Britain, despite the absence there of any mountains in which such beings might have hidden.

Oral and literate culture did not interact passively, but depended on each other for survival and development. We can see the importance of oral influences in the repetition, use of epithet, tortured rhymes, clichés and vague historical context displayed in much popular literature. For the rural masses, visual presentation of ideas was crucial to their reception, a fact which was not lost on religious propagandists at the time of the Reformation. In the early years of the sixteenth century, moral and political messages began increasingly to infiltrate popular festivals. Carnivals whose aim was to pillory parasitic clergy and a wordly and uncaring papacy were found in France and Germany, and one enterprising printer from Basel, Pamphilus Gengenbach, produced accompanying booklets which would carry the message of the festival beyond its immediate audience and also explain the more obscure allegorical references (Bercé 1976:65–6). Theatrical confraternities were founded to perform religious plays at festivals in a variety of countries. Some forms of theatre relied for their impact on the ability of the players to mix elements drawn from folk memory with comments on everyday life and motifs derived from printed literature. Ukrainian religious stage plays, performed by peripatetic students during their vacations from Orthodox Brotherhood schools or the Kiev Mohyla academy, used folk culture enriched with educated values and information derived from the products of literacy, fusing Scripture, theology, classics and foreign literature with folklore (Lewin 1977). Groups of English touring players performed Renaissance drama for noble patrons and others in central and eastern Europe between 1590 and 1660 (Limon 1985). As Harvey Graff (1987:5) has written, 'literacy was *formed, shaped,* and *conditioned* by the oral world that it penetrated'.

No area of early modern life was free of this complex interaction between oral and literate forms. Twentieth-century readers tend to assume that written documents and written communication will automatically be more important than verbal exchanges because they are fixed and unambiguous. The ultimate authority in any context will be the written or printed page. For early modern men and women, the reality was rather more complex. On the one hand, the products of literacy were not always of paramount importance as authentication and, on the other, books and writings had a symbolic or totemic significance which depended hardly at all on the words they contained.

Taking first the power of the written or printed word to command respect, many of the important events at which literacy was used contained acts and spoken words too. Scotland was one of the first European countries to instigate a centralised register of land transfers in 1617. The written 'instrument of sasine' was recorded in official volumes, but the actual transfer usually took place on the land itself, and involved the handing over of a clod of earth from the seller to the buyer before witnesses. For authenticating personal documents, a seal was counted as good as a signature in countries such as Poland until well into the early modern period, a practice which also says something about the aspirations of the magnates to royalty. The point of these examples is to show that ritual and symbol were often mixed with 'modern' bureaucratic, literate forms and that the importance of the former should not be underestimated. Written documents were an essential complement to public, personal acts rather than a substitute for them in many contexts. A document could be valued for its mystery and symbolism rather than as a record, authentication or replacement for memory (Franklin 1985:24-36).

Books too were used in a symbolic and instrumental way. Oaths on a Bible depended more on what the Bible symbolised than what it contained, and the cross which usually adorned the front of any large edition might be the sole focus of veneration for an illiterate peasant. In all European countries, the Bible's cultural significance went far beyond its textual content. Revered as the touchstone of the Protestant Reformation, it was used as an icon, a talisman, for social display, to cure illness, find lost goods and even forecast the names of future lovers. Martin Martin recorded in his 1703 account of a journey in the Highlands and Islands of Scotland that on Colonsay it was the custom to fan the faces of the sick with the pages of the Bible. Books were objects of awe, playing a role in eschatological expectations such as visions of the afterlife in which a 'Book of Life' is consulted to assess the soul's fate in Heaven or Hell. In sixteenth-century Italy, the legend of Santa Margherita was believed to possess healing powers and, if read out to or placed on the stomach of a pregnant woman, to help in childbirth. Books were useful gifts in sixteenth-century France because they were less heavy with meaning than flowers, animals or clothes (Cressy 1986; Martin 1703:248).

These examples of oral–literate interaction point towards an important feature of communication in early modern Europe. Information could only travel as quickly as the human beings responsible for disseminating it. This is an important point about all communications before the advent of electrically transmitted signals, and one made by the famous media guru, Marshall McLuhan (1973). Until the nineteenth century, communication and transportation were synonymous. Take the example of the fastest postal service in Europe, that for carrying diplomatic mail. Thurn und Taxis' imperial postal couriers did the journey from Augsburg to Venice in six days, two days faster than the town's official news service. Beacon chains and bells were potentially very fast but conveyed only one message: the former that invasion had occurred, the latter that fire had broken out or that someone important had died. Smoke signals, semaphore flags and pigeon posts were not fully developed until the nineteenth century. At its speediest, mail could travel only fifty miles a day on land and was utterly dependent on finding an individual who would carry it. There were few professional couriers and vital communication might rely on a chance meeting. Sir Edward Stafford, Elizabethan ambassador to France in 1584, saluted his queen in a letter posted 'out of an alehouse upon the river of Loire where I met with this bearer'. Crossing the Alps, other messengers might have to wear special studded boots while all had to avoid bandits and their country's enemies who might deprive them not only of their mail but also of their lives (Allen 1972). News travelled only as fast as a man on foot or horseback or in a boat.

Slow as a means of transmitting ideas – at least by modern standards – word of mouth was by no means inferior to the written or printed word where public opinion was concerned. The power of rumour and innuendo in small communities where an individual's reputation was vital to his or her social and economic welfare is well known. It could also create vigorous climates of opinion on more momentous events than, say, the production of an illegitimate child. Oral transmission was at least as fast as written, and in the form of rumour and gossip it could be faster and more influential. Public opinion on the central issues of the day was, after all, formulated not by slavish acceptance of newspaper reports and propaganda sheets, but by discussion among people as they tried to make sense of conflicting interpretations of events. The printed or written word might be more permanent than the spoken, but it lacked the speed of penetration and therefore immediate impact of oral communication. Climates of opinion on current affairs were created locally, dependent on personal contact, attendance at sermons or participation in acts of protest such as religious iconoclasm or riots about over-taxation or grain shortages (Scribner 1984:247).

Competing political, religious and military camps recognised the power of the pulpit in forming opinion. Indeed, in winning mass support for a cause, the voice of the clergy was often more powerful than the weight of printed propaganda. This was certainly the case in mid-seventeenth-century Scotland. The 'Scottish Revolution', a reaction to the religious changes proposed by Charles I's unpopular archbishop Laud, began in 1637. Between then and 1648 the Covenanters, as the reformers were called, presented a united front, but in 1648 a more moderate, Royalist group called the Engagers broke away from the Presbyterian, pro-Parliamentary Covenanters embodied in the Kirk and its General Assembly. The Covenanters retained control of the pulpit and used it to deadly effect against the

Engagers whose only propaganda weapon was the pamphlet and the newspaper, neither of which proved adequate to win over the hearts and minds of the majority of Scots. Realising that they were losing the propaganda battle, the Engagers set up a committee to investigate 'the fittest way how the publict conditioun of the affaires of the kingdome and of our Armie may be weiklie represented to the kingdome'. Unfortunately for the Engagers, there was no better method than the weekly sermon and they were defeated soon after (Stevenson 1981).

Spoken communication was quick and economical, conveying deep meaning in a few words by the use of inflection, intonation, gestures and facial expressions. Collating and printing urgent news was time-consuming and most transactions of information in great centres of exchange like Amsterdam or Venice would take place in personal conversations. Second, strangers and travellers must have played a vital part in disseminating information and ideas. This helps to explain the ambivalent position of travellers. Village and town authorities adopted a suspicious and censorious attitude towards people who spread ideas which might foment fear and unrest. Individuals might be apprehensive of a passing stranger as a potential robber, beggar or carrier of disease. But they might equally be eager for the news which a traveller could bring and certain innkeepers made a business of collecting stories from travellers and selling them to publishers (Scribner 1984). In eighteenth-century Germany,

> if a stranger comes travelling through, he will generally show up at the *Spinnstube* in order to share his store of novelties, and if a newspaper reader came from the village into the room, he was hardly allowed to catch his breath. Even if he did not bring the newspaper with him to read out loud, he had to describe the latest events in exact details
> (Medick 1984:334).

Oral communication and unwritten culture was of prime importance in the lives of ordinary people. Assessing just how significant is extremely difficult. For many purposes, folk knowledge and the wisdom of experience passed on from one generation to another in work and play was all that was needed. Charles Estienne's sixteenth-century agricultural manual assured the French landowner that reading and writing were superfluous to the productivity of his tenant farmers as long as they were experienced and receptive (Davis 1975:196). Women's knowledge of childbirth, babies, housewifery and farming must have come almost exclusively from experience or from discussion and explanation offered by older matrons.

Was it then the case that those steeped in oral culture thought differently to those who had mastered the art of reading and writing? This is a common assumption among observers in developed countries of the twentieth century. They view illiterates as intellectually impoverished, not to say pathological; societies without mass literacy are assumed to be backward, undeveloped and in need of help. Literacy, on the other hand, is held to be synonymous with modernity, receptivity to change, societal development and personal adequacy. To enter the mind of any early modern person, and particularly those who left no written record of their thoughts and deeds, is notoriously difficult. Gauging how broad and 'modern' the minds of literates were compared with illiterates is fraught with methodological problems, not least of which is the widespread assumption that the more recent a set of values or body of information is, the more rational and enlightened it must be. Despite these difficulties, it is possible to distinguish certain features which marked out different ways of thinking.

In the course of the eighteenth century, European society became more secular in its outlook and less dominated by religious concerns. From the end of the Thirty Years War (1648), if not sooner, religion played a much reduced role in international relations, and some historians have spoken of a 'dechristianisation' of Europe which was signalled by scientific advances, the decline of the belief in witchcraft and magic, and the growing dissatisfaction with bodies such as the Jesuits who were committed to a supranational religious ideal. A secular outlook is usually assumed to be connected with modernity, a religious one with a traditional set of mind. In Catholic countries, requests for masses after death became increasingly the preserve of those who could not sign their wills. Around 1710, testators from Marseille who asked for masses after their deaths were divided evenly between literates and illiterates, but by 1780 three illiterates made the request for every one who signed his will. Over the same period the number of wills which dedicated the testator's soul to God decreased appreciably for literates but hardly at all for those unable to sign their names. Continued adherence to this religious aspiration seems to have been increasingly the preserve of illiterates. For ordinary people, literacy and a lack of expressed concern for religion seem to have been equated (Vovelle 1975:136–7). Illiteracy might be linked with traditional attitudes, literacy with a greater receptivity to change, but it is also possible that literacy and a modern outlook both sprang from a similar set of social and economic circumstances and that literacy was not the most important determinant of attitudes. There were other differences. For those who were not steeped in literate ways of thought, time was perceived as blocks punctuated by significant festivals such as May Day and by important events such as harvest or a change of ruler. Literates tended increasingly to relate time to a documented continuum of years, months and days, and they turned more rapidly to watches and clocks when these became widely available. The sixteenth century was the most crucial period in the turnround from traditional to modern methods of dating in western Europe, and the transition was led by urban dwellers; in eastern Europe it took much longer, partly because the length of an hour, for example, was different in the province of Novgorod from that in the Moscow region, and notched sticks were only replaced by printed calendars in the eighteenth century (Moran 1981; Smith 1983).

The intellectual skills required by oral culture, including a highly retentive memory trained to store mnemonics, aphorisms and rhymes, were different from those needed fully to participate in the offerings of print and writing. The father of the eighteenth-century English poet John Clare knew more than a hundred ballads by heart. Oral culture was very much a culture of the senses. Its role in shaping the products of literacy and their impact was profound.

CHAPTER TEN
Conclusion

Education was a medium through which many prevalent social attitudes were conveyed and portrayed. Literacy for its part was an indicator of attitudes and opportunities created by social, economic, cultural and political factors. The ways in which education and literacy developed in the early modern period were complex and contingent on a wide variety of circumstances. Certain features were common to all parts of Europe and bear witness to the superficial similarity between the social organisation of the continent's diverse regions. Men were everywhere more literate than women, the upper classes more literate than the lower, and towns generally enjoyed less illiteracy than the deeply rural environment in which most people lived. Educational provision improved across Europe between the Renaissance and the Industrial Revolution and, partly as a result, so too did levels of literacy. A much larger proportion of the population could read and write in 1800 than had been the case three centuries before and the uses to which literacy could be put had increased greatly. Printed books became much more widely available in languages which ordinary men and women could understand after the middle of the sixteenth century, and literate ways of thinking and acting became more common. The control of secular authorities over education was growing and the presence of increasingly powerful states made demand for education and literacy more insistent.

Patterns there may be, but generalisations from them have to be made with caution. There is, for example, no simple and universal explanation of why men and women became more literate between the end of the fifteenth century and the start of the nineteenth. Schools were important to developments in France, England and the Netherlands but were marginal to the advances made in Scandinavian countries during the eighteenth century. Becoming literate was a complex process. Funding too made a difference to the availability of education to ordinary children. In Scotland and Baden in Germany, where taxation of landowners or the use of communal funds reduced the net cost of education to parents, literacy tended to be high, but comparable levels of signing can also be found in England where most schooling was paid for by fees or out of charitable funds. Protestants were usually more literate than Catholics in the sixteenth century, though the drive to christianise the masses and the fallout from the great religious conflicts of the period were important in raising the literacy of all denominations. High levels of economic development seem to have created resources to spend on education in areas like Holland or the towns of northern Italy, alongside a demand for learning among the commercial and artisan classes. On the other hand, there were valleys in the Alpine parts of south-east France or northern Italy which even by contemporary standards were economically backward but which had exceptionally high levels of literacy. A desire to improve their social and economic position through migration might explain this, but not all upland zones adjacent to more developed lowland ones were so blessed: Highland Scotland and the Pyrenees are examples. Illiterate zones generally had few schools, low demand for literacy, dialect or language differences, a dispersed or sparse population and limited economic development. Rising literacy cannot simply be attributed to schools, prosperity, environment or religion.

Just as the reasons for literacy differed between social groups and regions, so too did the implications of rising literacy for society and culture. Writing helped to objectify speech, fix it and extend communication over time and space, giving rise to more complex administrative forms which in turn help to integrate societies and further religious evangelism. By increasing the number of contacts an individual could have, writing and reading hastened the pace of life (Goody 1968:1–2). Print and writing further aided the growing distinction between the natural, divine and human orders, enlarged the choice of literature and furthered both the intellectual and physical 'division of labour' in early modern Europe. Some communities were already at home with these implications by the Renaissance (Goody & Watt 1968:62). In the cities of northern Italy, a 'literate mentality' was already present in the fifteenth century, but in the Russian empire verbal communication remained dominant until the nineteenth century. An extension of the ability to read and write sometimes helped to replace oral forms as the culture of the masses, as in England, while in southern France it reinforced and enriched those forms. Furthermore, print could divide as well as unify European culture. When books were printed in Latin they could be read by educated elites anywhere in Europe, thus unifying intellectual life. Vernacular printing reached a wider audience, provided it was in a typeface they could decipher and a version of their own everyday tongue they could recognise, but more languages were needed to gain access to what, in Latin, had been common intellectual property. It is important to recognise that in practical terms only a small minority of the population had access to the full spectrum of 'culture' since only they had knowledge of Latin. Even in the eighteenth century when vernacular publication expanded enormously, full understanding and enjoyment of scientific literature or the novel depended on high-quality education which was still restricted principally to men from the middling and upper classes. Basic literacy could be a base for approaching such culture, but we should not equate elementary reading and writing with automatic access to all the products of literacy. At the same time, the penetration of print and writing into everyday life could enrich experience, but it is also true that oral culture allows much wider participation by individuals in forming the total cultural tradition than does written since few people write creatively and reading tends to be more passive than writing. Oral forms of communication remained important to everyday life and shaped both the development of literate culture and the transmission of ideas. Using literacy was also a complex process.

Literacy did not necessarily involve a change of attitudes since printing, reading and writing might simply fix existing ideas rather than offering new ones even if the long-run potential was considerable. In England there was no major shift from communal to individual forms of economic and social organisation between the fourteenth and seventeenth centuries: the spread of literacy merely offered a different medium of transactions. Contrast this with the Burgundy region of France where the power of the *seigneur* and communal life in the village and fields, previously determined by custom and memory, became fixed in written leases and court records. By itself, literacy does nothing. Just as literacy and individuality are commonly linked, so too are literacy and rationality since the ability to read and write is said to break the mental mould of irrational custom. Printed texts offered a new view of the world during the seventeenth century, but they also provided a rationalisation and intellectualisation of witchcraft beliefs in the form of texts like Jean Bodin's *De la Démonomanie des Sorciers* of 1586. Long-established myths were reproduced in print as often as new discoveries in the literature of the sixteenth century, and the books which people may have read tended to perpetuate an old-fashioned world picture rather than forging a new one out of recent geographical and scientific discoveries. If literacy was used to strengthen and extend existing beliefs and attitudes, then its value as a liberator of minds should not be exaggerated. Basic literacy conferred few material benefits to ambitious individuals and in any case the inequalities of wealth and status were extensive enough to limit the advantages which modern societies expect to accrue to the literate. Finally, literacy is often associated with democracy since literate people are said to demand more political participation and are able to make more balanced choices of representative: literacy makes people more involved and better informed. This, of course, depends on the existing political structure, and early modern regimes were not noted for a commitment to 'democracy'. Some towns did have something approaching universal adult male suffrage in local elections but, in general, political participation was restricted to a tiny minority. Education was designed to transmit set information and approved viewpoints. It could open up the possibility of transmitting new ideas, for example between members of religious or secular groups who questioned the existing structures of power and authority, but this was very much a side-effect. The very act of individual choice of what was read was potentially subversive (if exercised) but it is hard to escape the conclusion that new ways of thinking and acting came about despite rather than because of education. There were numerous theorists who wrote about education and there was some tinkering with pedagogic practice, but those who tried to break away from the models established by groups like the Jesuits (the Piarists, for example) found themselves drawn back to existing methods. Local variations in educational practice are to be expected in view of the limited supervisory power of central authorities, but the ideology and practical reality of education was order, conformity and the reception of specified facts and interpretations.

The point is that literacy cannot be divorced from its social and ideological context. Education, literacy and print are not 'things' with identities of their own but are dependent on the environment in which they operate for their influence. What is taught, what is learned and how it is used and understood depends on social norms and conventions, on the context established by many factors in the material and intellectual environment. Literacy might create new possibilities for thought and action, but that was not the direct aim of most forms of education. By itself, then, literacy could do little. Its relative significance depended at any given period on the social class, gender and residence of the individual. To say this is not to indulge in an anachronistic running down of the achievements of educators and people in early modern Europe. It is simply to show how different their assumptions, their methods of teaching and their views of the uses of education and literacy were from the ostensible purposes of modern societies and to highlight the implications of these differences for the way we understand social and cultural change.

General texts are designed to make material accessible to non-specialist audiences in a straightforward way. This volume has hopefully succeeded in that task. However, there is no point in simplifying to the extent of distorting the complex reality of social life in early modern Europe. Patterns of development and general structures certainly existed, but the relative significance of different features making up those broad similarities was far from uniform across space and time. Nor were the implications of educational and cultural change uniform across Europe, but depended for their impact on existing social, political, economic and legal structures. We should not walk away with the impression that education and literacy achieved nothing nor with a vision of a cultural and historical morass from which it is impossible to escape. Literacy was a force for change but it was also both agent and indicator of continuities. The general features of education and literacy in the early modern period have lessons for the ways in which we understand those aspects of modern life, but they also highlight the significance of appreciating the complexity of historical experience. Ultimately, an awareness of the reasons why cultural characteristics differ from one country to another may prove more fruitful to an understanding of the present than a search for grand theories and interpretative frameworks. The study of education and literacy in early modern Europe shows how different meanings and understandings fit together to produce cultural characteristics, and it is that sense of context which history so perfectly provides.

Bibliography

Actes du 95e congrès national des sociétés savantes. Histoire de l'enseignement de 1610 à nos jours, 1974. Paris.

ADAM, W., 1985, 'Lesen und Vorlesen am Langenburger hof. Zur Lesefahigkeit und zum Buchbesitz der diener und beamten', in Brückner *et al.* (eds), 1985.

ADAMS, J. R. R., 1980, 'Reading societies in Ulster', *Ulster Folklife*, **26**:55–64.

ADDY, G. M., 1977, 'The first generation of academic reform in Spanish universities, 1760–1789', in Leith (ed.), 1977.

ADLER, P. J., 1974, 'Habsburg school reform among the Orthodox minorities, 1770–1780', *Slavic Review*, **33**:23–45.

ÅKERMAN, S., *et al.*, 1979, 'Splitting background variables: AID analysis applied to migration and literacy research', *Journal European Economic History*, **8**:157–92.

ALDIS, H. G., 1904, *A list of books printed in Scotland before 1700*. Edinburgh.

ALEXANDER, D. & STRAUSS, W. L., 1977, *The German single-leaf woodcut, 1600–1700*. 2 vols. New York.

ALLEN, E. J. B., 1972, *Post and courier service in the diplomacy of early modern Europe*. The Hague.

ALSTON, P., 1969, *Education and the state in Tsarist Russia*. Stanford.

ANDERSON, C. A. & BOWMAN, M. J., 1973, 'Human capital and economic modernization in historical perspective', in Lane, F. C. (ed.), *4th international conference of economic history, 1968*. Paris.

ANDERSON, C. A. & BOWMAN, M. J., 1976, 'Education and economic modernization in historical perspective', in Stone (ed.), 1976.

ANDERSON, R. D., 1983, *Education and opportunity in Victorian Scotland. Schools and Universities*. Oxford.

ANDREYEV, N., 1977, 'Literature in the Muscovite period (1300–1700)', in Auty & Obolensky (eds), 1977.

ANGLIN, J. P., 1980, 'The expansion of literacy: opportunities for the study of the three Rs in the London diocese of Elizabeth I', *Guildhall Studies in London History*, 3:63–74.

ARIES, P., 1962, *Centuries of childhood*. London. (First published Paris, 1960.)

ARMOGATHE, J. R., 1973, 'Les catéchismes et l'enseignement populaire au XVIIIe siècle', in *Images du peuple au XVIIIe siècle*. Paris.

ARNOVE, R. & GRAFF, H. J., (eds), 1987, *National literacy campaigns*. New York.

ART, J., 1980, 'Volksonderwijs in de Zuidelijke Nederlanden', *Algemene Geschiedenis der Nederlanden*, vol. 7. Haarlem.

ASTON, M., 1977, 'Lollardy and literacy', *History*, **62**:347–71.

ASTON, T. H., (ed.), 1983, *Social relations and ideas. Essays in honour of R. H. Hilton*. Cambridge.

AUTY, R., 1977a, 'The Russian language', in Auty & Obolensky (eds), 1977.

AUTY, R., 1977b, 'Russian writing', in Auty & Obolensky (eds), 1977.

AUTY, R. & OBOLENSKY, D., (eds), 1977, *An introduction to Russian language and literature*. Cambridge.

AVRICH, P., 1973, *Russian rebels, 1600–1800*. London.

BAILEY, C. R., 1977, 'Attempts to institute a "system" of secular secondary education in France, 1762–1789', in Leith (ed.), 1977.

BAIN, A., 1965, *Education in Stirlingshire from the Reformation to 1872*. London.

BAINTON, R. H., 1980, 'Learned women in the Europe of the sixteenth century', in Labalme (ed.), 1980.

BAJKÓ, M., 1977, 'The development of Hungarian formal education in the eighteenth century', in Leith (ed.), 1977.

BAKER, D. N. and HARRIGAN, P.J., (eds), 1980, *The making of Frenchmen: current directions in the history of education in France, 1679–1979*. Waterloo, Canada.

BALDO, V., 1977, *Alunni, maestri e scuole in Venezia alla fine del xvi secolo*. Como.

BANNERMAN, J., 1983, 'Literacy in the Highlands', in Cowan & Shaw (eds), 1983.

BÁRÁNY, G., 1966, 'The awakening of Magyar nationalism before 1848', *Austrian History Yearbook*, **2**:19–50.

BARBER, G., 1981, 'Who were the booksellers of the Enlightenment?', in Barber & Fabian (eds), 1981.

BARBER, G. & FABIAN, B., (eds), 1981, *Buch und Buchhandel in Europa im achtzehnten Jahrhundert*. Hamburg.

BARTNICKA, K., 1973, 'Les activités de propaganda de la commission d'éducation nationale', *Przeglad Historyczny*, **54**:518.

BARTON, H. A., 1977, 'Popular education in Sweden: theory and practice', in Leith (ed.), 1977.

BASCHWITZ, K., 1938, 'The history of the daily press in the Netherlands', *Bulletin of the International Committee of Historical Sciences*, **10**:96–113.

BAUER, M., 1982, 'Christoph Weigel (1654–1725), Kupferstecher und Kunsthändler in Augsburg und Nürnberg', *Archiv für Geschichte des Buchwesens*, **23**:693–1186.

BAUMANN, G., (ed.), 1986, *The written word. Literacy in transition.* Oxford.

BEALE, J. M., 1983, *A history of the burgh and parochial schools of Fife.* Edinburgh.

BECKER, P. J., 1980, 'Bibliotheksreisen in Deutschland im 18. Jahrhundert', *Archiv für Geschichte des Buchwesens*, **21**: 1361–1534.

BECKER-CANTARINO, B., 1977, 'Joseph von Sonnenfels and the development of secular education in eighteenth-century Austria', in Leith (ed.), 1977.

BECKETT, J. C., 1986, 'Literature in English, 1691–1800', in Moody & Vaughan (eds), 1986.

BEDNARSKI, S., 1933, *Upadek i Odrodzenie szkól Jezuickich w Polsce.* Cracow.

BENEDICT, P., 1980, *Rouen during the wars of religion.* Cambridge.

BENNASSAR, B., 1967, *Valladolid au siècle d'or.* Paris.

BENNASSAR, B., 1982, *Un siècle d'or Espagnol, 1525–1648.* Paris.

BERCÉ, Y-M., 1976, *Fête et révolte. Des mentalités populaires du XVIe au XVIII siècle.* Paris.

BERNARD, L., 1970, *The emerging city. Paris in the age of Louis XIV.* Durham, NC.

BEUTLER, C., 1973, 'Un chapitre de la sensibilité collective: la littérature agricole en Europe continentale au XVIe siècle', *Annales E.S.C.*, **28**:1280–1301.

BIEŃKOWSKI, T., 1981, 'Wiedza o przyrodzie w Polsce XVI-XVIII wieku', *Rozprawy z Dziejów Oświaty*, **14**:15–31.

BIRN, R., 1981, 'La contrabande et la saisie de livres à l'aube du siècle des lumières', *Revue d'Histoire Moderne et Contemporaine*, **28**:158–73.

BLACK, J. L., 1977, 'Citizenship training and moral regeneration as the mainstay of Russian schools', in Leith (ed.), 1977.

Literacy in early modern Europe

BLACK, J. L., 1979, *Citizens for the fatherland. Education, educators and pedagogical ideals in eighteenth-century Russia*. New York.

BLISS, A., 1976, 'The development of the English language in early modern Ireland', in Moody, Martin & Byrne (eds), 1976.

BLÜHM, E., 1985, 'Die ältesten Zeitungen und das Volk', in Brückner *et al.* (eds), 1985, 741–52.

BOLLÈME, G., 1965, 'Littérature populaire et littérature de colportage au 18e siècle', in Bollème (ed.), 1965.

BOLLÈME, G., (ed.), 1965, *Livre et société dans la France du XVIIIe siècle*, vol. 1. Paris.

BOLLÈME, G., 1969, *Les almanachs populaires aux XVIIe et XVIIIe siècles*. Paris.

BOLLÈME, G., 1971, *La bibliothèque bleue*. Paris.

DE BOOY, E. P., 1977, *De weldaet der scholen*. Haarlem.

DE BOOY, E. P., 1980a, 'Volksonderwijs in de Noordelijke Nederlanden', *Algemene Geschiedenis der Nederlanden*, vol. 7. Haarlem.

DE BOOY, E. P., 1980b, *Kweekhoven der wijsheid*. Zutphen.

BORDES, M., 1979, 'La réforme scolaire Sarde de 1729 dans le comté de Nice', *Annales du Midi*, **91**:415–22.

BORSAY, P., 1977, 'The English urban renaissance: the development of provincial urban culture, c1680–c1760', *Social History*, **3**:581–603.

BOUYSSY, M. T., (ed.), 1970, *Livre et société dans la France du XVIIIe siècle*, vol. 2. Paris.

BOYCE, G., CURRAN, J. & WINGATE, P., (eds), 1978, *Newspaper history from the seventeenth century to the present day*. London.

BOYD, W., 1961, *Education in Ayrshire over seven centuries*. London.

BRANCOLINI, J. & BOUYSSY, M. T., 1970, 'La vie provinciale du livre à la fin de l'ancien régime', in Bouyssy (ed.), 1970.

BREATNACH, R. A., 1961, 'The end of a tradition: a survey of eighteenth century Gaelic literature', *Studia Hibernica*, **1**:128–50.

BRIDGMAN, A., 1977, 'Aspects of education in eighteenth-century utopias', in Leith (ed.), 1977.

BROCKLISS, L. W. B., 1978, 'Patterns of attendance at the university of Paris, 1400–1800', *Historical Journal*, **21**:503–44.

BROCKLISS, L. W. B., 1987, *French higher education in the seventeenth and eighteenth centuries*. Oxford.

BROOKS, J., 1985, *When Russia learned to read. Literacy and popular culture, 1861–1917*. Princeton.

BROOKS, P. N., (ed.), 1980, *Reformation principle and practice. Essays in honour of A. G. Dickens*. London.

BROWN, J. C., 1982, *In the shadow of Florence. Provincial society in Renaissance Pescia*. Oxford.

BRÜCKNER, W., BLICKLE, P. & BREVER, D., (eds), 1985, *Literatur und Volk im 17.Jahrhundert. Probleme populärer Kultur in Deutschland*, vol. 2. Wiesbaden.

BUCHAN, D., 1972, *The ballad and the folk*. London.

BUKDAHL, J. (ed.), 1959, *Scandinavia past and present*. Copenhagen.

BURIAN, P., 1970-1, 'The state language problem in old Austria (1848-1918)', *Austrian History Yearbook*, 6-7:81-103.

BURKE, P., 1978, *Popular culture in early modern Europe*. London.

BURKE, P., 1986, 'The humanist as professional teacher', in Wilkes, J. (ed.), 1986, *The professional teacher*. Leicester.

BURKE, P., 1987, *The historical anthropology of early modern Italy*. Cambridge.

BURKE, P. & PORTER, R., (eds), 1987, *The social history of language*. Cambridge.

BURNET, M., 1965, *ABC of literacy*. Paris.

BUTEL, P., 1976, 'L'instruction populaire en Aquitaine au XVIIIe siècle: l'exemple de l'Agenais', *Revue d'Histoire Economique et Sociale*, 54:5-28.

BYLEBYL, J. L., 1979, 'The school of Padua: humanistic medicine in the sixteenth century', in Webster (ed.), 1979.

BYRES, T. J., 1976, 'Scottish peasants and their song', *Journal of Peasant Studies*, 3:236-51.

CAMIC, C., 1985, *Experience and enlightenment. Socialization for cultural change in eighteenth-century Scotland*. Edinburgh.

CANNY, N., 1982, 'The formation of the Irish mind: religion, politics and Gaelic Irish literature, 1580-1750', *Past & Present*, 95:91-116.

CAPP, B., 1979, *Astrology and the popular press. English almanacs, 1500-1800*. London.

CAPP, B., 1985, 'Popular literature', in Reay (ed.), 1985.

CARNIE, R. H., 1965, 'Scottish printers and booksellers, 1668-1775: a study of source-material', *Bibliotheck*, 4:213-27.

CARPANETTO, D. & RICUPERATI, G., 1987, *Italy in the age of reason*. London.

CARRATO, J. F., 1977, 'The enlightenment in Portugal and the educational reforms of the marquis of Pombal', in Leith (ed.), 1977.

CASTAN, Y., 1974, *Honnêteté et relations sociales en Languedoc, 1715-1780*. Paris.

CHARTIER, R., 1987, *Lectures et lecteurs dans la France de l'ancien régime*. Paris.

239

CHARTIER, R., JULIA, D. & COMPERE, M., 1976, *Education en France du XVIe au XVIIIe siècle*. Paris.

CHEVALIER, M., 1976, *Lectura y lectores en España de los siglos XVI y XVII*. Madrid.

CHISICK, H., 1981, *The limits of reform in the Enlightenment: attitudes towards the education of the lower classes in eighteenth-century France*. Princeton.

CHOJNACKI, S., 1974, 'Continuity and discontinuity in Italian culture, 1300-1800', *History of Education Quarterly*, 14:533-41.

CHOLVY, G., 1980, 'Une école des pauvres au debut du 19e siècle: "pieuses filles", béates ou soeurs des campagnes', in Baker & Harrigan (eds), 1980.

CHOPPIN, A., 1980, 'L'histoire des manuels scolaires: une approche globale', *Histoire de l'Education*, 9:1-25.

CHRISMAN, M. U., 1980, 'Lay response to the protestant reformation in Germany', in Brooks (ed.), 1980.

CHRISMAN, M. U., 1982, *Lay culture, learned culture. Books and social change in Strasbourg, 1480-1599*. New Haven.

CIPOLLA, C. M., 1969, *Literacy and development in the west*. Harmondsworth.

CIPOLLA, C. M., 1972, 'The diffusion of innovations in early modern Europe', *Comparative Studies in Society and History*, 14:46-52.

CLAEYSSEN, M., 1980, 'L'enseignement de la lecture au 18e siècle', in Baker & Harrigan (eds), 1980.

CLANCHY, M. T., 1979, *From memory to written record: England. 1066-1377*. London.

CLARK, P., 1976, 'The ownership of books in England, 1560-1640: the example of some Kentish townsfolk', in Stone (ed.), 1976.

CLARK, P., 1983, 'Visions of the urban community: antiquarians and the English city before 1800', in Fraser, D. & Sutcliffe, A. (eds), 1983, *The pursuit of urban history*. London.

COCHRANE, E. W., 1961, *Tradition and enlightenment in the Tuscan academies, 1690-1800*. Chicago.

CORVISIER, A., 1979, *Armies and societies in Europe, 1494-1789*. Bloomington.

COSTELLO, W. T., 1958, *The scholastic curriculum at early seventeenth-century Cambridge*. Cambridge, Mass.

COWAN, I. B. & SHAW, D., (eds), 1983, *The Renaissance and Reformation in Scotland*. Edinburgh.

CRAIG, D., 1961, *Scottish literature and the Scottish people, 1680-1830*. London.

CRAIG, D., (ed.), 1975, *Marxists on literature. An anthology.* Harmondsworth.

CRAIG, J. E., 1981, 'The expansion of education', *Review of Research in Education,* 9:151-213.

CRANFIELD, G. A., 1978, *The press and society: from Caxton to Northcliffe.* London.

CRAWFORD, P., 1985, 'Women's published writings, 1600-1700', in Prior, M. (ed.), *Women in English society, 1500-1800.* London.

CRESSY, D., 1980, *Literacy and the social order.* Cambridge.

CRESSY, D., 1986, 'Books as totems in seventeenth-century England and New England', *Journal of Library History,* 21:92-106.

CROIX, A., 1981, *La Bretagne aux 16e et 17e siècle,* vol. 2. Paris.

CSÁKY, M., 1978, 'Von der Ratio Educationis zur educatio nationalis', in Klingenstein et al. (ed.), 1978.

CULLEN, L. M., 1980, 'The social and cultural modernisation of Ireland, 1600-1900', in Cullen & Furet (eds), 1980.

CULLEN, L. M., 1981, *The emergence of modern Ireland, 1600-1900.* London.

CULLEN, L. M. & FURET, F., (eds), 1980, *Ireland and France, 17th-20th centuries. Towards a comparative study of rural history.* Paris.

DAHL, S., 1959, 'Travelling pedlars in nineteenth century Sweden', *Scandinavian Economic History Review,* 7:167-78.

DE DAINVILLE, F., 1947, 'Livres d'écoliers Toulousains à la fin du XVIe siècle', *Bulletin d'Histoire et Religion.* 9:129-40.

DE DAINVILLE, F., 1957, 'Collèges et frequentation scolaire au XVIIe siècle', *Population,* 12:467-94.

DARNTON, R., 1971a, 'Reading, writing and publishing in eighteenth-century France', *Daedalus,* 100:214-56.

DARNTON, R., 1971b, 'The high enlightenment and the low-life of literature in pre-revolutionary France', *Past & Present,* 51:81-115.

DARNTON, R., 1976, 'Trade in the taboo: the life of a clandestine book dealer in pre-revolutionary France', in Korshin (ed.), 1976.

DARNTON, R., 1984, 'The great cat massacre, 1730', *History Today,* 34:7-15.

DARNTON, R., 1986, 'First steps towards a history of reading', *Australian Journal of French Studies,* 23:5-30.

DAVIES, J., 1979a, 'Persecution and protestantism: Toulouse, 1562-1575', *Historical Journal,* 22:31-51.

DAVIES, J., 1979b, 'The libraries of some protestants of Toulouse in 1572: cultural influences and calvinism', *Bibliothèque d'Humanisme et Renaissance,* 41:555-66.

DAVIES, J., 1983, 'A student library in sixteenth-century Toulouse', *History of Universities*, 3:61–86.

DAVIS, N. Z., 1975, *Society and culture in early modern France*. London.

DAVIS, N. Z., 1980, 'Gender and genre: women as historical writers 1400–1820', in Labalme (ed.), 1980.

DAVIS, N. Z., 1983, 'Beyond the market: books as gifts in sixteenth-century France', *Transactions of the Royal Historical Society*, 5th series, 33:69–88.

DEDIEU, J-P., 1979, '"Christianisation" en Nouvelle Castille. Catéchisme, communion, messe et confirmation dans l'archevêché de Tolède, 1540–1650', *Mélanges de la Casa de Velazquez*, 15:261–94.

DELMASURE, A., 1973, 'L'enseignement primaire au XVIe siècle dans la partie française du diocèse de Tournai', *Revue du Nord*, 217:93–8.

VAN DEURSEN, A. TH., 1978, *Het kopergeld van de gouden eeuw. Volkskultur*. Amsterdam.

DEYON, P., 1967, *Amiens: capitale provinciale*. Paris.

DILWORTH, M., 1973, 'Literacy of pre-Reformation monks', *Innes Review*, 24:71–2.

DIXON, W., 1958, *Education in Denmark*. London.

DOYLE, W., 1978, *The old European order, 1660–1800*. Oxford.

DUGLIO, M. R., 1971, 'Alfabetismo e società a Torino nel seculo XVIII', *Quaderni Storici*, 17:485–509.

DUNN, P. P., 1976, '"That enemy is the baby": childhood in imperial Russia', in de Mause (ed.), 1976.

DUPRONT, A., 1965, 'Livre et culture dans la société française du 18e siècle: reflections sur une enquête', in Bollème (ed.), 1965.

DURKACZ, V. E., 1978, 'The source of the language problem in Scottish education, 1688–1709', *Scottish Historical Review*, 57:28–39.

DURKACZ, V. E., 1983, *The decline of the Celtic languages*. Edinburgh.

EECKAUTE, D., 1970, 'A propos de la pédagogie en Russie au début du XIXe siècle', *Cahiers du Monde Russe et Soviétique*, 11:244–58.

EHRARD, J. & ROGER, J., 1965, 'Deux périodiques français du 18e siècle', in Bollème (ed.), 1965.

EISENSTEIN, E. L., 1968, 'Some conjectures about the impact of printing on western society', *Journal of Modern History*, 40:1–56.

EISENSTEIN, E. L., 1979, *The printing press as an agent of change*. Cambridge.

EISENSTEIN, E. L., 1983, *The printing revolution in early modern Europe*. Cambridge.

EMERSON, R. L., 1977, 'Scottish universities in the eighteenth century, 1690–1800', in Leith (ed.), 1977.

ENGELSING, R., 1973, *Analphabetentum und Lektüre*. Stuttgart.

ETTINGHAUSEN, H., 1984, 'The news in Spain: *Relaciones de Sucesos* in the reigns of Philip III and IV', *European History Quarterly*, 14:1–20.

EVANS, R. J. W., 1974, 'Humanism and counter-reformation at the central European universities', *History of Education*, 3:1–15.

EVANS, R. J. W., 1975, *The Wechel presses: humanism and calvinism in central Europe*. Oxford.

EVANS, R. J. W., 1979, *The making of the Habsburg monarchy, 1550–1700*. Oxford.

EVANS, R. J. W., 1981, 'German universities after the thirty years war', *History of Universities*, 1:169–90.

FABER, J., 1980, 'Inhabitants of Amsterdam and their possessions, 1701–1710', in van der Woude, A. & Schuurman, A. (eds), 1980, *Probate inventories*. Utrecht.

FABIAN, B., 1976, 'English books and their eighteenth-century German readers', in Korshin (ed.), 1976.

FAIRCHILDS, C. C., 1976, *Poverty and charity in Aix-en-Provence, 1640–1789*. London.

FANFANI, A., 1951, 'La préparation intellectuelle et professionelle à l'activité économique en Italie du XIVe au XVIe siècle', *Le Moyen Age*, 57:327–46.

FEBVRE, L. & MARTIN, H-J., 1976, *The coming of the book*. London.

FÉLICIANGÉLI, D., 1980, 'Substrat éducatif dans le comté de Nice à l'arrivée des français en 1792', in Baker & Harrigan (eds), 1980.

FERRANTE, J. M., 1980, 'The education of women in the middle ages in theory, fact, and fantasy', in Labalme (ed.), 1980.

FERTÉ, P., 1980, 'La géographie statistique du recruitment des anciennes universités', in Baker ' Harrigan (eds), 1980.

FINNEGAN, R., 1973, 'Literacy versus non-literacy: the great divide', in Horton & Finnegan (eds), 1973.

FLANDRIN, J-L. & M., 1970, 'La circulation du livre dans la société du 18e siècle: un sondage à travers quelques sources', in Bouyssy (ed.), 1970.

FLETCHER, J. M., 1981, 'Change and resistance to change: a consideration of the development of English and German universities during the sixteenth century', *History of Universities*, 1:1–36.

FLEURY, M. & VALMARY, A., 1957, 'Les progrès de l'instruction élémentaire de Louis XIV à Napoleon III d'après l'enquête de Louis Maggiolo (1877-1879)', *Population*, 12:71-92.

FOURNEL-GUERIN, J., 1979, 'Le livre et la civilisation écrite dans la communauté morisque aragonaise', *Mélanges de la Casa de Velazquez*, 15:241-59.

FOXON, D., 1964, *Libertine literature in England, 1660-1745*. London.

FRANKLIN, S., 1985, 'Literacy and documentation in early medieval Russia', *Speculum*, 60:1-38.

FREEZE, G. L., 1974, 'Social mobility and the Russian parish clergy in the eighteenth century', *Slavic Review*, 33:641-62.

FRIEDRICHS, C. R., 1979, *Urban society in an age of war: Nördlingen, 1580-1720*. Princeton.

FRIEDRICHS, C. R., 1982, 'Whose house of learning? Some thoughts on German schools in post-Reformation Germany', *History of Education Quarterly*, 22:371-7.

FRIJHOFF, W., 1979, 'Surplus ou déficit? Hypothèses sur le nombre réel des étudiants en Allemagne à l'époque moderne (1576-1815)', *Francia*, 7:173-218.

FRIJHOFF, W. & JULIA, D., 1976, 'L'éducation des riches. Deux pensionnats: Belley et Grenoble', *Cahiers d'Histoire*, 21:105-31.

FURET, F. & OZOUF, J., 1982, *Reading and writing. Literacy in France from Calvin to Jules Ferry*. Cambridge.

FURET, F. & SACHS, W., 1974, 'La croissance de l'alphabétisation en France XVIIIe-XIXe siècle', *Annales ESC*, 29:714-37.

FUSSELL, G. E., 1932, 'Early farming journals', *Economic History Review*, 3:417-22.

GADD, F., 1981, 'Læse- og skrivekyndigheden indtil 1814, belyst ved det grønlandske materiale'. *Ur Nordisk Kulturhistoria. Studia Historica Jyväskyläensiä*, 22:73-86.

GADD, F., 1985, 'Læse- og skrivekyndigheden i 1700- og 1800- tallet indtil 1880. Grønland', in Skovgaard-Petersen (ed.), 1985.

GALENSON, D., 1979, 'Literacy and the social origins of some early Americans', *Historical Journal*, 22:75-91.

GALENSON, D., 1981, 'Literacy and age in pre-industrial England: quantitative evidence and implications', *Economic Development and Cultural Change*, 29:813-29.

GARDEN, M., 1976, 'Ecoles et maîtres: Lyon au XVIIIe siècle', *Cahiers d'Histoire*, 21:133-56.

GAWTHROP, R. & STRAUSS, G., 1984, 'Protestantism and literacy in early modern Germany', *Past & Present*, 104:31-55.

GEORGELIN, J., 1978, *Venise au siècle des lumières*. Paris.

GESSLER, J., (ed.), 1931, *Le livre des mestriers de Bruges et ses dérivés. Quatre anciens manuels de conversation*. Bruges.

GIBBS, G. C., 1971, 'The role of the Dutch republic as the intellectual entrepot of Europe in the seventeenth and eighteenth centuries', *Bijdragenen Medelingen ... der Nederlanden*, 86:323-49.

GINZBURG, C., 1980, *The cheese and the worms*. London.

GOLD, C., 1977, 'Educational reform in Denmark, 1784-1814', in Leith (ed.), 1977.

GOLDTHWAITE, R., 1972, 'Schools and teachers of commercial arithmetic in Renaissance Florence', *Journal of European Economic History*, 1:418-33.

GOLDTHWAITE, R., 1980, *The building of Renaissance Florence*. Baltimore & London.

GOODY, J., (ed.), 1968, *Literacy in traditional societies*. Cambridge.

GOODY, J., 1977, *The domestication of the savage mind*. Cambridge.

GOODY, J. & WATT, I., 1968, 'The consequences of literacy', in Goody (ed.), 1968.

GOUBERT, P., 1973, *The Ancien Régime. French society, 1600-1750*. London.

GRAFF, H. J., 1975, 'Literacy in history', *History of Education Quarterly*, 15:467-74.

GRAFF, H. J., 1979, *The literacy myth*. New York.

GRAFF, H. J., (ed.), 1981, *Literacy and social development in the west: a reader*. Cambridge.

GRAFF, H. J., 1987, *Legacies of literacy. Continuities and contradications in western culture and society*. Bloomington.

GRAFTON, A. & JARDINE, L., 1986, *From humanism to the humanities. Education and the liberal arts in fifteenth- and sixteenth-century Europe*. London.

GRAMBO, R., 1977, 'Folkloristic research in Norway, 1945-76', *Norveg*, 20:221-86.

GRAMBO, R., 1983, 'Folkloristic research in Norway, 1977-1982', *Norveg*, 26:107-55.

GREEN, L., 1979, 'The education of women in the Reformation', *History of Education Quarterly*, 19:93-116.

GRENDLER, P. F., 1975, 'The Roman inquisition and the Venetian press, 1540-1605', *Journal of Modern History*, 47:48-65.

GRENDLER, P., 1977, *The Roman inquisition and the Venetian press, 1504-1605*. Princeton.

GRENDLER, P. F., 1978a, 'Books for Sarpi: the smuggling of prohibited books into Venice during the interdict of 1606-1607', in

Bertelli, S. & Ramakus, G. (eds), 1978, *Essays presented to Myron P. Gilmore. Vol. 1. La nuova Italia*. Florence.

GRENDLER, P. F., 1978b, 'The destruction of Hebrew books in Venice, 1568', *Proceedings of the American Academy of Jewish Studies*, 45:103–30.

GRENDLER, P. F., 1981, *Culture and censorship in late Renaissance Italy and France*. London.

GRENDLER, P. F., 1982, 'What Zuanne read in school: vernacular texts in sixteenth-century Venetian schools', *Sixteenth Century Journal*, 13:41–54.

GRENDLER, P. F., 1984, 'The schools of christian doctrine in sixteenth-century Italy', *Church History*, 53:319–31.

GREVET, R., 1985, 'L'alphabétisation urbaine sous l'ancien régime: l'exemple de Saint-Omer (fin XVIIe début XIXe siècle)', *Revue du Nord*, 67:609–32.

GRIFFIN, A., 1637, *The English, Latin, French, Dutch, scholemaster. Or, an introduction to teach young gentlemen and merchants to travell or trade*. London.

GROBELAK, L., 1979, 'Les premises de l'enseignement du français en Pologne aux XVIe-XVIIe siècles', *Acta Poloniae Historica*, 40:175–82.

GROSPERRIN, B., 1976, 'Faut-il instruire le peuple? La réponse des physiocrates', *Cahiers d'Histoire*, 21:157–69.

GRUNDMANN, H., 1958, 'Litteratus–illiteratus. Der Wandel einer Bildungsnorm vom Alterum zum Mittelalter', *Archiv für Kulturgeschichte*, 40:1–65.

GUTTON, J-P., 1970, *La société et les pauvres. L'exemple de la généralité de Lyon, 1534–1789*. Paris.

GUTTORMSSON, L., 1981, 'Læsfærdighed og folkeuddannelse, 1540–1800', *Ur Nordisk Kulturhistoria. Studia Historica Jyväskyläensiä*, 22:123–92.

GUTTURMSSON, L., 1985, 'Skrivefærdighed i et skoleløst samfund (ca.1800–1880)', in Skovgaard-Petersen (ed.), 1985.

HALLGRÍMSSON, H., 1925, *Íslensk Alþýðumentum á 18.öld*. Reykjavik.

HAMLYN, H. M., 1946–7, 'Eighteenth-century circulating libraries in England', *The Library*, 5th series, 1:197–222.

HANEBUTT-BENZ, E-M., 1983, 'Studien zum deutschen Holzstich im 19. Jahrhundert', *Archiv für Geschichte des Buchwesens*, 14:581–1266.

HARDING, A., (ed.), 1980, *Law–making and law–makers in British history*. London.

HARRIS, J. R., 1985, 'Industrial espionage in the eighteenth century',

Industrial Archaeology Review, 7:127-38.

HARRIS, M., 1978, 'The structure, ownership and control of the press, 1620-1780', in Boyce *et al.* (eds), 1978.

HEISS, G., 1978, 'Konfession, Politik und Erziehung', in Klingenstein *et al.* (eds), 1978.

HERMANNSSON, H., (ed.), 1914, 'The story of Griselda in Iceland', *Islandica*, 7:xviii, 1-48.

HERMANNSSON, H., 1916, 'Icelandic books of the sixteenth century', *Islandica*, 9:xii, 1-72.

HERMANNSSON, H., 1918, 'The periodical literature of Iceland down to the year 1874: an historical sketch', *Islandica*, 11:1-100

HERMANNSSON, H., 1922, 'Icelandic books of the seventeenth century', *Islandica*, 14:xiii, 1-121.

HERMANNSSON, H., 1929, 'Icelandic manuscripts', *Islandica*, 19:1-80.

HERMANNSSON, H., 1958, 'The Hólar Cato. An Icelandic schoolbook of the seventeenth century', *Islandica*, 39:xxxiv, 1-91.

HITTLE, J. M., 1979, *The service city. State and townsmen in Russia, 1600-1800*. London.

HORN, P., 1980, *The rural world, 1780-1850. Social change in the English countryside*. London.

HORN, P., 1981, 'The contribution of the propagandist to eighteenth-century agricultural improvement', *Historical Journal*, 25: 313-29.

HORTON, R. & FINNEGAN, R., (eds), 1973, *Modes of Thought*. London.

HOUDAILLE, J., 1977, 'Les signatures au mariage de 1740 à 1829', *Population*, 32:65-90.

HOUSTON, R. A., 1983, 'Literacy and society in the west, 1500-1850', *Social History*, 8:269-93.

HOUSTON, R. A., 1985, *Scottish literacy and the Scottish identity*. Cambridge.

HØYER, S., 1982, 'Recent research on the press in Norway', *Scandinavian Journal of History*, 7:15-30.

HUFTON, O., 1974, *The poor of eighteenth-century France*. Oxford.

HUNT, C. J. & ISAAC, P. C. G., 1977, 'The regulation of the booktrade in Newcastle upon Tyne at the beginning of the nineteenth century', *Archaeologia Aeliana*, 5th series, 5:163-78.

HUPPERT, G., 1984, *Public schools in Renaissance France*. Urbana.

HYDE, J. K., 1979, 'Some uses of literacy in Venice and Florence in the thirteenth and fourteenth centuries', *Transactions of the Royal Historical Society*, 5th series, 29:109-28.

IVINS, W. M., 1953, *Prints and visual communication*. London.

JAKOBSON, R., 1955, 'Ivan Fedorov's primer', *Harvard Library Bulletin*, 9:5–39.

JAROSZ, I., 1978, 'Książki szkolne w Polsce w wieku XVI', *Rozprawy z Dziejów Oświaty*, 21:3–14.

JEWELL, H. M., 1982, '"The bringing up of children in good learning and manners": a survey of secular educational provision in the north of England, c1350–1550', *Northern History*, 18:1–25.

JOHANSSON, E., 1981, 'The history of literacy in Sweden', in Graff (ed.), 1981.

JOHNSON, F. R., 1946, 'Printers' "copy books" and the black market in the Elizabethan book trade', *The Library*, 5th series, 1:97–105.

JONES, R. E., 1979, 'Book owners in eighteenth century Scotland: a note on subscription lists in books edited by John Howie', *Local Population Studies*, 23:33–5.

JOYCE, W. L., HALL, D. D., BROWN, R. D. & HENCH, J. B., (eds), 1983, *Printing and society in early America*. Worcester, Mass.

JULIA, D., 1970, 'L'enseignement primaire dans la diocèse de Reims à la fin de l'ancien régime', *Annales Historiques de la Révolution Française*, 200:233–86.

JULIA, D., 1980, 'Les professeurs, l'église et l'état après l'expulsion des Jesuites, 1762–1789', in Baker & Harrigan (eds), 1980.

JULIA, D., REVEL, J. & CHARTIER, R., (eds), 1986, *Les universités européenes du XVIe au XVIIIe siècle. Histoire sociale des populations étudiantes. Tome 1*. Paris.

KAESTLE, C. F., 1976, '"Between the Scylla of brutal ignorance and the Charybdis of a literary education": elite attitudes towards mass schooling in early industrial England and America', in Stone (ed.), 1976.

KAGAN, R., 1974, *Students and society in early modern Spain*. London.

KAGAN, R., 1975, 'Law students and legal careers in eighteenth-century France', *Past & Present*, 68:38–72.

KAGAN, R., 1986, 'Universities in Italy, 1500–1700', in Julia *et al.* (eds), 1986.

KAHAN, A., 1985, *The plow, the hammer and the knout. An economic history of eighteenth-century Russia*. London.

KAISER, T. E., 1983, 'The abbé de Saint-Pierre, public opinion and the reconstitution of the French monarchy', *Journal of Modern History*, 55:618–43.

KAMEN, H., 1965, *The Spanish inquisition*. London.

KAMEN, H., 1984, *European society, 1500–1700*. London.

KANIEWSKA, I., 1986a, 'Les étudiants de l'université de Cracovie aux XVe et XVIe siècles (1433-1560)', in Julia *et al.* (eds), 1986.

KANIEWSKA, I., 1986b, 'La conjuncture étudiante de l'université de Cracovie aux XVIIe et XVIIIe siècles', in Julia *et al.* (eds), 1986.

KEEP, J. L. H., 1985, *Soldiers of the Tsar.* Oxford.

KESSLER, W., 1976, 'Buchproduction und Lektüre in Zivilkroatien und -Slawonien zwischen Aufklärung und "nationaler Weidergeburt" (1767-1848)', *Archiv für Geschichte des Buchwesens*, 26:339-790.

KLAITS, J., 1976, *Printed propaganda under Louis XIV.* Princeton.

VON KLARWILL, V., 1970, *The Fugger news letters.* Freeport, NY. (Reprints of 1924 and 1926 volumes.)

KLEPIKOV, S., 1971, 'Russian block books of the seventeenth and eighteenth centuries', *The Papers of the Bibliographical Society of America*, 65:213-24.

KLINGENSTEIN, G., LUTZ, H. & STOURZH G., (eds), 1978. *Bildung, Politik und Gesellschaft.* Vienna.

KNIGHT, K. G., 1985, 'Populärliteratur und Literaturgeschmack in den achtziger Jahren des 17. Jahrhundert', in Brückner (ed.), 1985.

KOHLER, A., 1978, 'Bildung und Konfession', in Klingenstein *et al.* (eds), 1978.

KORSHIN, P., (ed.), 1976, *The widening circle. Essays on the circulation of literature in eighteenth-century Europe.* Pennsylvania.

KRUKOWSKI, J., 1979, 'Szkoły pokątne w Krakowie w okresie komisji edukacji narodowej', *Rozprawy z Dziejów Oświaty*, 22:69-82.

KRUPA, M., 1981, 'Szkoła ludowa w Galicji w latach 1772-1790', *Rozprawy z Dziejów Oświaty*, 14:57-82.

KUKK, H., 1982, 'Tartu university library through three centuries', *Journal of Baltic Studies*, 13:349-63.

VAN DER LAAN, H., 1977, 'Influences on education and instruction in the Netherlands, especially 1750 to 1815', in Leith (ed.), 1977.

LABALME, P. H., (ed.), 1980, *Beyond their sex. Learned women of the European past.* London.

LABARRE, A., 1971, *La livre dans la vie Amiénoise du seizième siècle.* Paris.

LAGET, M., 1971, 'Petites écoles en Languedoc au XVIIIe siècle', *Annales ESC*, 26:1398-1418.

LANGER, H., 1978, *The thirty years war.* Poole.

LAQUEUR, T. W., 1976, 'The cultural origins of popular literacy in England, 1500-1850', *Oxford Review of Education.* 2:255-75.

LARQUIÉ, C., 1981, 'L'alphabétisation à Madrid en 1650', *Revue D'Histoire Moderne et Contemporaine*, 28:132–57.

LASLETT, P., 1969, 'Scottish weavers, cobblers and miners who bought books in the 1750s', *Local Population Studies*, 3:7–15.

LASLETT, P., 1971, *The world we have lost*. London.

LAURET, A. M., 1970, 'Contribution à l'histoire de l'enseignement et de l'éducation aux Pays-Bas et principalement l'oeuvre des Soeurs de la Charité de Tilborg', *Acta Historiae Neerlandica*, 4:170–83.

LA VOPA, A. J., 1980, *Prussian schoolteachers. Profession and office, 1763-1848*. Chapel Hill, NC.

LAW, A., 1965, *Education in Edinburgh in the eighteenth century*. London.

LEBRUN, F., 1984, 'Le contenu idéologique de la littérature "populaire" du XVIe au XIX siècle d'après "L'enfant sage à trois ans"', in Croix, A., Jacquiart, J. & Lebrun, F. (eds), 1984, *La France d'ancien régime*, vol. 1. Toulouse.

LEHMANN, H., 1985, 'Die Kometenflugschriften des 17. Jahrhundert abs historische Quelle', in Brückner *et al.* (eds), 1985.

LEITH, J. A., (ed.), 1977, *Facets of education in the eighteenth century. Studies on Voltaire and the eighteenth century*, 167. Oxford.

LE ROY LADURIE, E., 1974, *The peasants of Languedoc*. Urbana.

LE ROY LADURIE, E. & DEMONET, M., 1980, 'Alphabétisation et stature: un tableau comparé', *Annales ESC*. 35:1329–32.

LEVINE, D., 1979, 'Education and family life in early industrial England', *Journal of Family History*, 4:368–80.

LEWIN, P., 1977, 'The Ukrainian popular religious stage of the seventeenth and eighteenth centuries on the territory of the Polish commonwealth', *Harvard Ukrainian Studies*, 1:308–29.

LEWIN, P., 1981, 'The Ukranian school theatre in the seventeenth and eighteenth centuries: an expression of the Baroque', *Harvard Ukrainian Studies*, 5:54–65.

LIEBREICH, A. K., 1985, 'Piarist education in the seventeenth century', *Studi Secenteschi*, 26:225–78.

LIEBREICH, A. K., 1986, 'Piarist education in the seventeenth century', *Studi Secenteschi*, 27:57–89.

LIMON, J., 1985, *Gentlemen of a company. English players in central and eastern Europe, 1590-1660*. Cambridge.

LINDBERG, S. G., 1981, 'The Scandinavian book trade in the eighteenth century', in Barber & Fabian (eds), 1981.

LITAK, S., 1973, 'The parochial school network in Poland prior to the establishment of the Commission of National Education', *Acta Poloniae Historica*, 27:45–65.

LITAK, S., 1978, 'Das Schulwesen der Jesuiten in Polen', in Klingenstein *et al.* (eds), 1978.

LITAK, S., 1983, 'Z działalności szkolnej Michała Jerzego Poniatowskiego na Mazowszu', *Rozprawy z Dziejów Oświaty*, **25**: 15-36.

LOCKRIDGE, K. A., 1974, *Literacy in colonial New England*. New York.

LOCKRIDGE, K. A., 1981, 'Literacy in early America, 1650-1800', in Graff (ed.), 1981.

LONGUET, Y., 1978, 'L'alphabétisation à Falaise de 1670 à 1789', *Annales de Normandie*, **28**:207-23.

LOTTIN, A., *et al*, 1983, *Etudes sur les villes en Europe occidentale. Milieu du XVIIe siècle à la veille de la révolution française. Tome 2. Angleterre, Pays-Bas et Provinces Unies, Allemagne Rhénane.* Paris.

LOTTIN, A. & SOLY, H., 1983, 'Aspects de l'histoire des villes des Pays-Bas méridionaux et de la principauté de Liege', in Lottin *et al.* (eds), 1983.

LOUBÈS, G., 1983, 'Ecoles en Gascogne centrale au XVe siècle', *Annales du Midi*, **95**:309-20.

LUCCHI, P., 1978, 'La Santacroce, il Salterio e il Babuino: libri per imparare a leggere nel primo secolo della stampa', *Quaderni Storici*, **38**:593-630.

LUPPOV, S. P., 1981, 'Die Nachfrage nach Büchern der Akademie der Wissenschaften und nach auslandischen Veröffentlichungen in Petersburg und Moskau in der mitte des XVIII. Jahrhundert', *Archiv für Geschichte des Buchwesens*, **22**:257-300.

LUTTINEN, R., 1985, 'Skrivkunnigheten i Finland fram till början av 1900- talet', in Skovgaard-Petersen (ed.), 1985.

LYNCH, M., 1981, *Edinburgh and the Reformation*. Edinburgh.

McARDLE, F., 1978, *Altopascio. A study in Tuscan rural society, 1587-1784*. Cambridge.

McCLELLAND, C. E., 1977, 'German universities in the eighteenth century: crisis and renewal', in Leith (ed.), 1977.

McCLELLAND, C. E., 1980, *State, society and university in Germany, 1700-1914*. Cambridge.

McDONALD, W. R., 1966, 'Scottish seventeenth-century almanacs', *The Bibliotheck*, **4**:257-322.

MACINNES, J., 1950, 'Gaelic religious poetry, 1650-1850', *Records of the Scottish Church History Society*, **10**:31-53.

MACKENNEY, R., 1987, *Tradesmen and traders. The world of the guilds in Venice and Europe, c1250-c1650*. London.

MACKINNON, K. M., 1972, 'Education and social control: the case of Gaelic', *Scottish Educational Studies*, 4:125–37.

McLUHAN, M., 1973, *Understanding media*. London.

MACLYSAGHT, E., 1969, *Irish life in the seventeenth century*. Dublin, 3rd edition.

McMULLEN, N., 1977, 'The education of English gentlewomen, 1540–1640', *History of Education*, 6:87–101.

MAJOREK, C., 1973, 'Podręczniki komisji edukacji narodowej w aspekcie rozwiązań dydaktycznych', *Rozprawy z Dziejów Oświaty*, 16:69–140.

MALCOLMSON, R. W., 1981, *Life and labour in England, 1700–1780*. London.

MAMONTOWICZ-ŁOJEK, B., 1968, 'Szkoła artystyczno-teatralna Antoniego Tyzenhauza, 1774–1785', *Rozprawy z Dziejów Oświaty*, 11:36–98.

MANDROU, R., 1975, *De la culture populaire aux 17e et 18e siècles*. Paris, 2nd edition.

MARCO, J., 1977, *Literatura popular en España en los siglos XVIII y XIX*. Madrid.

MARKER, G., 1982, 'Russia and the "printing revolution": notes and observations', *Slavic Review*, 41:26–83.

MARKUSSEN, I. & SKOVGAARD-PETERSEN, V., 1981, 'Læseindlærning og læsebehov i Danmark, ca1550–ca1850', *Ur Nordisk Kulturhistoria. Studia Historica Jyväskyläensiä*, 22:13–72.

MARQUES, A. H. DE OLIVEIRA, 1971, *Daily life in Portugal in the late middle ages*. London.

MARQUES, A. H. DE OLIVEIRA, 1972, *History of Portugal*, vol.1. New York and London.

MÁRQUEZ, A., 1980, *Literatura e inquisición en España, 1478–1834*. Madrid.

MARTEL, A., 1938, *La langue polonaise dans les pays ruthènes, ukraine et russie blanche, 1569–1667*. Lille.

MARTENS, W., 1975, 'Leserezepte fürs Frauenzimmer', *Archiv für Geschichte des Buchwesens*, 25:1143–1200.

MARTIN, H-J., 1969, *Livre, pouvoirs et société à Paris*. Geneva.

MARTIN, H-J., 1978, 'The *bibliothèque bleue*', *Publishing History*, 3:70–103.

MARTIN, H-J., 1981, 'Livre et lumières en France. A propos de travaux récents', in Barber & Fabian (eds), 1981.

MARTIN, M., 1703, *A description of the western islands of Scotland*. London.

MARVICK, E. W., 1976, 'Nature versus nurture: patterns and trends in seventeenth-century French child-rearing', in de Mause (ed.), 1976.

MARZAC, N., 'The note-books of Pierre Gautier: the academic and social life of a sixteenth-century student in Paris and Burgundy', *Bulletin d'Histoire et Religion*, **36**:621–8.

MATERNICKI, J., 1974, 'L'enseignement de l'histoire en Pologne au XVIIIe siècle', *Acta Poloniae Historica*, **29**:161–79.

MATHEW, W. M., 1966, 'The origins and occupations of Glasgow students, 1740–1839', *Past & Present*, **33**:74–94.

MATHIAS, P., 1975, 'Skills and the diffusion of innovations from Britain in the eighteenth-century', *Transactions of the Royal Historical Society*, 5th series, **25**:93–114.

DE MAUSE, L., (ed.), 1976, *The history of childhood*. London.

MAYNES, M. J., 1979, 'The virtues of archaism: the political economy of schooling in Europe, 1750–1850', *Comparative Studies in Society and History*, **21**:611–25.

MAYNES, M. J., 1980, 'Work or schools? Youth and the family in the Midi in the early nineteenth century', in Baker & Harrigan (eds), 1980.

MEDICK, H., 1984, 'Village spinning bees: sexual culture and free time among rural youth in early modern Germany', in Medick, H. & Sabean, D. W. (eds), *Interest and emotion. Essays on the study of family and kinship*. Cambridge.

LE MENN, G., 1985, 'Une "bibliothèque bleue" en langue Bretonne', *Annales de Bretagne et des Pays de l'Ouest*, **92**:229–40.

MEYER, J., 1974, 'Alphabétisation, lecture et écriture. Essai sur l'instruction populaire en Bretagne du XVIe au XIXe siècle', in *Actes du 95e congrès national des sociétés savantes*, vol.1. Paris.

MILLETT, B., 1976, 'Irish literature in Latin, 1550–1700', in Moody, Martin & Byrne (eds), 1976.

MOODY, T. W., MARTIN, F. X. & BYRNE, F. J., (eds), 1976, *A new history of Ireland, vol. 3. Early Modern Ireland, 1534–1691*. Oxford.

MOODY, T. W. & VAUGHAN, W. E., (eds), 1986, *A new history of Ireland, vol. 4. Eighteenth-century Ireland*. Oxford.

MOORE, C. N., 1985, 'Mädchenlektüre im 17. Jahrhundert', in Brückner *et al.* (eds), 1985.

MORAN, G. T., 1981, 'Conception of time in early modern France: an approach to the history of collective mentalities', *Sixteenth Century Journal*, **12**:3–20.

MORGAN, V., 1978, 'Approaches to the history of the English universities in the sixteenth and seventeenth centuries', in Klingenstein *et al.* (eds), 1978.

Literacy in early modern Europe

MUCHEMBLED, R., 1985, *Popular culture and elite culture in France, 1400–1750*. London.

NASH, C. S., 1981, 'Educating new mothers: women and the enlightenment in Russia', *History of Education Quarterly*, 21:301–16.

NEUBURG, V. E., 1971, *Popular education in eighteenth century England*. London.

NEUGEBAUER, W., 1985, *Absolutistischer Staat und Schulwirklichkeit in Brandenburg-Prussen*. Berlin.

NIETO, J. C., 1974, 'Juan de Valdés on catechetical instruction: "The dialogue on christian doctrine" and "The christian instruction for children"', *Bulletin d'Histoire et Religion*, 36:253–72.

NORTON, F. J., 1958, *Italian printers, 1501–1520*. London.

NORTON, F. J., 1966, *Printing in Spain, 1501–20*. Cambridge.

NORTON, F. J. & WILSON, E. M., (eds), 1969, *Two Spanish verse Chapbooks*. Cambridge.

O'BRIEN, G. M., 1970, 'Maria Theresa's attempt to educate an empire', *Paedagogica Historica*, 10:542–65.

Ó'CUÍV, B., 1976, 'The Irish language in the early modern period', in Moody, Martin & Byrne (eds), 1976.

Ó'CUÍV, B., 1986, 'Irish language and literature, 1691–1845', in Moody & Vaughan (eds), 1986.

O'DAY, R., 1982, *Education and society, 1500–1800*. London.

Ó'TUATHAIGH, M. A. G., 1980, '"Early modern Ireland, 1534–1691": a reassessment', in Drudy, P. J. (ed.), 1980, *Irish studies, vol. 1*. Cambridge.

OKENFUSS, M. J., 1973, 'Technical education in Russia under Peter the Great', *History of Education Quarterly*, 21:325–45.

OKEY, R., 1986, *Eastern Europe, 1740–1985. Feudalism to communism*. London, second edition.

ÓLASON, V., 1982, *The traditional ballads of Iceland*. Reykjavik.

OLCZAK, S., 1974, 'Le réseau d'écoles paroissiales dans le diocèse de Poznan (première moitié du XVIIe siècle)', *Miscellanea Historiae Ecclesiasticae*, 5:323–6.

ONG, W. J., 1982, *Orality and literacy*. London.

ONG, W. J., 1986, 'Writing as a technology that restructures thought', in Baumann (ed.), 1986.

OVERTON, M., 1985, 'The diffusion of agricultural innovations in early modern England: turnips and clover in Norfolk and Suffolk, 1580–1740', *Transactions of the Institute of British Geographers*, new series 10:205–21.

OVSYANNIKOV, Y., 1968, *The lubok. 17th–18th century Russian broadsides*. Moscow.

PALMER, R. R., 1980, 'The central schools of the first French republic: a statistical survey', in Baker & Harrigan (eds), 1980.

PARKER, G., 1979, *The Dutch revolt*. Harmondsworth.

PARKER, G., 1980, 'An educational revolution? The growth of literacy and schooling in early modern Europe', *Tijdschrift voor Geschiedenis*, 93:210–20.

PARTNER, P., 1976, *Renaissance Rome, 1500–1559. A portrait of a society*. Berkeley.

PERREL, J., 'Les écoles de filles dans la France d'ancien régime', in Baker & Harrigan (eds), 1980.

PERROT, J-C., 1981, 'Les dictionnaires de commerce au XVIIIe siècle', *Revue d'Histoire Moderne et Contemporaine*, 28:36–67.

PERRY, M. E., 1980, *Crime and society in early modern Seville*. London.

PESET, M. & MANCEBO, M. F., 1986, 'La population des universités espagnoles au XVIIIe siècle', in Julia *et al.* (eds), 1986.

PETRAT, G., 1985, 'Der Kalender im Haus des Illiteraten und Analphabeten', in Brückner *et al.* (eds), 1985.

PETSCHAUER, P., 1976, 'Improving educational opportunities for girls in eighteenth-century Germany', *Eighteenth Century Life*, 3:56–62.

PHILLIPS, C. R., 1977, 'Education in the service of the Spanish state', *History of Education Quarterly*, 17:345–51.

PHILLIPSON, N. T., 1980, 'The social structure of the faculty of advocates in Scotland, 1661–1840', in Harding (ed.), 1980.

PHILLIPSON, N. T. & MITCHISON, R., (eds), 1970, *Scotland in the age of improvement*. Edinburgh.

POLLOCK, L. A., 1983, *Forgotten children. Parent–child relations from 1500 to 1900*. Cambridge.

PORTER, R., 1982, *English society in the eighteenth century*. Harmondsworth.

POŚPIECH, A. & TYGIELSKI, W., 1981, 'The social role of magnates' courts in Poland (from the end of the 16th to the 18th century)', *Acta Poloniae Historica*, 43:75–100.

POTKOWSKI, E., 1979, 'Ecriture et société en Pologne du bas moyen age (XIVe–XVe siècles)', *Acta Poloniae Historica*, 39: 47–100.

POUTET, Y., 1971, 'L'enseignement des pauvres dans la France du XVIIe siècle', *XVIIe Siècle*, 90–1:87–111.

PRICE, J. L., 1974, *Culture and society in the Dutch republic during the 17th century*. London.

QUÉNIART, J., 1974, 'Deux exemples d'alphabétisation: Rouen et Rennes à la fin de XVIIe siècle', in *Actes du 95e congrès* .... Paris.

RAINE, J., (ed.), 1845, *Depositions and other ecclesiastical proceedings from the courts of Durham*. Durham.

RAINE, J., (ed.), 1861, *Depositions from the castle of York*. Durham.

RANUM, O., (ed.), 1975, *National consciousness, history and political culture in early modern Europe*. Baltimore and London.

RAPPAPORT, S., 1983, 'Social structure and mobility in sixteenth century London, part 1', *London Journal*, 9:107-35.

RAUN, T., 1979, 'The development of Estonian literacy in the 18th and 19th centuries', *Journal of Baltic Studies*, 10:115-26.

REAY, B., 1983, 'Popular literature in seventeenth-century England', *Journal of Peasant Studies*, 10:243-9.

REAY, B., (ed.), 1985, *Popular culture in seventeenth-century England*. New York.

RICHARDSON, R. C. & JAMES, T. B., (eds), 1983, *The urban experience: a sourcebook. English, Scottish and Welsh towns, 1450-1700*. Manchester.

RICUPERATI, G. & ROGGERO, M., 1977, 'Educational policies in eighteenth-century Italy', in Leith (ed.), 1977.

RICUPERATI, G. & ROGGERO, M., 1978, 'Istruzione e società in Italia. Problemi e prospettive de ricerca', *Quaderni Storici*, 38:640-65.

RIES, P., 1982, 'Staat und Presse im 17. Jahrhundert in England', *Daphnis*, 11:351-75.

RIES, P., 1987, 'Der Inhalt der Wochenzeitungen von 1609 im Computer', in Blühm, E., & Gebhardt, H. (eds.), *Presse und Geschichte, band II*. Munich.

RINGER, F. T., 1977, 'Problems in the history of higher education: a review article', *Comparative Studies in Society and History*, 19:239-55.

ROBERTS, M., 1953, *Gustavus Adolphus. A history of Sweden, 1611-1632*, vol.1. London.

ROBERTS, M., 1967, *Essays in Swedish history*. London.

ROBERTS, M., 1968, *The early vasas. A history of Sweden, 1523-1611*. Cambridge.

ROCHE, D., 1965, 'Milieux académiques provinciaux et société des lumières', in Bollème (ed.), 1965.

RODRIGUEZ, M-C. & BENNASSAR, B., 1978, 'Signatures et niveau culturel des témoins et accusés dans les procès d'inquisition du ressort du tribunal de Tolède (1525-1817), et du ressort du tribunal de Cordoue (1595-1632)', *Cahiers du Monde Hispanique et Luso-Brésilien*, 31:17-46.

ROGERS, P., 1972, 'Book subscriptions among the Augustans', *Times Literary Supplement*, 15 December 1972:1539–40.

ROGERS, P., 1985, *Literature and popular culture in the eighteenth century*. Brighton.

ROSS, J. B., 1976, 'The middle-class child in urban Italy, fourteenth to early sixteenth century', in de Mause (ed.), 1976.

RUCIŃSKI, H., 1974, 'La confrérie "litteraire" de Koprzywnica en tant qu'image de la structure sociale d'une petite ville dans les années 1694–1795', *Przeglad Historyczny*, 55:282–3.

RUWET, J. & WELLEMANS, Y., 1978, *L'analphabétisme en Belgique (XVIIIe–XIXe siècles)*. Louvain.

SANDERSON, M., 1983, *Education, economic change and society in England, 1780–1870*. London.

SAUNDERS, D., 1985, *The Ukrainian impact on Russian culture, 1750–1850*. Edmonton.

SCHENDA, R., 1985, 'Orale und Literarische Kommunikationsformen im Bereich von Analphabeten und Gebildeten im 17. Jahrhundert', in Brückner *et at.* (eds), 1985.

SCHILLING, M., 1985, 'Das Flugblatt als Instrument gesellschaftlicher Anpassung', in Brückner *et al.* (eds), 1985.

SCHINDLING, A., 1976, 'Landesschule', *Handwörterbuch zur Deutschen Rechtsgeschichte*, 14:1408–12.

SCHMITT, C. B., 1974, 'The university of Pisa in the Renaissance', *History of Education*, 3:3–17.

SCHOFIELD, R. S., 1968, 'The measurement of literacy in pre-industrial England', in Goody (ed.), 1968.

SCHOFIELD, R. S., 1981, 'Dimensions of illiteracy, 1750–1850', in Graff (ed.), 1981.

SCHUBERT, E., 1975, '"Bauerngeschrey". Zum problem der öffentichen Meinung im spätmittelalterlichen Franken', *Jährbuch für Fränkische Landesforschung*, 34/35:883–907.

SCHULTE, H. F., 1968, *The Spanish press, 1470–1966. Print, power, and politics*. Urbana.

SCHUTTE, A. J., 1980, 'Printing, piety and the people in Italy: the first thirty years', *Archiv für Reformationsgeschichte*, 71: 5–20.

SCHUTTE, A. J., 1986, 'Teaching adults to read in 16th century Venice: Giovanni Antonio Tagliente's *Libro Maistrevole*', *Sixteenth Century Journal*, 17:3–16.

SCHUTZ, A. H., 1955, *Vernacular books in Parisian private libraries of the sixteenth century according to the notarial inventories*. Chapel Hill, NC.

SCRIBNER, R. W., 1981a, *For the sake of simple folk. Popular propaganda for the German Reformation.* Cambridge.

SCRIBNER, R. W., 1981b, 'Flugblatt und Analphabetentum. Wie kam der gemeine Mann zu Reformatorischen Ideen', in Köhler, H-J. (ed.), 1981, *Flugschriften als massenmedium der Reformationszeit.* Stuttgart.

SCRIBNER, R. W., 1984, 'Oral culture and the diffusion of Reformation ideas', *History of European Ideas*, 5:237–56.

SEIDLER, G. L., 1977, 'The reform of the Polish school system in the era of the enlightenment', in Leith (ed.), 1977.

SIDDLE, D. J., 1987, 'Cultural prejudice and the geography of ignorance: peasant illiteracy in south-eastern France, 1550–1790', *Transactions of the Institute of British Geographers*, new series 11:1–10.

SIMMONS, J. S. G., 1977, 'Russian printing', in Auty & Obolensky (eds), 1977.

SIMONE, R., 1978, 'Scrivere, leggere e capire', *Quaderni Storici*, 38:666–82

SIMPSON, I. J., 1947, *Education in Aberdeenshire before 1872.* London.

SINCLAIR, A., 1984, *Madrid newspapers, 1661–1870. A computerised handbook.* Leeds.

SINCLAIR, J., 1826, *Analysis of the statistical account of Scotland*, part 2. London.

SKOVGAARD-PETERSEN, V., (ed.), 1985, *Da menigmand i norden lærte at skrive – en sektionsrapport fra 19 nordiske historiker-kongres, 1984.* Copenhagen.

SLACK, P., 1979, 'Mirrors of health and treasures of poor men: the uses of vernacular medical literature in Tudor England', in Webster, C. (ed.), 1979.

ŠMAHEL, F., 1986, 'L'université de Prague de 1433 à 1622: recrutement géographique, carrières et mobilité sociale des étudiants gradués', in Julia *et al.* (eds), 1986.

SMITH, A., 1979, *The newspaper. An international history.* London.

SMITH, R. E. F., 1983, 'Time, space and use in early Russia', in Aston (ed.), 1983.

SMITH, W. D., 1984, 'The function of commercial centers in the modernization of European capitalism: Amsterdam as an information exchange in the seventeenth century', *Journal of Economic History*, 44:985–1005.

SOLÉ, J., 1973, 'Lecture et classes populaires à Grenoble au XVIIIe siècle. Le témoignage des inventaires après décès', in *Images du peuple au dix-huitième siècle*. Paris.

SOLOMON, H. M., 1972, *Public welfare, science and propaganda in seventeenth-century France*. Princeton.

SPORHAN-KREMPEL, L., 1975, 'Das nürnberger Nachrichten- und Zeitungswesen', *Archiv für Geschichte des Buchwesens*, **25**: 999–1026.

SPRANDEL-KRAFFT, L., 1983, 'Über das Verhältnis von Autorund Druckherr in der Inkunabelzeit', *Archiv für Geschichte des Buchwesens*, 14:353–84.

SPUFFORD, M., 1981, *Small books and pleasant histories. Popular fiction and its readership in seventeenth-century England*. London.

STEINBERG, S. H., 1974, *Five hundred years of printing*. Harmondsworth edition.

STEPHENS, C. B., 1980, 'Belgorod: notes on literacy and language in the seventeenth-century Russian army', *Russian History*, 7:113–24.

STEVENSON, D., 1981, 'Scotland's first newspaper, 1648', *The Bibliotheck*, 10:123–6.

STONE, L., 1964, 'The educational revolution in England, 1560–1640', *Past & Present*, 28:41–80.

STONE, L., 1969, 'Literacy and education in England, 1640–1900', *Past & Present*, 42:69–139.

STONE, L., (ed.), 1976, *Schooling and society*. Baltimore.

STONE, L., 1977, *The family, sex and marriage in England, 1500–1800*. London.

STONE, L. & STONE, J. F., 1984, *An open elite? England, 1540–1880*. Oxford.

STRAUSS, G., 1976, 'The state of pedagogical theory c1530: what Protestant reformers knew about education', in Stone (ed.), 1976.

STRAUSS, G., 1978, *Luther's house of learning. Indoctrination of the young in the German Reformation*. London.

STRAUSS, G., 1980, 'The mental world of a German pastor', in Brooks (ed.), 1980.

STREET, B. V., 1984, *Literacy in theory and practice*. Cambridge.

SÜHRIG, H., 1979, 'Die Entwicklung der niedersächsischen Kalender im 17. Jahrhundert', *Archiv für Geschichte des Buchwesens*, **20**:329–794.

SÜHRIG, H., 1981, 'Kalender – zur Publizistik eines Massenkommunikationsmediums vom 18. bis 20. Jahrhundert', *Archiv für Geschichte des Buchwesens*, **22**:1981.

SÜHRIG, H., 1985, 'Zur unterhaltungsfunktion des Kalenders im Barock', in Brückner *et al.* (ed.), 1985.

TARKIAINEN, K., 1972, 'Rysstolkarna som yrkeskår, 1591–1661', *Historisk Tidskrift*, **92**:490–522.

TAZBIR, J., 1982, 'Polish national consciousness in the 16th–18th centuries', *Acta Poloniae Historica*, **46**:47–72.

THIRSK, J., 1983, 'Plough and pen: agricultural writers in the seventeenth century', in Aston (ed.), 1983.

THOMAS, D. M., 1979, 'Printing privileges in Spain', *Publishing History*, **5**:105–26.

THOMAS, K., 1986, 'The meaning of literacy in early modern England', in Baumann (ed.), 1986.

THOMSEN, N., 1982, 'Why study press history?', *Scandinavian Journal of History*, **7**:1–13.

THOMSON, S. H., 1967, 'The Czechs as integrating and disintegrating factors in the Habsburg empire', *Austrian History Yearbook*, **3**:203–22.

TILLY, C., 1973, 'Population and pedagogy in France', *History of Education Quarterly*, **13**:113–28.

TOMPSON, R. S., 1977, 'English and English education in the eighteenth century', in Leith (ed.), 1977.

TRENARD, L., 1974, 'Culture, alphabétisation et enseignement au XVIIIe siècle', *XVIIIe Siècle*, **6**:147–58.

TRENARD, L., 1977, 'Histoire des sciences de l'éducation (période moderne)', *Revue Historique*, **257**:429–72.

TRENARD, L., 1980, 'L'enseignement de la langue nationale: une réforme pédagogique, 1750–1790', in Baker & Harrigan (eds), 1980.

TRENARD, L., 1985, 'Alphabétisation et scolarisation dans la région lilloise. Les effets de la crise révolutionnaire, 1780–1802', *Revue du Nord*, **67**:633–48.

TRIAL, G. T., 1975, *History of education in Iceland*. Cambridge.

TUCKER, M. J., 1976, 'The child as beginning and end: fifteenth and sixteenth century English childhood', in de Mause (ed.), 1976.

TUDOR, P., 1984, 'Religious instruction for children and adolescents in the early English reformation', *Journal of Ecclesiastical History*, **35**:391–413.

TVEIT, K., 1981, 'Lesekunne og undervisning før folkeskolevesenet', *Ur Nordisk Kulturhistoria, Studia Historica Jyväskyläensiä*, **22**:87–122.

TVEIT, K., 1985, 'Skrivekyndighet i Norden i det 18. og 19. århundre. Norge', in Skovgaard-Petersen (ed.), 1985.

URBAN, W., 1977, 'La connaissance de l'écriture en Petite Pologne dans la seconde moitié du XVIe siècle', *Przeglad Historyczny*, **68**:257. [French summary of an article in Polish].

VAN ROEY, J., 1968, 'De correlate tussen het sociale-beroepsmilieu en de godsdienstkeuze te Antwerpen op het einde der XVIe eeuw', in *Sources de l'Histoire Religieuse de la Belgique*, 1968. Louvain.

VAN UYTVEN, R., 1968, 'Invloeden van het sociale en professionele milieu op de godsdienstkeuze: Leuven en Edingen', in *Sources de l'Histoire Religieuse de la Belgique*, 1968. Louvain.

VAN DER WOUDE, A. M., 1980, 'De alfabetisering', in *Algemene Geschiedenis der Nederlanden*, vol.7. Haarlem.

VASSBERG, D. E., 1983, 'Juveniles in the rural work force of sixteenth-century Castile', *Journal of Peasant Studies*, 11:62–75.

VIAZZO, P. P., 1983, *Alagna Valsesia, una comunita walser*. Borgosesia.

VIGO, G., 1972-3, 'Istruzione e società nel regno Italico. II caso di Vigevano (1806–1814)', *Bolletino della Società Pavese di Storia Patria*, 22-3:125–39.

VĪKSNIŅŠ, N., 1973, 'Some notes on the early histories of Latvian books and newspapers', *Journal of Baltic Studies*, 4:155–8.

VINCENT, D., 1981, *Bread, knowledge and freedom. A study of nineteenth-century working-class autobiographers*. London.

VOGLER, B., 1975, 'La politique scolaire entre Rhin et Moselle: l'example du duché de Deux Ponts (1556–1619)', *Francia*, 3:236–320.

VOGLER, B., 1976, 'La politique scolaire entre Rhin et Moselle: l'example du duché de Deux Ponts (1556–1619)', *Francia*, 4:287–364.

VOGLER, B., 1983, 'La Rhénanie', in Lottin *et al.* 1983.

VOSS, V. B., 1980, 'Onderwijs en opvoeding: inleiding', *Algemene Geschiedenis der Nederlanden*, vol.7. Haarlem.

VOVELLE, M., 1975, 'Y a-t-il eu une révolution culturelle au XVIIIe siècle? A propos de l'éducation populaire en Provence', *Revue d'Histoire Moderne et Contemporaine*, 22:89–141.

WALVIN, J., 1984, *English urban life, 1776–1851*. London.

WARD, A., 1974, *Book production, fiction and the German reading public*. Oxford.

WATT, I., 1972, *The rise of the novel. Studies in Defoe, Richardson and Fielding*. Harmondsworth edition.

WATTS, S. J., 1984, *A social history of western Europe, 1450–1720*. London.

WEBSTER, C., (ed.), 1979, *Health, medicine and mortality in the sixteenth century*. Cambridge.

WEYRAUCH, E., 1985, 'Die Illiteraten und ihre Literatur', in Brückner *et al.* (eds), 1985.

WHITTAKER, D. J., 1984, *New schools for Finland. A study in educational transformation*. Reports from the institute for educational research, university of Jyväskylä, 352.

WIDE, S. M. & MORRIS, J. A., 1967, 'The episcopal licensing of schoolmasters in the diocese of London, 1627-1685', *Guildhall Miscellany*, 2:392-406.

WILES, R. M., 1976, 'The relish for reading in provincial England two centuries ago', in Korshin (ed.), 1976.

WIŚNIOWSKI, E., 1973, 'The parochial school system in Poland towards the close of the middle ages', *Acta Poloniae Historica*, 27:29-43.

WIŚNIOWSKI, E. & LITAK, S., 1974, 'L'enseignement paroissial en Pologne jusqu'au XVIIIe siècle à la lumière des plus récentes recherches', *Miscellanea Historiae Ecclesiasticae*, 5:320-3.

WITHERS, C., 1984, *Gaelic in Scotland, 1698-1981*. Edinburgh.

WOOD, M. W., 1981, 'Paltry peddlers or essential merchants? Women in the distributive trades in early modern Nuremberg', *Sixteenth-Century Journal*, 12:3-14.

WOOLF, S., 1979, *A history of Italy, 1700-1860*. London.

WORMALD, J., 1981, *Court, kirk, and community. Scotland, 1470-1625*. London.

WRIGHTSON, K., 1982, *English society, 1580-1680*. London.

WYCZANSKI, A., 1974, 'L'alphabétisation et structure sociale en Pologne au XVIe siècle', *Annales ESC*, 29:705-13.

YASUMOTO, M., 1973, 'Urbanization and population in an English town: Leeds during the industrial revolution', *Keio Economic Studies*, 10:61-94.

Index